THE WAXING MOON

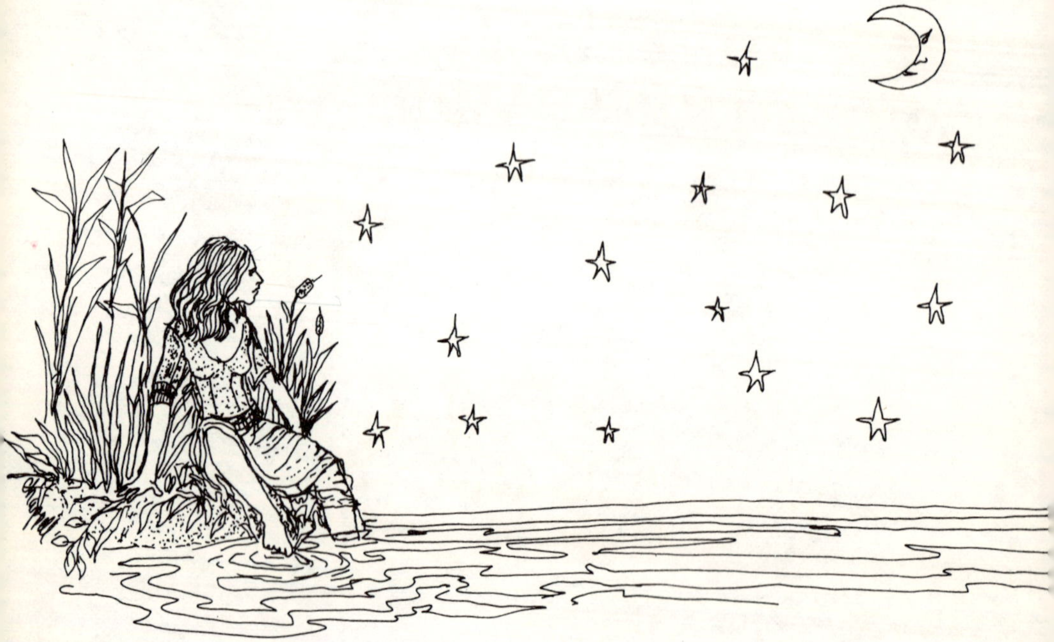

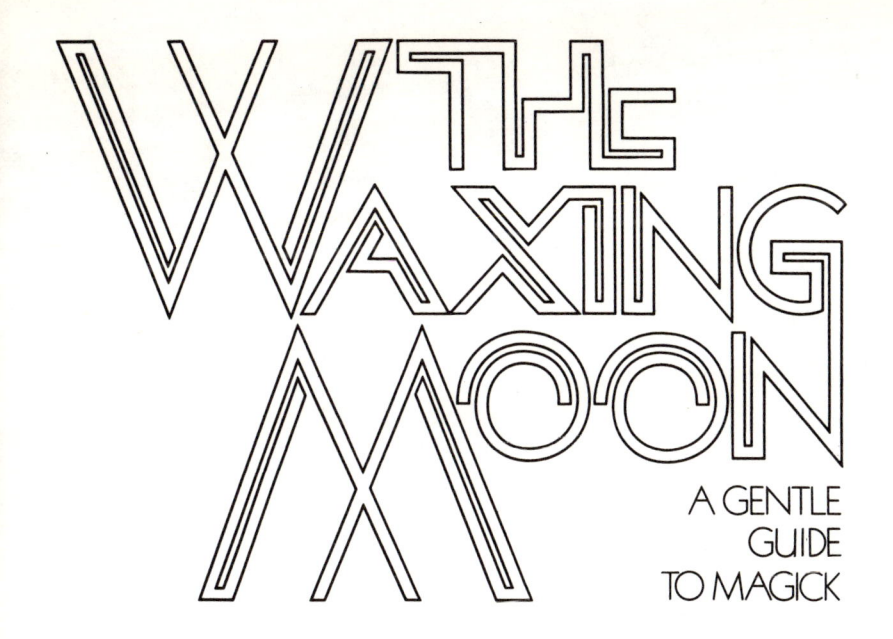

THE WAXING MOON

A GENTLE GUIDE TO MAGICK

TEXT AND ILLUSTRATIONS
BY HELEN CHAPPELL

NEW YORK   links   LONDON

Copyright © 1974 by Helen Chappell
All rights reserved
including the right of reproduction
in whole or in part in any form
Published by Links Books
33 West 60 Street, New York 10023 and
78 Newman Street, London W. 1
Distributed by Quick Fox, Inc.
33 West 60 Street, New York 10023 and
Quick Fox Limited, 40 Nugget Avenue, Unit 11,
Agincourt, Ontario Canada

First printing
Standard Book Number: 0-8256-3032-0
Library of Congress Catalog Card Number: 73-89670
Printed in the United States of America

Back cover photograph by A. Delaney Walker

Book and cover design by Holly McNeely

☆ THIS BOOK
IS
DEDICATED
TO
THE ONES I LOVE

The Waxing Moon is a book for ♡ my parents, who love and support me through all my changes; for Dr. L. E. Chappell and Helen B. Chappell ♡ From Yr. daughter with love ☆ And of course, Judy Brown, best pal and good friend who is always there ♡ ☆ Phoebe Larmore, agent superb, who believed in the work ♡ Thanks, love and long and happy lives to all of you ☆ Love and kisses to the people who helped me put it together ♡ For you Felicia Donofrio =KISS= =KISS= for Joan Browne-Kendal who typed and corrected my spelling (thank yew J.B.K.) for down home people from the year one: Carol B., Bette Meredith, Ms. Bunny Lamb, Da Punk, Bushy, Nancy, and dat old gang of mine ☆ Fun couples and blood kin ♡ Leo & Helen Daiuta ☆ ♡ Ashby and Catherine Larmore ♡ Max and Dorothy Brown ☆ Uncle Finnie and Aunt Wahalla who brought me up as one of their own =KISS= =KISS= For city folk and canyon dwellers ♡ Audrey Daiuta (we're hi-skool pals) ♡ For those fine folk Joan & Michael, for Baltimore days, S.V.A. daze and one of the kindest offers to come at a bad time ♡ Tommy Calcagno (of X-Tommy & Tommy Fame) kisses and laughter and the shared experiences ♡ Paulette Strachman, poet!!!

☆ Sherry Hochstein for art supplies and good vibes ♥ Josh Martin, for Sunday afternoons and endless raps ☆ The Divine Ms. Shirley Solomon for the Los Angeles nightmare and other curios ☆ Charles and Nancy Perini (and Nonka) ☆ Susan Leonard ☆ Alice Delaney Walker, Chicago poet ☆ Michael ☆ Judy Fahey ♥ Connie Chappell, a true and real sister ♥ Save the Children ♥ Kimmie, Christy, Miss P.K. Kendall ♥ Jenny ☆ Kit, Marnie & Michael ☆ The Light Bringers ☆ Eileen Molner scholar and Goliard poet ☆ Tom Clancy ☆ Yes, Barry Cohen ☆ Nick Howe and Ken Westhaver ☆ Franconia folk (remember those fabulous sixties?) Sally, Laura, Yvonne, Art, Bill Tucker, Duff, Jack & all the boys at Dow, including the Torch, the Ladies of Desolation Row, Justine, Cathy ★ and you too, Digby Brown, ★ For Boston daze and fat city weirdness. Ms. Vivian Video ★ friends, lovers and comedians ★ 25 ♥ Albert the Mystic ♥ ☆ Crazy Dave from N.H. ♥ The boy from Brooklyn who found home at last—Billy ♥ Brecker, who made a contribution to the illustrations ☆ Long-gone Bob; tee hee ☆ T.E. wherever he may be ☆ Uncle Daddy Badmouth in California ☆ Friend James Whitehead, Pisces-cynic and good old boy-Gentleman and scholar ☆ present at the creation ☆ Special thanks to: Danny Moses, Long suffering editor and truly organic human! Carol Fein 😊 a lady who knows 👧 Certainly Bert Snyder, who was back there in Atlantis ♥ (Thanks, Bert) ☆ and of course, Holly McNeely ☆ Capricorn ideal and designer extraordinaire ♥ I mean Holly is a great person & a great book designer ☆ Thank yew all for time and love on the book ☆ And last, but certainly not least, astrologer, reader and fellow practitioner of the Work who helped this book so much—Patricia Draut ♥ You done good, Pat ☆ To the memory of Rebecca Chappell and past and future together ♥ Thanks to L. Simon Jennings, Tippy Raackee and Wendy Wolfe of New Orleans ☆ Fr. S. O'Connell, S.J. ♥ Oxissi ♥ And for the whole sick crew ☆ For the Watcher in the Shadows and Janis Joplin ☆ And for you—the reader ♥ this book is dedicated ♥

AN IMPERFECT CIRCLE

☆Today I studied Egyptian artifacts and Early-American furniture in the Brooklyn Museum ♡ Tonight I found myself reading Tarot for the waiters and waitresses of a neighborhood watering hole ☽ For me, that is a good day, for I took something from my world and gave something back to it ☉ Writing an introduction to this book is one of the hardest things I have ever tried to do, for it closes a circle in my life ☆As another human being plodding along through my three score and ten on planet Earth, I do not pretend to know it all ❀There are no straight lines in nature and no one can draw a perfect circle ☆ But we can try to do the best we can and keep on our own journeys by fate or free will ☆ For me, the act of creating this book was an attempt to draw one perfect circle in the two media I understand best ☆ Where words failed to find their place, I would turn to the images I saw ♡ The Waxing Moon is a labor of love ♡ I've laughed over it, defended it, sweated over it, froze over it, traveled for it, bit my nails, studied, argued, bled and have witnesses to prove that I've even cried over it in frustration and joy ☆ For me, it's a book that's been a long time comin' and will be a long time gone ☉ Twelve or fourteen or more years of my life this trip around have been with the fascination of magic in all its forms; and I know that I shall never know or understand all there is to learn and un-learn in the journey ♡ And this is the hardest part—to close an imperfect circle ☆

☆The Waxing Moon is given to you as a beginner's guide to magick ♡ It has been said that you pays your money and you takes your choice ☉ I hope this book will show you what some of your choices are ☆ When I first went to books for some word on what magick was all about, I found nothing to tell me the difference between Voodoo and Witchcraft, or even how they are, in many ways, alike ☉ The *Waxing Moon* is like an old explorer's map, filled with blank spaces marked *terra incognita* and *here bee sea serpents*. ෴ make friends with the *sea serpents*; fill in the blank spaces ☉ Listen, I don't want you to take my word for it ♡ Read further, experiment to find your own path through the unknown world ♡ The *Waxing Moon* will only show you how and why and where ☉ It's a starting point ☆ How far you want to go is up to you ♆ I wrote this as a guide book, and like any tourist or explorer, you'll never know unless you strike out on your own with guide book, camera and a light lunch ☆ ☽ Even if magick isn't your cup of tea leaves, I hope you'll enjoy the ride ♡ ☆ My only advice would be to follow your own instincts ☐ Do your own thing as long as you don't hurt anyone else in its doing ♡ All the bastards get their own, if you wait long enough, and that may include your own Karma ☉ Magick is not a parlor game, but a part of the study of the cosmic nature ☆ Never take anything for granted and be tolerant of others' beliefs and ways of exploration ♡ Always look at your path logically; if it still *feels* right, you'll know you're not lost, just backpacking on new terra incognita ☉ ☽ Above all, I want you to enjoy this magickal mystery tour on my imperfect circle ♡ The unexplored life ain't worth the fare ☉ ← STARTING POINT.

Helen Chappell
☉
NYC
11/11/73

CONTENTS

1
FOLK MAGICK—BEGINNINGS AND ENDS
13

2
HERB MAGICK—LADY'S SLIPPER AND DRAGON'S BLOOD
33

3
DIVINATION—HEXAGRAMS AND STARS
55

4
THE PERFECT OBJECT—AMULETS AND TALISMANS
81

5
GYPSY MAGICK—PEOPLE OF EARTH AND STARS
105

6
VOODOO—DAMBALLA AND LE GRAND ZOMBI
125

7
WICCA—THE LADY AND THE HORNED GOD
145

8
SATANISM—THE BLACK MASS AND THE DEVIL'S TUNE
165

9
RITUAL MAGICK—ANGELS AND DEMONS IN THE CIRCLE
189

WHERE TO FIND IT
209

BIBLIOGRAPHY
211

Chappell

1

FOLK MAGICK—BEGINNINGS AND ENDS

Imagine that you are a small child, suddenly abandoned on a strange planet. You must survive in a strange world, populated with odd animals and strange plants. Water falls out of the sky. Sometimes a yellow ball comes up into that sky and there is light. Then the big yellow ball crosses the heavens and disappears. A pale white ball appears. It doesn't give off any light. In fact, the sky is very dark. Stranger still, this silver ball appears and disappears in regular cycles. Sometimes, it gets unbearably hot; othertimes, it is unbearably cold. You must contend with fierce animals who are out to make a meal of you, and try to trap smaller, more helpless ones to eat yourself. In the winter, you grub for roots and what animals you can find. You try to stay warm and away from the weather.

After a few years or millenniums of this sort of life, you begin to notice something. Everything is moving in an order. A cycle. A pattern. But just when you think you've got all that figured out, and you're scraping by, there's something new. A drought or a flood. Some totally new and inexplicably hostile animal that seems to think you're filet mignon. Or an erupting volcano. There's always something to watch out for, some unexpected thing that might snuff your life, so arduously fought for, out.

Because it's the only life you know, you learn how to cope. You learn how to survive everything except the anxiety.

When you have a chance to sit and think, you begin to notice certain things. That big yellow ball in the sky, for instance. Sort of like an eye, watching you. When the eye goes away, so does light and life. But when the smaller silver ball is in the sky, darkness surrounds you. And strange things happen in the dark. Noises. Rustlings, rumblings. Chirps. Roars. Screams. Squeals. Sometimes it seems like a pair of horns. You notice this silver ball affects your moods, your menses, and all the other living things in your environment. The animals seem to have some strange affinity with this silver ball too. They move about under its influence.

Because you live very closely with your world, for your survival depends entirely on the whims of the environment, you feel a great affinity with all the other things that are living with you. Rocks and bushes, flowers and animals all seem to be motivated by a personality, by a force very close to your own spirit. You learn to respect them, to accept them as beings possessed with a soul like your own.

Another strange thing catches your attention. There seem to be two kinds of everything. And one of them has the ability to produce, from some mysterious recess in its body, miniature replicas of itself. And these miniature replicas grow up. Birth is a mysterious thing. In your observations, you feel that even rocks and plants can give birth.

And then you see something die. A deer lies down on its side gasping for air, then becomes very still. Cautiously, you walk over and poke at it. It doesn't move. You yell, kicking at it. It doesn't move. In the course of your wanderings, you notice that as the land gets colder, the plants and trees seem to die also. They lose their leaves and foliage, wither away, and like the deer, sort of molder back into the earth.

Gradually, you begin to notice that things move in cycles. You realize your survival and the survival of the things you need for food and shelter depend on the movement of the sun and the moon, those two strange eyes that always seem to be watching you from the sky.

You draw some analogies in your mind. The sun is like a father, nourishing and bringing light to the world. The moon is like the mother, giving birth, swelling and receding every twenty-eight lights and darks. You begin to see them as personalities, capricious and unpredictable as humans. Perhaps they are the great father and mother, and they came together to make you and put you here. But suppose they get mad and refuse to continue traveling across the sky as they are supposed to? Then what are you going to do?

One day you are running away from an angry saber-tooth, or watching a volcano erupt, and it suddenly occurs to you that maybe you've done something to offend Father or Mother. Or, perhaps you've just found a whole field of really nice juicy berries lying in the sun, and you wonder if the Father and Mother made them just for you. Well, if they're like you, if they were sitting right there with you, you'd want to offer them some to express your gratitude, wouldn't you? So, you look up into the sky, hold up a handful of berries, and offer your thanks.

One terrible winter, the deer are few and far between. You've gotten to rather like eating meat, and you miss your food supply. Could it be that the spirit governing all the deer has taken offense at you for killing too many of his people? You finally find a deer, half starved and weak, but food. Before you kill it, you offer your thanks to the deer spirit for allowing you one last chance to eat.

So the first gods are born, from a sense of helplessness and a sense of great wonder. The sun and moon put you here. If you are good to them, they will allow you to stay, and keep you from starving or being eaten by something larger than you. Just as the Deer Spirit must look like a deer, or the Tree Spirit is a big tree, so Mother must look like a woman, and Father must look like a man. After all, you are their child, and children look like their parents.

Maybe, by this time, you've found a mate and settled into a tribe of relatives. Grandmother, who has that amazing ability to give birth to most of the members of the community, is treated with a great deal of respect. After all, wasn't it her idea to start planting seeds to grow corn and quit moving all over the place? So, Grandmother is in charge of making sure that the Great Mother stays happy, makes everything fruitful and multiply. And Grandmother has much wisdom, because she is old and has seen a lot. Wasn't she the one who gathered together the herbs and plants that cured wicked bites from marauding tree sloths? Grandmother's word settles all disputes. And if she gets mad at you, don't you get sick, just a little? And when your sister couldn't get pregnant, wasn't it Grandmother who went out and talked to the Great Mother about the necessity of impregnating Oga? And Grandmother's dream that gave you the rituals and charms for catching game?

And Grandfather is no slouch either. After hunting the woods for years, he knows every rock and every tree by name. The Great Father, he assures everyone, directs his hunting. When the Grandmother confers with the Corn Spirit, Grandfather can parlay with the Spirit of the Bison. He knows how to bring in the meat, and the best times to attack the tribe over the hill. When he speaks around the campfire on long winter nights, he is speaking with the power of the Great Father Sun. Life is still nasty, brutish, and short, but at least you know where you stand.

But most important, the elders are the keepers of knowledge. They direct and head the rituals of passage. Life, birth, and death are all attended by certain prescribed ceremonies. These rites make sure that the dead do not walk, that they do not bother the living; they insure that couplings lead to fertility and birth, and they pro-

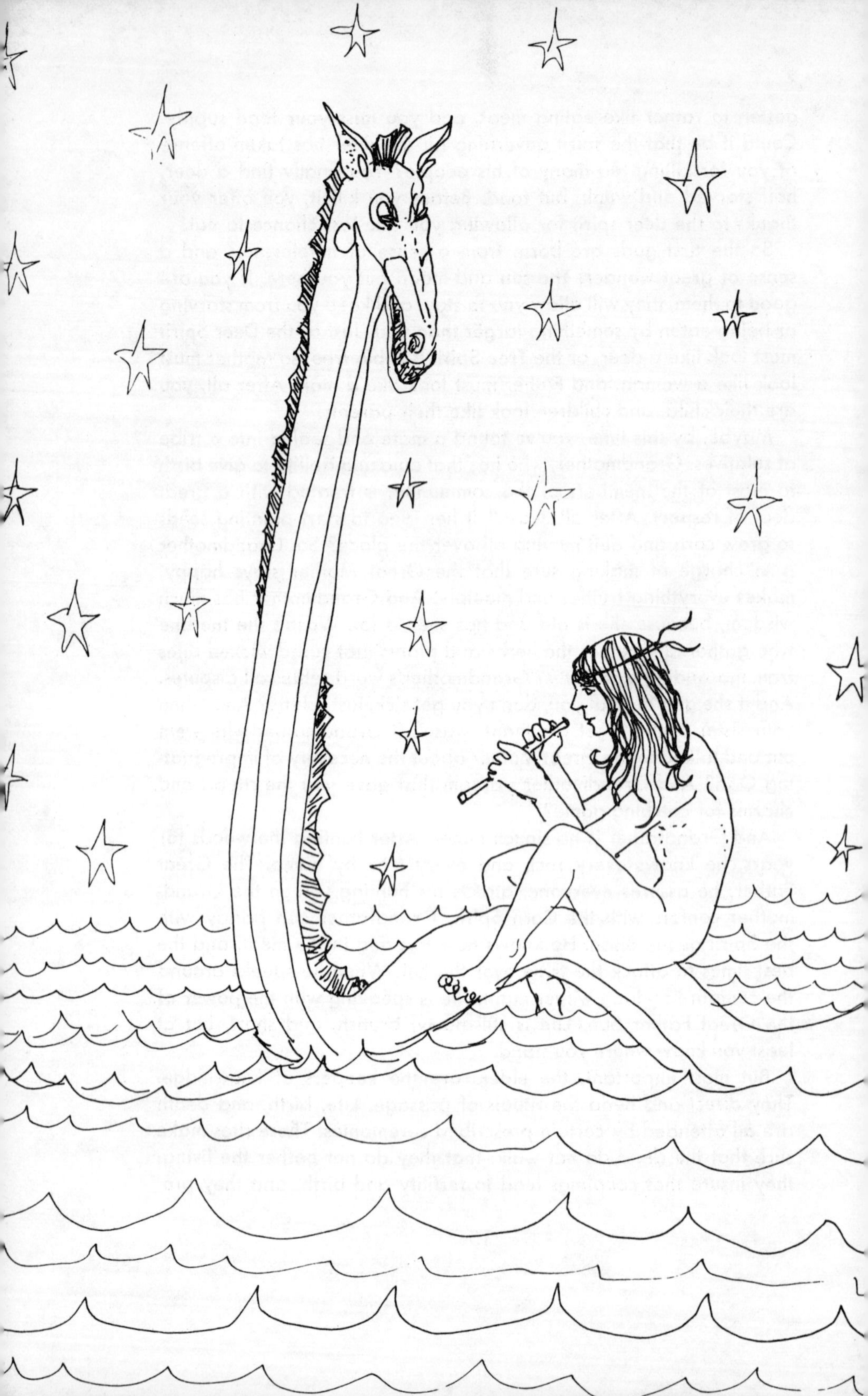

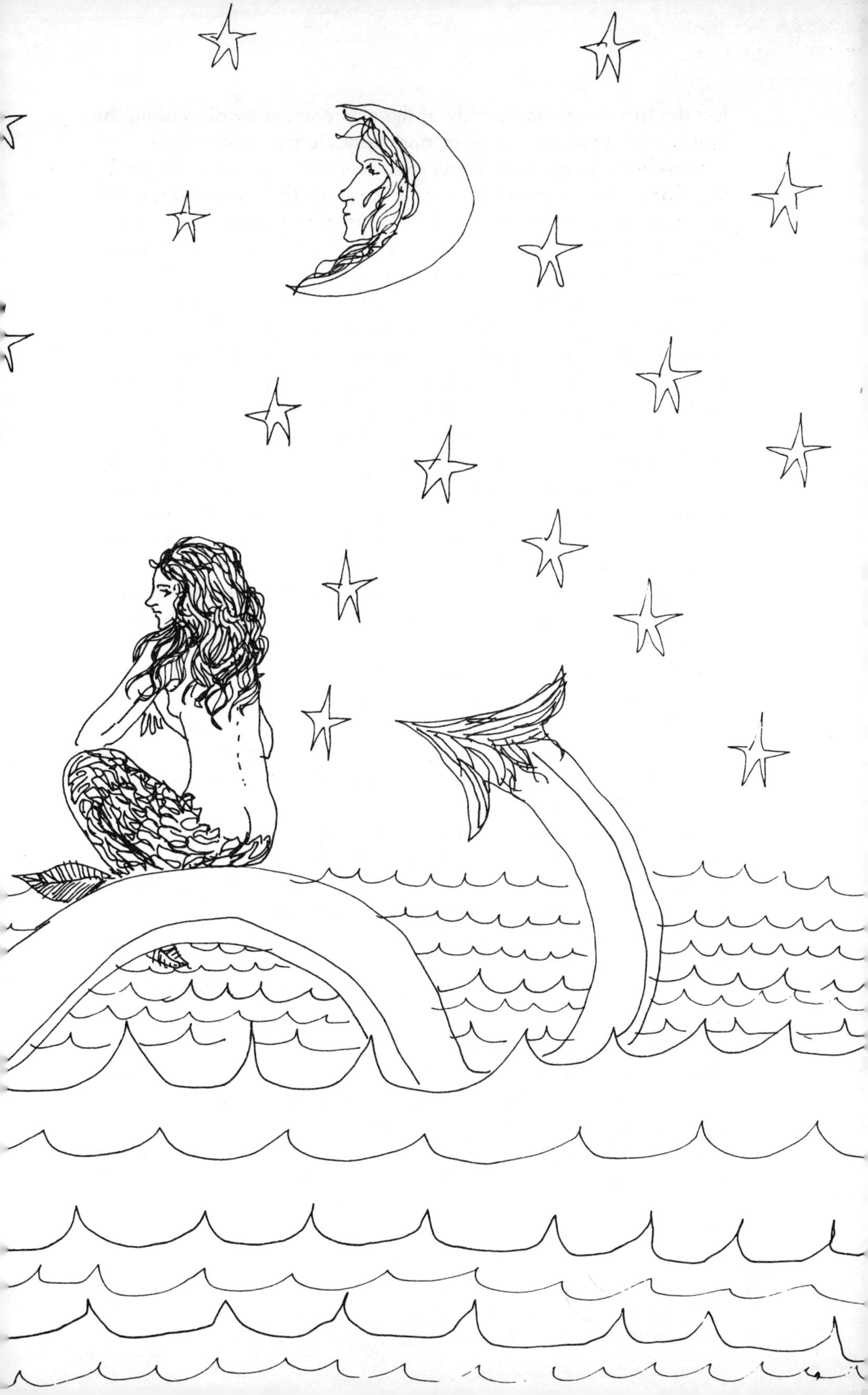

tect the tribe from the hostility of the environment by dispensing the appropriate sacrifices, prayers, and thanks to the right people.

Provided you manage to survive, eventually you are taught by the elders and initiated how to receive all their knowledge. The secrets and mysteries are carefully handed to you by your parents and grandparents; in turn it will be your duty to pass the legends and ancient secrets on to your own children.

Now it is your role to settle disputes, to read the omens of the spirits and the gods, to make sure that proper protocol is observed, to choreograph the dances and ceremonies that mark the rites of passage, to study the properties of medicine and religion, and to use your power to influence the ecology for the good of the tribe.

You learn that art should imitate nature to insure a successful hunt or a bumper crop; you direct everyone to go out into the corn fields right after the spring planting and copulate on the ground to show the Moon Goddess what you need. You learn to dress up in the skins of animals and rehearse tomorrow's hunt so that there will be meat for dinner. You make a doll of an ailing person and treat the object as if it were the person so that the evil spirits causing the disease will go from the real person into the doll, which you will then burn, trapped full of evil spirits.

To insure your sexual potency, you carry about your neck a small stone in the shape of a phallus. To appease the anger of the gods, you offer one of your number to them as a sacrifice; you learn that hair, blood, and urine are essences of your body, and they must be very carefully disposed of lest they should fall into the hands of an enemy, who, by destroying them, will destroy you.

You realize the power of the spirits of air, earth, fire, and water, and you learn how to make them your allies with ceremonies and chants. You observe the taboos that might offend a helpful spirit and the ways of protecting yourself against evil spirits.

As you sit around the campfire at night, you tell the old stories of the dead who walk by night and drink the blood of the living. You tell of men who have gone mad, possessed by the spirit of a wolf or bear whose spirit they did not offer the proper thanks to in the hunt. You learn the fear of the night and the power of the gods of earth and stars. You watch the cycles and the behavior of the animals, the rocks, and the plants and you learn to understand their spirits, for they are your allies and aid your work.

Caves make way for straw huts, and straw huts make way for clusters of wooden shacks. The wheel is invented, and what we call civilization begins. But the old ways still survive, sometimes half forgotten in the passage of time, sometimes supplanted by new beliefs and new rituals. But time moves slowly, and the old ways are comfortably secure. Art continues to awesomely imitate nature, and even with the arrival of the one god, the old ways are remembered because they worked.

What once made perfect sense when you lived in a cave attains a great mystery when you live in a walled town, drinking ale and slumbering by the fireplace on a winter's night. And, yet, the mystery adds to the faith. Ideas travel slowly, and the idea of someone being able to make marks on a piece of paper for another person to understand is astounding. There may still be wolves outside the walls but the corn is planted in neat rows that grow to touch the sky. There is time now to think of things that are of the spirit and not of the flesh; yet the old ways still survive, long after the original meaning has been lost.

Now there is time for study. It is noticed that the stars move in a certain way, and the gods speak with new voices. Food can be tamed; it no longer has a spirit. The dead still may walk, or perhaps they are the invention of a being whose sole purpose is to harass humanity. The protocol of the wilderness gives way to the protocol of the town and then to the court etiquette of the city. Old trees, rooted deep in the earth, do not die out quickly, though they put out new branches.

And these mysteries are the beginnings of all magicks; even while humanity changes from natural ritual to philosophical ritual in answer to the question of Why Are We Here?, people still retain their gods in their own images. And while the gods may change their masks and have a whole set of different passports, even to the extent of merging into one androgynous omnipotent deity, humanity still bribes, supplicates, blackmails, and cajoles them for succor.

Even as a single cell must carry some memory of its origins in the muck of time, so do men and women come into the world vaguely remembering some fear and joy from the primeval past. When the walled towns become skyscraper cities, humanity still feels small, impotent, and helpless in the face of nature—those primeval insecurities are still remembered, still feared. Just as certain basic concepts of clothing do not change, so do certain basic instincts remain the same, generation after generation. Only the ornaments and the cut will change to suit.

Our feeling of alienation from the world we live in has never really left us. To conquer our fears, we attach ourselves to the rituals of the past, and even the most revolutionary of us still harbors some trace of the old cave dweller's uneasiness with the future. Our instincts for survival are strong, and they are balanced by our paranoia concerning the unknown.

That which we have not been able to explain we have called magick, and we have turned to it when every other recourse fails, for our fear of nature is matched only by our fascination with the inevitability of its cycles of life, birth, and death. In a world where the only constant is change, it is not unnatural that we have managed to retain the motions, if not the logic, behind what have become meaningless rituals to us. After all, we can understand the origins, relate their relevance to our own condition, and perhaps in this way take off the last masks of the gods and the last masks of our souls.

When you look carefully at a spell, such as making a wish on the first evening star (that's a very basic one that every child knows) you may begin to look past its "weirdness" to the underlying reasons for it. The stars twinkling in the darkness of night are like small reassurances that the sun will come up in the morning, for even in the darkest hours of night, there is still light, still hope. What you hope for is your wish; and you want it to come true.

Most magick is simply an abstract imitation of something that happens in nature. Since nature is constant, even when she is fickle and angry, an imitation of her mysteries is a sort of dress rehearsal for your desires. When you perform an act of magick, you are assuming the role of the most powerful form in the universe—nature—in hopes that your imitation will produce the same inevitable effect that she has.

Consider: "What is all this meaningless dribble I'm reciting here?" Well, each of these sounds (abracadabra) corresponds to some sound in nature . . . ahhh. Rapport. Now you begin to understand.

A spell can be a two-year complexity, or it can be a two-second utterance of a single word, yet it carries a powerful symbolism rooted deep in the consciousness of your culture. Why do you think they always show vampires recoiling in horror at a silver cross? In Christian society, the cross is a symbol of good. If you tried the same thing on a Taoist vampire, he'd probably just laugh at you and keep coming, sharpening his fangs as he approached. Hence, it is up to you to make sure that you understand the symbolism behind each spell you cast.

All magicks are folk magicks. I doubt that you will ever see a horse sitting out in the woods under a full moon reciting some enchantment. Folk magick is the last remnant of the ancient nature beliefs that were once the basis of all religion, medicine, philosophy, and survival.

To accept a superstition as a firm belief is not enough. You must understand where it has come from, what changes it has gone through with each succeeding culture, and how it relates to you—if it does, and what emotional response its symbolism has for you.

We all know as surely as stepping on a crack would break your mother's back that horseshoes were good luck charms, that black cats were to be avoided, along with thirteen and walking under ladders. We knew that wishes made on falling stars would be granted, and if you dropped a knife, you would have a visitor. We all grew up with those half-serious superstitions, and thousands more like them. But we never knew why.

For instance, did you know that thirteen has always been an unlucky number because it was one more than twelve? Twelve is four groups of three, and both four and three have always been lucky numbers, for they relate to the genitals and fertility. Strength was added to this belief when there were thirteen at the Last Supper of Christ. The thirteenth was, of course, Judas, who betrayed Christ. In the Middle Ages, when the devil was making more personal appearances than he seems to be doing these days, it was firmly believed that he lurked in corners and under bridges and ladders just waiting to trap unwary souls. The Egyptians venerated cats; they also had a reputation for being evil magicians. Black cats were commonly assumed to be the familiars of witches, who were bent upon some unbearable evil. To touch wood was to assure oneself of good luck from the very beginning, for the spirits that lived in trees were known to be friendly to humans. Spiders will bring rain if stepped on, for spiders were once considered sacred to the rain gods.

All folk beliefs are based on some ancient logic of sympathetic magick, but sometimes they are so shopworn that you cannot begin to even determine origins. Why would your lover come to you if you dropped a dishcloth? Or, for that matter, what has dropping a knife, fork, or spoon have to do with the arrival of respectively a man, a woman, or a child?

Of course, a new-born child should be carried to the top of the house as soon as possible so it will grow up high-minded; but why in the world would a frog tied around its neck ease its teething pain? Could it be the primitive belief that pain can be transferred from one living thing to another by physical contact?

Frogs and toads play a large part in folk magick. For instance, everyone knows that handling toads is the best way to get warts, but how many people know in this day and age that a live frog, sliced open and tied around an aching, arthritic joint, will dry out the pain? Killing toads will make the cows go dry, however, so watch it if you've got arthritis and you're living on a dairy farm. I knew a man who could read frogs. He could tell what tomorrow's weather would be by the way the bullfrogs and needeeps were singing. High whining trills, he said, meant a day of rain, while low contented croaks meant it would be warm and sunny. Toads and frogs appear quite frequently in fairy tales as bewitched princes and other great dignitaries. They were once thought to be associates of witches and friends of the devil. Ancients saw them as personifications of the spirits that lived in creeks and streams. Anyone who has dissected a frog in biology will remember how very close to human anatomy theirs is supposed to be. Until a few hundred years ago, frogs were supposed to be mysteriously self-generating creatures who were born in mud from nothing; no one made the connection between tadpoles and frogs. They did think that frogs and toads were familiars of witches and demons.

Many common superstitions concern birds. Whip-poor-wills, for instance, are said to gather around a house where there is a death. A bird flying in the window is an omen that a death will soon take place in the house. If you hear a mourning dove before breakfast, it will rain before evening.

Birds defy all the laws and fly. Although it still amazes me that one can get a big metal box off the ground and into the air, it is easy to see how soaring into the sky would place birds closer to the gods, would make them the messengers and servants of the deities. There is also a primitive belief that the spirit of the dead should travel upward toward the gods, probably in the form of a bird; thus, the bird becomes symbolic of the souls of the dead. Winged men are fairly common in mythology, perhaps expressing all those secret desires to get closer to the bringers of life. Angels in medieval paintings are rather soft, luminous non-sexual beings with white, softly feathered doves' wings, bringing tidings from the Lord or carrying on some divine business.

Conversely, Satan and his demons always have ugly-looking leathery wings like bats. Bats are not well beloved. A spell to curse someone includes grinding up baked bat's wings into their food. Because they are nocturnal creatures who like to live in dark places like caves, they were regarded as Satan's pets.

Bats are associated with another universal archetype, the vampire. Aside from Bela Lugosi's Dracula, based on Bram Stoker's novel, whose vampire was based on a real man named Vlad Tepes, who was not a vampire but a minor Wallachian warlord (are you still following me?) whose favorite method of executing people who incurred his anger was impaling them on large stakes, which gave rise

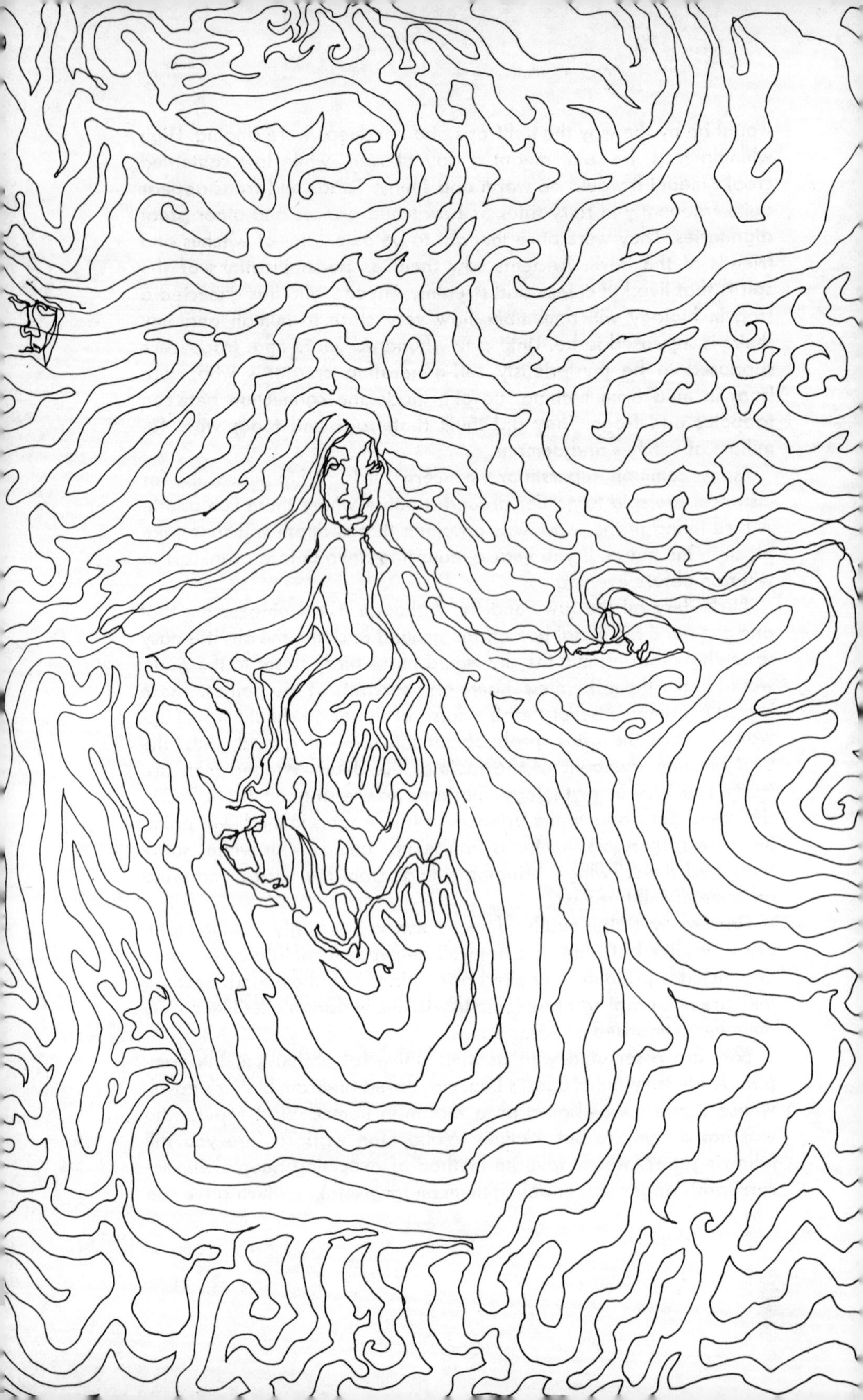

to the legend that he was a vampire . . . well, vampires seem to have been with us as long as death and the fear of the dead. From ancient China to twentieth-century London, the belief in this strange creature has prevailed. Now, a vampire may be called many different things and appear in many different forms, but there is always one single thread; someone dies, but they are not dead; they rise up from the dead to drink the blood of the living; they lead a sort of half-life. Ground rules for vampires vary from place to place, of course, but there is always an antidote for getting rid of them. Sometimes a corpse is dug up, and a wooden stake of oak, hawthorn, or ash is struck through the heart (Vlad Tepes's favorite execution). Sometimes the vampire is permitted to move about only in darkness, sunlight turning him into a charcoal brick. Silver daggers, bullets, or crosses will also put the poor thing permanently out of his misery.

The power of metals appears frequently in folk magick. Silver, probably because of its ability to reflect light, is supposed to be an excellent charm against illnesses and disease. Silver is also the metal sacred to the Lunar Goddess, the Great Mother and protectress. Another metal frequently mentioned as having great protective powers is iron. Until quite recently, iron was the hardest metal known. It is the symbol of strength and power, for both weapons and plowshares are made from it. A Pennsylvania German superstition advises one to keep an iron bar or horseshoe bar above the windows and doors to keep away witches. In the Ozarks, some people will wear an iron ring made from a nail to ward off the spavins. Silver bullets and iron stakes will kill the werewolf.

Were-animals are as common as vampires. There are werewolves, werecats, werepanthers, werelions, werebears, and even a wereseal. Unlike the vampire myth, which has some origins in the similarity of sex and death, the were-animal myth concerns a human possessed by the spirit of an animal. Sometimes this change is brought about by offending the god of the animal, sometimes it is *sought* as a means of adopting the fierce qualities of the animal in order to assure success in hunting or battle or whatever. By becoming the animal, one assumes the strength and attributes of the animal.

However, both the vampire and were-animal legends concern a form of cannibalism, rooted in the primitive belief that to consume the enemies' hearts or livers or brains is to assume the courage and intelligence of the enemy. The magick of blood is very potent, for blood is the life force, the precious essence of birth and death, and the shedding of blood is considered a great charge of energy.

Hence the necessity of sacrifice. It has been noted that in certain times and cultures, the ruler of the tribe was expected to reign only for a certain amount of time. At the end of that time, when his life essences had been drained by the responsibility of power, he was ceremonially sacrificed to the gods, so the letting of his blood and release of his life essence would appease the gods and insure fertility.

This awe of blood extends to the menses of women. Even in our society today, menstruation is regarded as strange and sometimes repulsive, even by women themselves. The dread of menses is expressed in the fear of losing blood and life force, and it is connected with the lunar cycle and the Great Mother. In some societies, women are excluded from all activity during their menses in the belief that they are polluted or dangerous because of this loss of the life force. However, menstrual blood is often an ingredient in magick potions, especially aphrodisiacs.

Sigmund Freud, bless his male chauvinist heart, pointed out that grief was a selfish thing, attached to guilt feelings about how badly the mourner felt he had treated the deceased. It was always important to see the dead off with a proper show and enough goodies to sustain them on through the next world, where, it was assumed, things were pretty much as they are here. The rituals attached to death almost always emphasize great pomp and ceremony. While we no longer feel it necessary to pack a suitcase for the dead, we seem to be leaving a lunch bag by laying the corpse out in its best outfit, carefully cosmetized, coiffed, and coffined to meet the Last Judgment. A suitable piece of marking stone is placed over the burial spot and sometimes once or twice a year some relative will lay flowers on the grave, even with the most serious doubts about the survival of the soul into heaven or hell or anyplace else. The idea that the dead will do what they are not supposed to do—walk around and annoy the living, possibly even revenge themselves—is as ancient as the mystery of death itself. Fear of the dead—of ghosts—is an old and honorable practice. It seems to be an instinct we are born with, although there are trance mediums who consider communication with the souls of the departed as a perfectly normal occupation. Indeed, whole religions are organized upon the firm belief that the dead continue their existence on another plane and are ready and willing to help the living out. Presumably, by virtue of being dead, one receives special powers and honors. The ancient Roman saying *Di mortis ni nisi bonum*—"speak no ill of the dead"—is quite wise. You never know who might be listening, or from where. I have a marvelous aunt who consoled me as a child by saying I shouldn't fear the dead but the living. Wise advice from a wise woman. But it is said that one who dies violently or is buried in unhallowed ground or without the proper ceremonies will return as a ghost to plague the living until they do something about this negligence.

Whole books have been devoted to debating the existence of ghosts, and they occupy a great deal of the world's literature and folklore. The belief, the need to believe that there is survival after we have outworn our flesh, expresses man's need to feel that life has more point than just being nasty, brutish, and short. However, if you want someone to merely pass to the other side and leave you alone, you should clip a piece of the corpse's hair, tie it up, and put it up somewhere. That way you will always know where the person's spirit is. If you want to haunt someone else, give them the lock of hair.

I've never seen a werewolf, I've known some people who, while not exactly bloodsuckers in the literal sense, could pass as *psychic* vampires. They just seem to have something about them that sucks away your will power, your energy, and your identity. Sort of living vampires. But the genuine bloodsucking sort, no. Ghosts, I'm not too sure of. It has been said that practically everyone will see a ghost at some time in his life. Usually they don't appear as The Woman in White or the Skeleton in Chains, but look just as they did when they were alive. They may speak or not, or they can be as solid or as filmy as they want.

It might be fun to be a ghost, at least for a while, before going on to reincarnation as a toothbrush in Des Moines or whatever lies after death. But a werewolf or a vampire, no. In the Middle Ages, it was popularly believed that one need only perform the following ritual to become a werewolf: Go to a crossroads under a full moon. Remove your clothing and place them in a pile. Walk three times around them while urinating and you'll be off and howling till sunrise. Becoming a vampire is a bit more difficult. Do you have red hair and green eyes? Hair on the palms of your hands? Strange-looking canines? Have you been hanging around with gentlemen in long opera cloaks? (Look, Count, it's the middle of the day, why are you running around in that tuxedo?) Any or all of the above could have qualified you for a stake through the heart and a quick cremation. As a matter of interest, there are forms of psychosis in which a person will act like an animal (lycanthropy) to the extent of crawling around on all fours and trying to attack anything that moves, and other forms of mental illness where a human develops a ravenous craving for human blood and flesh, living or dead. These cases are rare, but they do exist. Doctors say such diseases are forms of sado-masochism coupled with necrophilia. Another interesting argument for the vampire-werewolf-ghost syndrome is a genetic abnormality that results in the human body being covered with an overabundance of hair. This syndrome is by no means uncommon, and in a mild form is known as Fraser's Syndrome.

Supernatural beings have very little function in the art of practical magick, but it is better to know what *may* be out there lurking around the next corner when you're dealing with the occult. The belief in the existence of these creatures is by no means dead, as they are supposed to be. It is very much a part of the tradition and folklore of many parts of this country. Two hundred miles south of New York City, there are people who will swear on the Bible that they have seen a strange loping creature with wings flittering through the cranberry bogs, usually dragged up in the summer season and called the Jersey Devil. The yeti, also called the Satchsquach, or the missing link, is supposed to be running around out there somewhere, and there is no particular reason to doubt that either. A supernatural being, like an arrested man, should be deemed innocent until proven guilty.

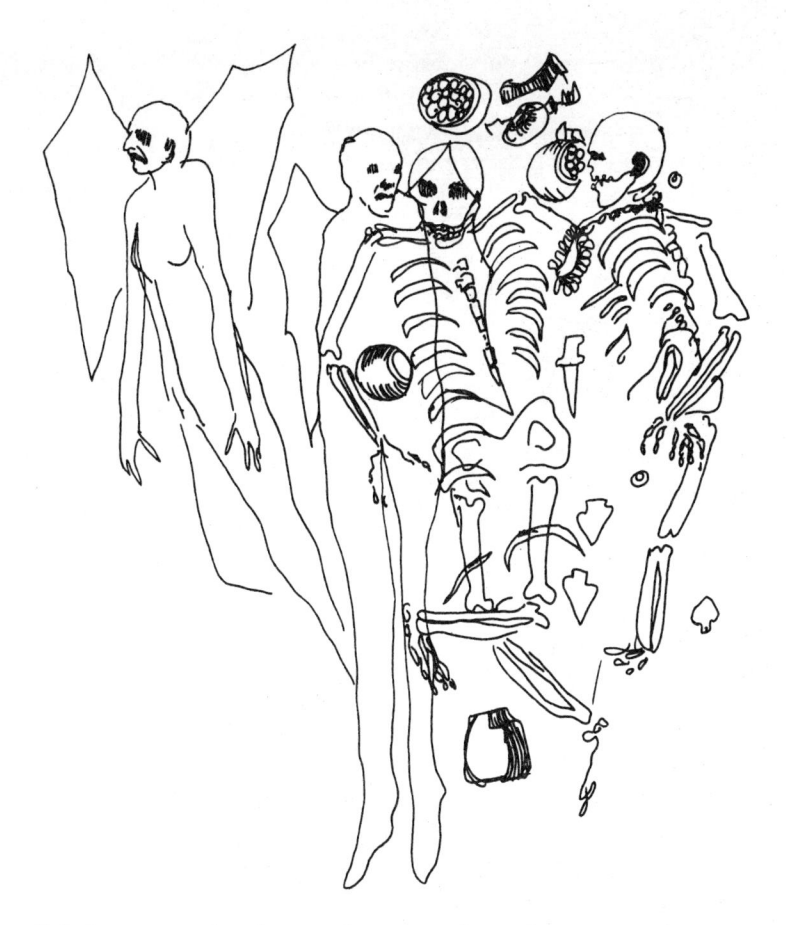

    To get back to where we once belonged is to return to a fear and awe of nature. Is a belief that magick will work, based on the theory that art must imitate nature, any more difficult to accept than this: You, that same five-year-old deposited in a strange land at the beginning of time, are now a five-year-old deposited in a world where you can turn a knob on a box and get little pictures moving around the surface? Is it stranger than having some man come on the screen to reassure you in an omnipotent tone that spraying something from a metal container into your armpits will get you flooded with Hollywood contracts and proposals from Greek shipping magnates?

While searching for ways to protect ourselves from nature, we have isolated ourselves from its very essence. Sophisticated urban-educated folk have always looked down on rural people, be they farmers in the Ozarks or Masai cattle herders in Kenya as primitives, because they lack the technology that isolates them from nature, regarding their beliefs as unenlightened and illogical. Childlike, in fact.

But these so-called primitive people do not cower in doubt and fear any more than we do, and perhaps less so. It is man's nature to seek a logical explanation to any problem that besets him. People who are engaged in a day-by-day fight for survival do not have the time to indulge themselves in senseless fantasies or illogical beliefs. To live in constant contact with the natural world is to be attuned to its cycles. Inevitably, one culture will absorb and transmute the basic principles of another it comes into contact with. Yet, certain cultural beliefs seem to be basic, at one time or another in all cultures of the world, as illustrated by the universal belief in vampires, werewolves, and ghosts.

Most cultures have looked to the sun and moon as deities in charge of the fertility and continuance of the earth's cycles; they have harbored a belief that there is a life force, or essence, in everything on earth, living and non-living, and that these essences could be appealed to for good or evil. There has been a universal belief that a sympathetic imitation will produce a real effect.

When we left nature for technology, we left the operative principles of spellcasting behind, to take up a more mechanized form of magick.

Only if we understand the roots of magick will we be able to understand the trunk and work with its many branches.

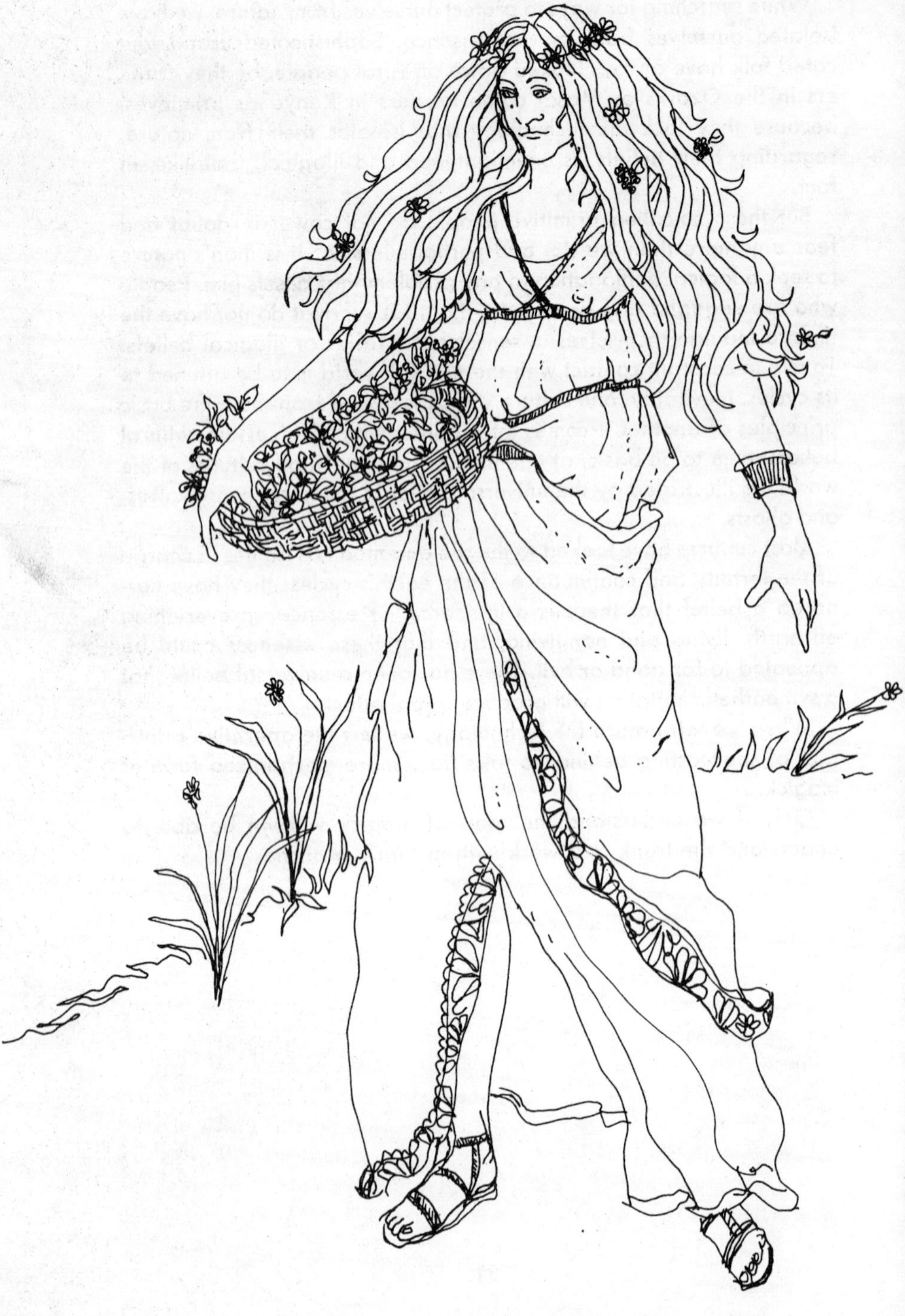

2
HERB MAGICK—LADY'S SLIPPER AND DRAGON'S BLOOD

Much virtue in herbs; little in men.
OLD GERMAN PROVERB

The ancient and honorable affinity between man and plant is one of the primary elements of magick. From the earliest times, humans have depended on the vegetative environment for food, clothing, shelter, and beauty. Becoming civilized, however you want to define *that*, is the direct result of tribes staying in one place in order to cultivate plants.

Even canyon dwellers tend their walkup jungles with the devotion the Vestal Virgins lavished on the temple fires. There is a need to have green living things, even when the earth is covered with cement... and some people even talk to their plants to make them grow. The Backster Effect confirmed an idea that sorcerers and witches have felt for centuries—that plants, like other living things, have feelings and do respond to kind thoughts and love just like animals and people. Bless their little nervous systems, plants have a sort of soul. And now that same theory is being extended to cover non-living things, like rocks and machines. It is one of the operative tenets of magick that was common knowledge to any Stone Age dweller, an idea presented to Plato by Socrates as the theory of the forms, and to occultism by such learned men as Cornelius Agrippa, whose *Occult Philosophie* notes the occult virtue of herbs in magick, based on neo-Platonic theory.

Plants, trees, and flowers have so fascinated man that every culture has had its own particular myths, gods, and legends assigned to the creation of vegetation. Athena invented the olive tree as a gift for the citizens of her city. The Virgin's tears fell to the ground as lily-of-the-valley. The old calendars turned on the planting and harvesting seasons. No festivals were more important than those dedicated to the Goddess of the Earth. Cereals were sacred plants to the ancient Greeks, while the Druids saw their gods as the spirits that dwelt in oak trees. Both Horus and Brahma are represented by the lotus flower. There was a popular legend in the Middle Ages about a

Ragged Robin

MANDRAKE

secret race of plant men. Mandrakes lived in the deepest forests and ate human flesh. Peyote and mescalin were sacred plants of the Central American Indians, who ingested them as a part of their religious ceremonies. The visions produced by these magick plants are those of the gods. When intrigue was plentiful and adultery a capital crime, women would signal their lovers by the type of flowers they carried to a ball or party, and no Victorian lady was without a *Language of Flowers* to interpret her beaux' bouquets. A single red rose was present in the secret tribunals of the Inquisition as a reminder that the proceedings were *sub rosa*, or below the flower, whose meaning is silence.

The medicinal value of plants is both venerable and prehistoric. Until a century ago, almost all elixirs, tonics, salves, and compounds were based on plants. *Culpeper's Herbal*, a charming and informative book written by a London apothecary in the mid-1600's, is still a classic on medicinal and cosmetic herbs. In addition to being an apothecary, Nicholas Culpeper was also an herbalist of fierce dedication and a good astrologer. To each of the more than five hundred herbs listed in his book he assigned a ruling planet and described not only the plant but also where to find it, its virtues, and its medicinal effects. In addition to giving excellent descriptions of plants, Culpeper advised on their ruling planets, when to gather them, how to dry and keep them, giving very good instructions for compounding elixirs and oils that can then be made from roots, barks, berries, and leaves.

The ancient doctors often decided that a plant resembling an organ of the human body held the means to cure it. Lungwort, for instance, looks like a pair of lungs and was often prescribed for the disorders of breathing.

In a time when it was solemnly recorded that Queen Elizabeth took a bath once a year "whether she needed it or nay," scented plants became very important to mask the rather strong odors that clung to houses, clothes, and people. Sweet perfumes and pomanders were much in fashion among people of both sexes and all classes. The whole movement toward the East was more a mercantile quest for spices than a real attempt to do battle with the Moors and Turks.

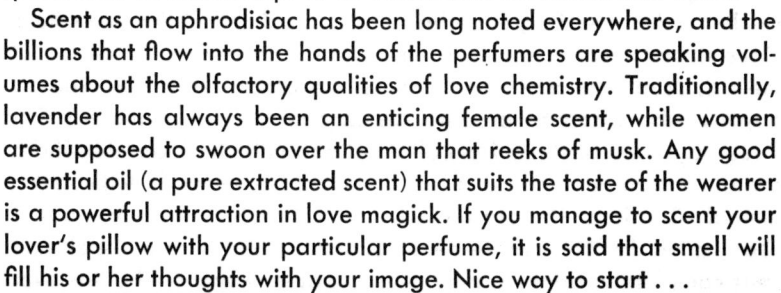

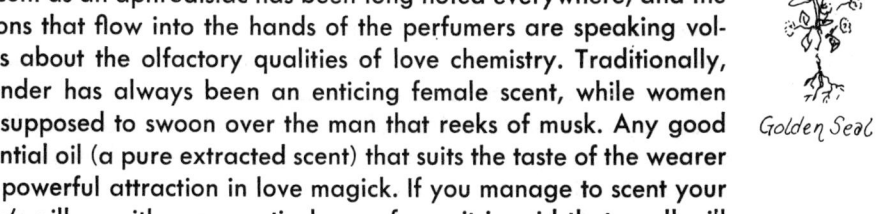

Scent as an aphrodisiac has been long noted everywhere, and the billions that flow into the hands of the perfumers are speaking volumes about the olfactory qualities of love chemistry. Traditionally, lavender has always been an enticing female scent, while women are supposed to swoon over the man that reeks of musk. Any good essential oil (a pure extracted scent) that suits the taste of the wearer is a powerful attraction in love magick. If you manage to scent your lover's pillow with your particular perfume, it is said that smell will fill his or her thoughts with your image. Nice way to start . . .

While liberally dousing herself with rosewater and musk, Madame de Montespan, who knew quite a bit about magick, consumed and fed her lover, Louis XIV, all sorts of aphrodisiacs to keep them *both* turned on. Her list of aphrodisiacs included chocolate, lettuce, chicory, carrots, peppers, celery, and asparagus. It was, she said, the asparagus that really did the number, but Louis liked oysters seasoned with dill, sweet basil, and bergamont. He must have been a very sexy Sun King, for he is said to have fathered two hundred children.

It is really too bad that Madame de Montespan didn't know about *cannabis sativa*, also known as grass, pot, or marijuana. This currently popular and illegal herb was used for centuries to stimulate love, increase the appetite, and ease pain. A modern sorceress I know saves her seeds and grinds them liberally into her dinners with her lover.

The anti- and pro-drug factions of occult practitioners may squabble forever, but one old spell book advises the magician to strain hempseeds into wine as an excellent tonic potion to be taken before consulting with demons. The "witches' flying ointment" (did you really think they flew on broomsticks?) smeared on the body before the Sabbath was a salve compounded of nightshade, aconite, and cinquefoil—all of which are known for their narcotic properties. Nightshade or belladonna is particularly good at inducing hallucinations of flying, but all of the ingredients in the flying ointments can be deadly poison if ingested. Ritual drugtaking has had a fairly respectable history. Its purpose was never to get high, but to break down the barriers between realities of the seen and the unseen. Stricter occultists say that even caffeine, tobacco, and wine are drugs forbidden to the magician. Equally studious practitioners argue that hallucinations have always held a valid place in magick, and indeed are tools for perception and understanding of all the forces.

A very good way to crack open the doors of perception, as Aldous Huxley called the drug experience, is a ritual called the Black Fast. Once it was used by sorcerers who wanted to perform some act of the art, usually a death spell: hence the *black*. Now it is used by anyone who wants to prepare for any major act of the art. For three days, one abstains from all meat and milk. Both of these foods contain a high percentage of fats. They are heavy foods, with strong animal vibrations. The old reasoning was that heavy foods made a heavy mind. For the next three days, one meditates on the spell and fasts completely, drinking only a little water. Anyone who has ever been on a crash diet knows the giddiness and wavery, hysterical imbalance that result from fasting, together with a very acute tuning of all the senses. When all energy is directed toward one thought, under such intense emotions, there must be some correspondence with action.

Even though I grew up in the country, I really didn't start to understand herbs until I moved into the city and had to cook for myself; then I learned to experiment with herbs and spices. For me, there is a certain charm in all those neat little bottles labeled and lined up on the shelf. But while I was spending a fortune in the supermarket, someone pointed out to me that if I bought my own herbs, or gathered them directly from nature, I'd be saving myself a lot of movie money.

In magick, environment is all-important, and stores that specialize in herbs and spices have more feeling than some white tin container from the A&P. Besides, could you buy Yohimbee from the A&P? There is no fresh clover in the produce section, either. Knowing where to find the first spring violets or finding an oak tree that harbors mistletoe and is growing at a crossroads in a cemetery is a good thing. Gathering or growing your own herbs is not only economical, it also assures you that they're intended for what you want. Besides, getting out there with nature is good for your soul.

The deeper into magick and herb lore you get, the more herbs you find grow only in Tibet or Africa. Here is where you really need a good spice store, a place that understands the needs of magicians and stocks Yohimbee and lotus root, or can get them for you without a lot of embarrassing questions. Too many questions may be embarrassing on both sides, for health food and herb stores cannot prescribe cures or sell herbs for magickal purposes without appending "as curios only" to their lists. I've been trying for two years to convince my favorite herb store that I'm anything but an FDA inspector in drag. What I do with my herbs is my own silent business. Spice stores are usually less expensive, you can buy in bulk, and they have a charm all their own. I get off sometimes just looking at all the big jars of exotica and sniffing the air. And the mystique—well, it goes a long way when you're spellcasting just to make a journey for the ingredients in your spells, does that mystique of the spice store.

The ceremony of herb gathering is nice too. Arm yourself with a field guide to the plants and trees of the area, a knife, a trowel, and some bags to carry your goodies. Old-time herbalists always gathered their plants when the moon was full, for maximum strength. Plants should always be gathered from the high ground, where they don't have soggy roots. You should know if you want a spring, summer, or fall plant. Decide if you need shoots, blooms, or seeds. Roots and barks should be taken in the early spring or late fall. Herb collecting can start in the very early spring and continue right into the first snowfall. Middle and late spring are the best times to gather blossoming plants; early summer is good for leaves.

To dry out your plants, spread them in the sunshine, or hang them upside down in a cool, dry place. For fast drying, spread them out on a cookie sheet and let them bake out in a warm oven. Roots and barks should be taken in dry weather and turned in the oven. Store them in earthenware containers.

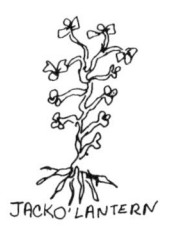

The trick to herb gathering is to take just what you need. To take too much is greedy, and damaging to most plants, which offends the Earth Goddess mightily. Usually, a few ounces of any one thing is enough to get you through a whole year's practicing.

Store your herbs in earthenware crocks and glass jars. Be sure to label them, or you'll end up flavoring your pasta with sassafras tea —uncool. It's also a nice idea to have a mortar and pestle to grind things into powder. There's a nice rhythm about chanting over a mortar that you just don't get with a blender, and it's good to keep in mind your spell while you're making the ingredients, by consecrating the herbs as you work.

All cultures and all magicks have placed a rather special dependence on the occult virtues of herbs and spices. They're a universal panacea for everything from bad luck to appeasing the gods. The closer a people are to nature, the more they know about the virtues of herbs and herb magick. Each plant has some special virtue of its own that may be released by brewing it into a tea, wearing it in a sack around the neck, burning it as incense, keeping it in a drawer or under a pillow, sprinkling it over food, stuffing your magick dolls with them, bathing in it, nursing yourself with it, or using it in cosmetics.

Once you're into herbs and herb magick, you're hooked. You start flavoring your Trix and taking three or four baths a day in chamomile and rosemary just because it feels so good. You hang orange balls in your closet and scent your drawers with lavender. You give up English Leather and Chanel for pure oils. You begin to collect little glass and crockery containers and shriek at the driver to stop in the middle of the turnpike because you've just spotted a whole clump of devil's paintbrush growing behind those beer cans back there. You make up little herb bags to give to your hairdresser when you can't tip him; your friends begin to complain about all those stupid weeds you have hanging up all over the house; and your mother refuses to visit you unless you stop telling her friends to use mint leaves as a facial.

No one ever said that herb incense will smell great, but the point of compounding incense has always been to attract the attention of the gods to the supplicant. As smoke drifts upward, your prayers are seen by the gods, carried on the sacred element of fire. In spellcasting, making the right atmosphere is important, and clouds of perfumed scent stir the olfactory senses. Choose herbs and spices that come under the influence of the gods and planets you want to influence, grind them together on a mortarboard, and burn the powder on charcoal during the spellcasting.

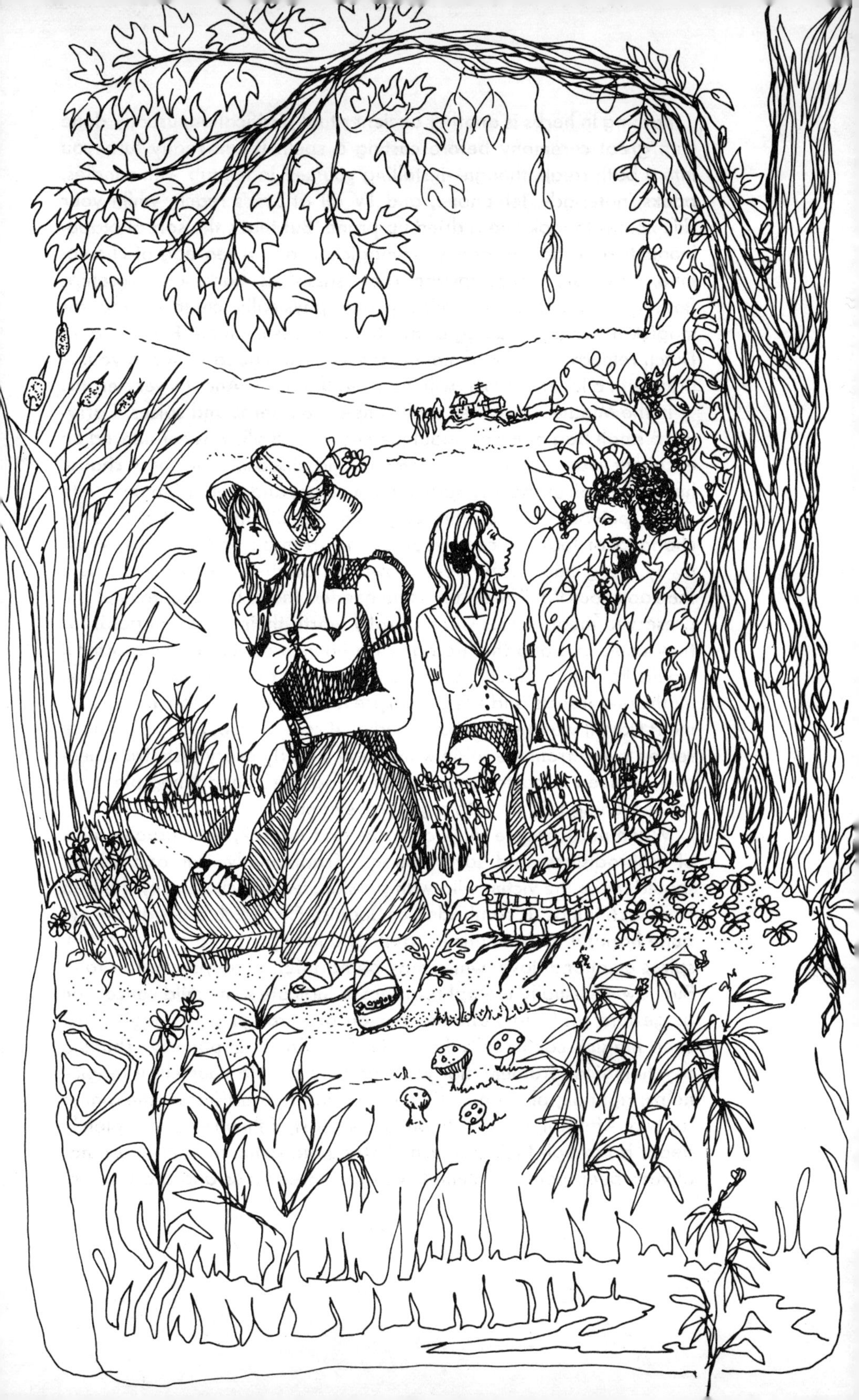

Bathing in herbs is another ancient ritual purification, usually done with great ceremony before casting a spell. It can really turn you into a bath freak, though—installing yourself in the tub with candles, books, notepads, telephone, and TV all at arm's reach, while your skin comes to look like a dried-up prune. But that's the sort of Napoleonic luxury that restores your magickal soul. A tea egg of chamomile, rosemary, mint, lovage root, sassafras bark, and rosehips floating in the tub symbolically and physically cleanses you for magickal work. A tea egg of five-finger grass is an old Pennsylvania Dutch remedy for lack of money, for it attracts good things to you. A bath with a lover in herbs will insure faithfulness. And it's very erotic.

In the Middle Ages, they really knew their herbs and spices. Carrying a small bag of herbs about the neck in red silk was considered an excellent way to ward off demons and disease. You must choose herbs and spices that are suited to your sign, and then grind them into a fine powder and sew the bag with red silk thread. It should be changed at least twice a year as the strength of the herbs wears away. Long ago, herbs were grown beside the kitchen door, where the cook could pull them up as he needed them. In those days of unpreserved meat, spices were literally worth their weight in gold, for they could prolong the lifespan of a haunch of venison long after it would have gone foul. Herbs were essential to preserve fabric from moths and insects and keep a corpse looking presentable until Judgment Day. If we are to believe medieval cookbooks, diners must have reeled away from the table with ulcers. Nearly every dish, from peacock sauteed in partridge gravy to rhubarb and hedgehog pie, calls for seasoning laid on with a generous hand.

When most people think of herbs and magick, they usually think of aphrodisiacs and love potions. Traditionally, an aphrodisiac should make the victim wild with passion, usually chemically induced from such things as canthrides, or Spanish Fly, which is nearly always quite harmful and sometimes fatal, or a love philtre, a potion that inspires emotional love, which may be harmful to the psyche if it fails. But now we usually use aphrodisiacs to indicate some mild concoction or gesture that turns another person on through pure magick. But even magick can't really help with frigidity or impotency. That's a psychological problem that you'll have to handle yourself. If magick helps, right on, play on... One of the best aphrodisiacs is the dinner for two. After all, the way to anyone's heart, if they're not completely dead, is through their stomach. Getting the victim to your house has always been your problem. If you ask three times and are refused, forget it. You could live in the Taj Mahal and be offering that peacock aspic with a side of filet mignon for the main course and it wouldn't help. Always take the third turndown as a definite omen to interest yourself elsewhere, for what we are planning is the seduction supper.

In the first few years I had my very own apartment, I really got into cooking. I made curries and chili, and once even turned out a beef stroganoff for twenty-six people. Since I've discovered the business lunch and the fondue pot, I'll never pull that kind of mess again.

The joy and simplicity of fondue is that it looks so exotic and it's so easy. You have a single pot, a clove of garlic, and a bayleaf (both love herbs). From one simple pot you can make an intimate supper for two, or you can feed a ravenous coven of twelve. It is really the answer to a sorceress's prayer, this little cauldron.

Once you're sure the victim is really coming (Friday, at seven—the day and hour of Venus), you clean up the house from top to bottom. Messy houses are not good for planned seductions. Casual pickups, yes—you look busy and productive; but tonight, clean, clean, clean . . . including yourself, with your herb bath. Set the scene dramatically, with cushions on the floor around a low table. Only candlelight, please . . . lots of red candles. And wine. Lay in at least two bottles of good red wine.

Make an aphrodisiac salad, using lettuce, celery, carrots, chicory, and onions, with a safflower-green pepper dressing. All love herbs.

While the fondue is cooking, ply your victim with wine and talk, music and red candlelight and salad. Sprinkle a bit of marijuana seed into the fondue and the salad for flavoring.

If you manage to make it through to the dessert course, serve bright red apples, pomegranates, and mangoes. And if that doesn't turn your victim on to the fact that you're mad about him or her, drop three coriander seeds into the last of the wine. Indian ladies swear that's the best of all.

Now that you're on your way to becoming well versed in the arts of magick, here's a list of herbs, roots, berries, and spices that should start you out.

ADAM AND EVE ROOTS: Traditionally, these roots come in male and female pairs. Voodoos say that if you exchange them with your lover, you will be bound to each other forever. They can be bought from occult suppliers or herb stores. A love charm from Louisiana.

ANGELICA: Usually used to protect households from ghosts and hexes. Added to the bath, it removes curses and jinxes. Powdered angelica sprinkled around the altar prevents demons from entering the Circle.

ANISETTE: Used as a flavoring in cooking aphrodisiacs, it also comes in handy when taken with a little Cognac for headcolds. Burned as incense, it is dedicated to Habondia.

ASAFOETIDA: A houseplant with a really strong smell. Powdered root is burned to place a curse. In the Victorian era, a bag of it was hung around the neck to ward off diphtheria.

BALM OF GILEAD: Pressed into an oil, it makes a good cosmetic for dry skin. The gypsies say that it can ease the pain of a broken heart.

BASIL: A common herb for salads, Italian food, and venison. This common herb has lots of uses. Indian women believe that it insures fertility, and it makes a great love charm when administered in the food of a lover. Voodoos carry it against hexes.

BAY LEAVES: Also known as Bay Laurel, Bayberry. The traditional laurel crown of the Greeks. The leaves make a powerful spice, and are hung on branches around the doors and windows of a house to ward off vampires and witches of the not-too-nice type. The berries can be crushed into an oil for bathing or made into candles of the art.

BELLADONNA: Literally means "beautiful lady." Spanish ladies used to chew the leaves to make the pupils of their eyes very large, which they thought was very attractive. Also known as nightshade, it is another ingredient in Flying Ointment. The leaves and roots are boiled into a poultice for sprains and swellings, and the berries can be crushed into a magickal ink. The plant grows wild all over the East Coast, and is distilled into medicines. It is very poisonous and you cannot buy it without a prescription. It makes an interesting dye, a very good cursing incense, and doll stuffing, but I would not recommend trying to ingest it or giving it to anyone. People who have used it as a drug say it really produces a rotten trip.

BERGAMONT: Popular with German sorcerers for controlling people. A little bit of the plant under the bed or desk of a person you want to see things your way is very effective. It also makes an interesting tea.

BETHEL: Orientals say that if you chew it, it gives you second sight. It also gives you black teeth. Voodoos believe two bethel nuts have the power to grant a wish if thrown into running water.

BLOOD ROOT: A protective herb. Burn as incense, scatter on the doorstep, and wear a bit on the person.

BUCKEYE ROOT: Wrap a dollar bill around a piece of this and it will make your money increase.

BUGLE: Dried and powdered on a grave, it will make you dream of the deceased, who is obligated to tell you the future.

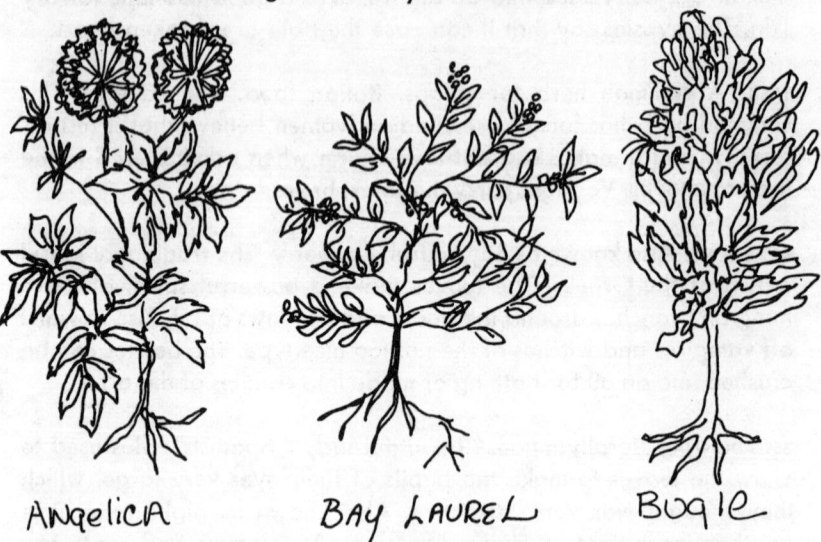

ANGELICA   BAY LAUREL   BUGLE

BURDOCK: Made into a tea, it is purifying water to bathe in and wash instruments of the art.

CACTUS: Peyote buttons are, of course, a powerful drug, much used in American Indian religious ceremonies. A friend of mine who chose to live in the old ways told me that peyote made him feel clairvoyant. Cactus thorns are supposed to be better than pins when you're sticking them into a doll.

CALAMUS ROOT: Mixed with Goofer Dust and burned as incense, it is a good spell to gain control of another person.

CARAWAY SEEDS: A German charm against Lilith, the first wife of Adam, who steals children from the crib. Caraway seeds on fresh baked rolls, given to the children on Christmas Day, is supposed to keep them from harm all year. In cakes, it is an aphrodisiac.

CELERY SEEDS: Chewed to help concentration. Much favored by mediums as an ingredient in incense.

CHAMOMILE: A popular herb tea for the nerves. Used as a wash it is good for gambler's luck. In the bath, it relaxes and soothes the skin. A good all-purpose incense.

CLOVER: Four-leaf clovers bring good luck, as everyone knows. Red clover carried in a red flannel bag keeps away evil. White clover ground into a powder is good to scatter around the room before a spring ritual.

CLOVES: Burned in incense, it is said to stop people from gossiping about you. (Hear that, Rona Barrett?) Chewed, cloves have the power to make your lover think of you while you think of him or her. Added to oo long and orange peel it makes a great tea. The Elizabethans, making pomander balls from oranges stuck with cloves, used to exchange these balls at New Year's to protect their loved ones from disease.

COMFREY: A bit carried on the person and in the luggage while traveling is supposed to keep you safe. Sometimes worn in a red flannel bag on the chain with a Saint Christopher's medal. I've given it to friends who do lots of hitching.

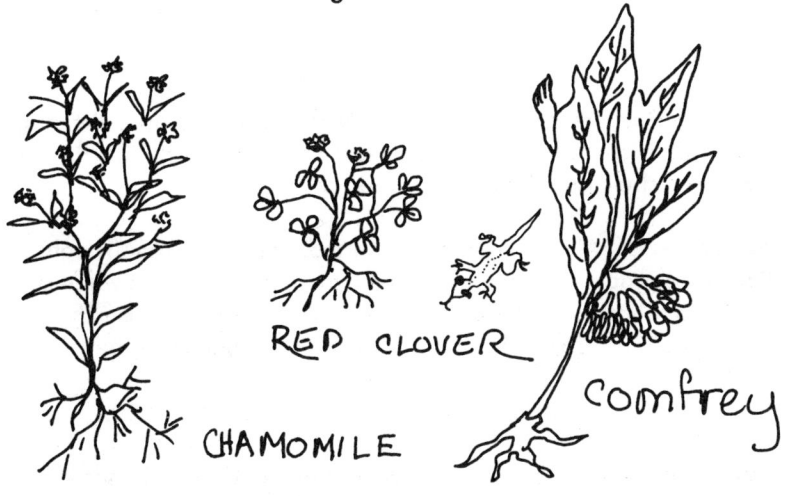

CORIANDER SEED: A popular and ancient love potion. Brew a little coriander seed into wine as a sure-fire aphrodisiac. It has a pungent taste and smell. The whole plant dried and crushed into a bath tea is good for cramps and colds.

CORN: Corn hung by the door or hearth is supposed to insure the fertility of the household through the winter. The custom of scattering corn at Halloween goes back to the old pagan fertility days, and was meant as a curse—that if the seed was scattered the crop would not grow the next year. Corn meal is used to draw veves in voodoo ceremonies.

CUMIN SEED: Mixed with salt, it makes a good protection powder scattered around the property. Many sources say it brings peace of mind.

DAMIANA: An aphrodisiac if there ever was one—mix with wine.

DANDELION GREENS: Are good for you. They make a good tea. Dandelion wine is supposed to increase clairvoyance and make those who drink it speak the truth of all matters. The fuzzy heads can be wished on, by closing the eyes, making the wish, and blowing hard on the head. If all the fuzz is gone, the wish will come true.

DEVIL'S SHOESTRING: Wards off evil. Powdered and scattered in the path of the enemy, it is supposed to hex them. A piece is carried as a talisman for gambler's luck.

DILL SEED: Another aphrodisiac.

DOGWOOD: Because of its association with the Crucifixion, the dogwood tree is sacred. If something must be buried in the earth as a part of the spell, bury it under a dogwood tree.

DRAGON'S BLOOD: A resin from a tree in Indonesia, it is usually sold in sticks as a good luck charm. A little of it ground to powder and added to whatever incense you are burning will increase the potency. Also a good cure for impotence if placed under the bed.

DULSE HERB: An aphrodisiac.

ELDER FLOWERS: Protects against psychic attacks by hostile sorcerers. Place a little in each corner of the room.

ELM BARK: A cure-all tea.

ERYNGO HERB: Brings travelers luck and success. Sometimes packaged in sachets for wedding presents, as it is supposed to keep a couple from quarreling.

FENNEL: A pretty effective lust-arouser.

FERN: All ferns are good protectors of the household. They make good houseplants. Dried and rubbed on the head, they are good for migraines.

FIVE-FINGER GRASS: A sure Pennsylvania Dutch talisman for attracting money and luck when carried in the pocket. Burned in incense with a green candle at the turn of the moon, it assures money coming in. Potent.

GENTIAN ROOT: A bathing herb to attract new lovers.

GINSENG: Considered by the Orientals to assure a long and lusty life. Widely available in health food stores, it is taken best as a tea. Supposed to be a great aphrodisiac for middle-aged lovers. Widely popular and very potent.

GOLDEN SEAL HERB: Made into a tea and wash, it is much used by prostitutes and others whose livelihood depends on having a steady clientele coming into the place of business.

GRAIN OF PARADISE: Also paradise seed. A voodoo aphrodisiac.

HERBA MATE: Makes a great tea, flavored with lemon and honey, for fasting. Used to keep lovers at home, where they belong.

HIGH JOHN THE CONQUEROR (ROOT): One of the most powerful talismans of voodoo. Kept in a red flannel bag, it gives luck in success, love, gambling, business, and the arts. Keeps away depression and confusion. If you can get an intended lover to hold it, while you are in bed together, he's (she's) yours for life.

HYDRANGEA ROOT: A courtroom charm to get a person released from jail. Marie Laveau's best-known spell.

IRISH OAK MOSS: Carried or burned for good luck and money.

JAMAICA GINGER ROOT: Ginger is supposed to be a good aphrodisiac. The root brings luck at the racetrack.

JIMSON WEED: A highly toxic herb much used in cursing. Makes a powerful doll stuffing—powder, incense, and water. I have been advised not to try and ingest it.

JOB'S TEARS: Kept in the pillow for luck; sewn into dolls for healing power.

KAVA KAVA: A tea to be shared by lovers to increase affection.

KHUS-KHUS: A friend of mine swears by this perfume extracted from the herb.

LAVENDER: As a perfume, it is supposed to attract men. In ancient Rome, it was used by prostitutes of both sexes to announce their trade. Today, it is used in sachets and in bathing teas to arouse the passions of a shared bath.

LEEKS: Shared by two people, they are a good love charm. As a talisman, they protect the wearer from evil.

LEMON VERBENA: Crushed into sachets to perfume the sheets and linens, it is a sexy love charm for people who are turned on by lemon. It makes a stimulating tea that enhances the creative mind.

LICORICE: Slyly offered to a person, it will induce them to change their minds in your favor. An interesting addition to baked goods.

LIFE EVERLASTING HERB: A popular Ozark tea among old people. Said to prolong healthy life and sexual vitality.

LINDEN: The tree branches are a charm against evil sorcerers, especially when hung about the house. Linden wood makes good wands of the art. The flowers make a nice bath tea.

LOVAGE ROOT: Considered a love stimulant when added to food; it is very good with chicken soup. It is also good for bathing and clairvoyance.

MAGNOLIA ROOT: Used as a charm to keep your lover faithful. Also makes a good healing herb in dolls.

MANDRAKE ROOT: In the Americas, this is the May apple. It protects its wearer as a talisman, and is used as a part of the Flying Ointment. The European mandrake is much more potent. Because it is toxic, it can only be obtained by prescription. As an incense, the root is very powerful in black magick ceremonies. The Indians used to eat the fruit of the American mandrake. It tastes terrible.

MARIGOLD: The flowers of the marigold make a good bathing tea. Attracts others to you. A medieval cookbook suggests that pressed marigolds added to fowl stimulate a lagging appetite.

MISTLETOE: The Druids considered the mistletoe a sacred plant. They used to harvest it from oak trees with a golden sickle. Having my own private source of mistletoe, I can testify to the fact that it is indeed a powerful all-purpose charm.

LEEK MARIGOLD MISTLETOE

MYRTLE: Strewn in the path of a loved one, it is supposed to be able to guide his feet to your door.

NETTLE: Sprinkled around the room or used as a doll stuffing, it removes curses or throws them back on the originator. Boiled down into a pulp, it makes a rather good astringent for the skin.

NUTMEG: A bit of freshly ground nutmeg makes an interesting stimulant.

OLIVES: Green olives are very sexy according to tradition. Olive oil is often used as a body rub and a base for fragrances.

ORANGE BLOSSOMS: Carried by brides as a symbol of love and fertility. Orange blossom perfume was considered a very powerful love stimulant when I was growing up. Crushed orange blossoms are burned as incense to attract a marriage proposal.

ORRIS ROOT: Carried as a love talisman in its whole form. Powdered orris root is burned as an incense in love rituals.

PARSLEY: Considered as a restorative by early herbalists, it was one of the favored herbs of Madame de Pompadour, who ate large quantities of it to make herself more appealing to Louis XV.

PASSION FLOWER: Despite its name, passion flowers are used in teas and powders to soothe angry tempers and restore peace to the home.

PERIWINKLE: Considered to be a powerful aphrodisiac by Renaissance magicians; powdered together with earthworms, it was supposed to be slipped into the lover's food. Voodooists use it as an incense when calling on the loa.

PINE: Traditionally a Christmas decoration, pine needles make a good winter incense and a house purifier. Pine cones are a household charm against evil spirits. For worshippers of the Great God Pan, pine trees are sacred.

PISTACHIO NUTS: The Arabians believed that pistachio nuts were an antidote to philtres. Often given to zombies to bring them out of their trance.

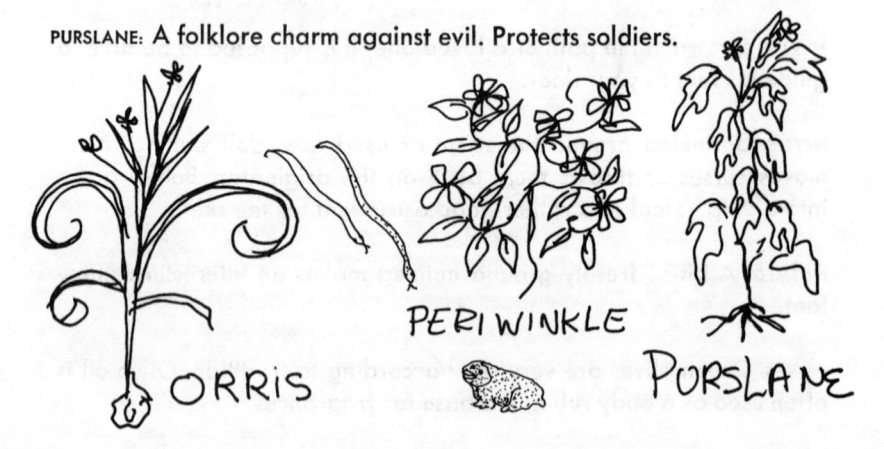

PURSLANE: A folklore charm against evil. Protects soldiers.

ORRIS

PERIWINKLE

PURSLANE

QUEEN OF THE VALLEY: Also known as Lily-of-the-Valley. Symbolizes virginity. The root is carried by those who wish to protect their virginity, or preserve their chastity. Interestingly enough, the flowers are supposed to make one able to see faeries, if placed under the tongue.

RHUBARB: If your lover is wandering, serve him rhubarb pie. Rhubarb syrup is supposed to be good for loss of blood.

ROSEMARY: Brings good dreams when laid under the pillow. A good spice, and a mild and charming addition to bathing teas; rosemary in the garden is a sign of bounty.

ROSES: Rose petals are scattered around the room during a spring or summer love ritual. Dried and crumbled, they make a nice pinch of bath herbs. Rose oil is considered very compelling by some, and rosebud tea is said to produce clairvoyant dreams. Rose hips make an interesting tea, full of vitamin C, and sexually stimulating. A dozen red roses coming from a lover is a sign of devotion. Gently squeeze the heads of one or two of them. If they have a hollow core, they are "soft" and therefore second-rate roses. That's a sign that he's cheap.

RUTABAGA: Used to curse people. If you want to get rid of someone, feed them some rutabagas.

SAFFRON: A good doll stuffing for healing dolls. Saffron oil makes a good perfume base.

SKULLCAP: Brewed with raspberry leaves and added to a mate's food, it stops him or her from philandering.

SKUNK CABBAGE: Burned in cursing ceremonies. Smells worse than its namesake.

SNAKE ROOT: Very popular sexual stimulant. A good all-purpose herb.

SPEARMINT: All mints are good additions to teas and sweet things, but spearmint is considered a particularly effective doll stuffing for curing lung diseases. Chewed fresh, it is supposed to give you the gift of beautiful speech. It dries and preserves very easily for later use as astringents and bath additives, and it makes a strong syrupy tea.

ROSEMARY   SPEARMINT   SKUNK CABBAGE

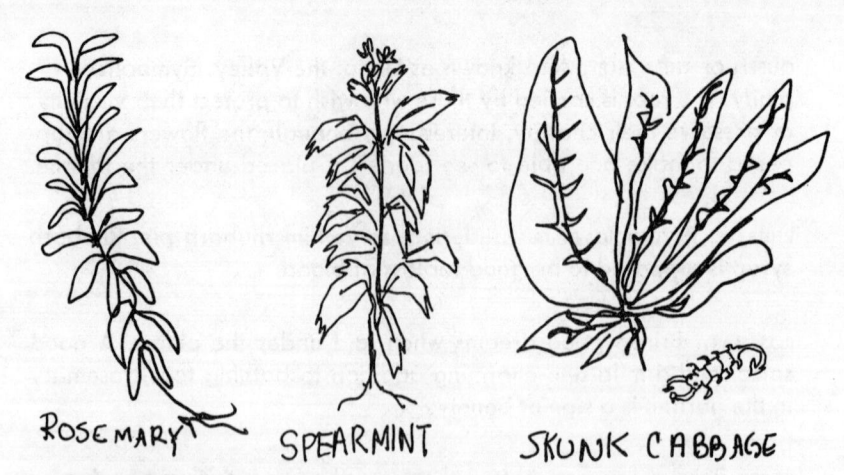

SPIKENARD: Brew and sprinkle on the picture of a person you want to return. Turn the picture face down and backward to the wall.

TANNIS: Roots, barks, and berries burned as an incense.

THYME: Said to give clairvoyant powers.

TOADSTOOLS: Also called faery rings. All mushrooms are interesting, even the poisonous ones. Some are beautiful and good to eat for the health; the Death Angel and other toxic varieties should be powdered and used as stuffing and incense for cursing. Always carry a field guide when gathering wild mushrooms.

TONKA BEANS: A love charm.

VALERIAN: Soothes the nerves and aids in calling up the gods.

VANILLA BEANS: Burned as an offering to the gods.

VETIVERT: I swear by this perfume. It has a thick, woodsy scent with just enough pine essence. As an herb, it is burned to keep away thieves and unwanted people. It removes hexes and curses.

VIOLET FLOWERS: Lavender and violet mixed together make a powerful love stimulant. Violets bring a change of luck and fortune.

WAHOO BARK: Brewed into a tea and rubbed on the head of a person possessed by evil spirits, it is a charm of exorcism.

WINTERGREEN: Makes a soothing syrup. The bark of the wintergreen protects children when placed in their bedroom.

WONDER OF THE WORLD: This root was very much in demand during the Depression, for it was used to locate buried treasure. In general, it attracts good luck and helpful spirits.

WORMWOOD: Also known as absinthe, it is burned to bring back the spirits of the dead. It is supposed to be a very strong aphrodisiac.

YELLOW DOCK ROOT: Makes a floor wash that attracts customers to a place of business. A good bathing herb for sallow skin.

YOHIMBEE: Burned to cross and hex people in Voodoo, it is also known to be a sexual stimulant among ceremonial magicians.

ZEBROVKA: Carried as a charm against witches in the Middle Ages.

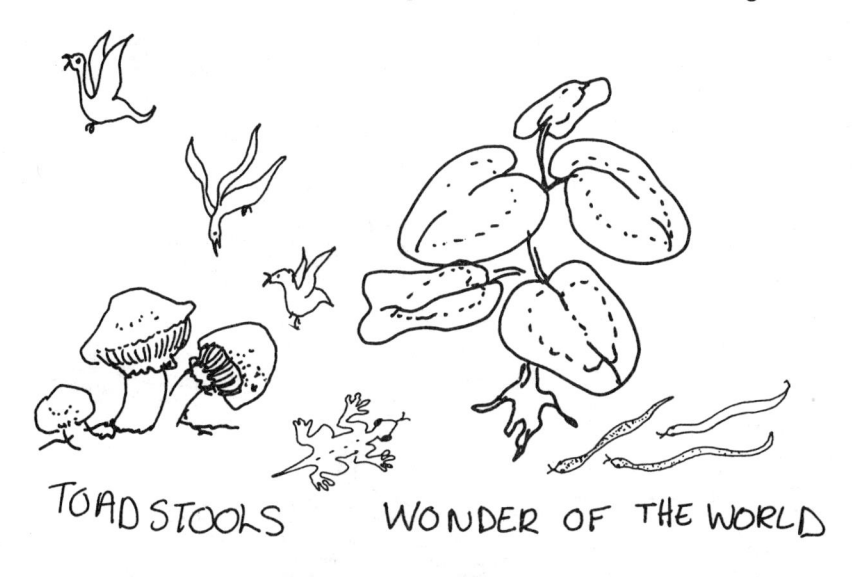

TOADSTOOLS   WONDER OF THE WORLD

And that's about the Half of It. What I have given you is just a sampling of the herbs used in magick. I don't know all of them—and I suppose I never will. There are too many plants in the world to be able to know the virtues of all of them. Yet sometimes I think that every plant, like every other living and non-living thing, and their actions, must have some purpose or it just wouldn't be there.

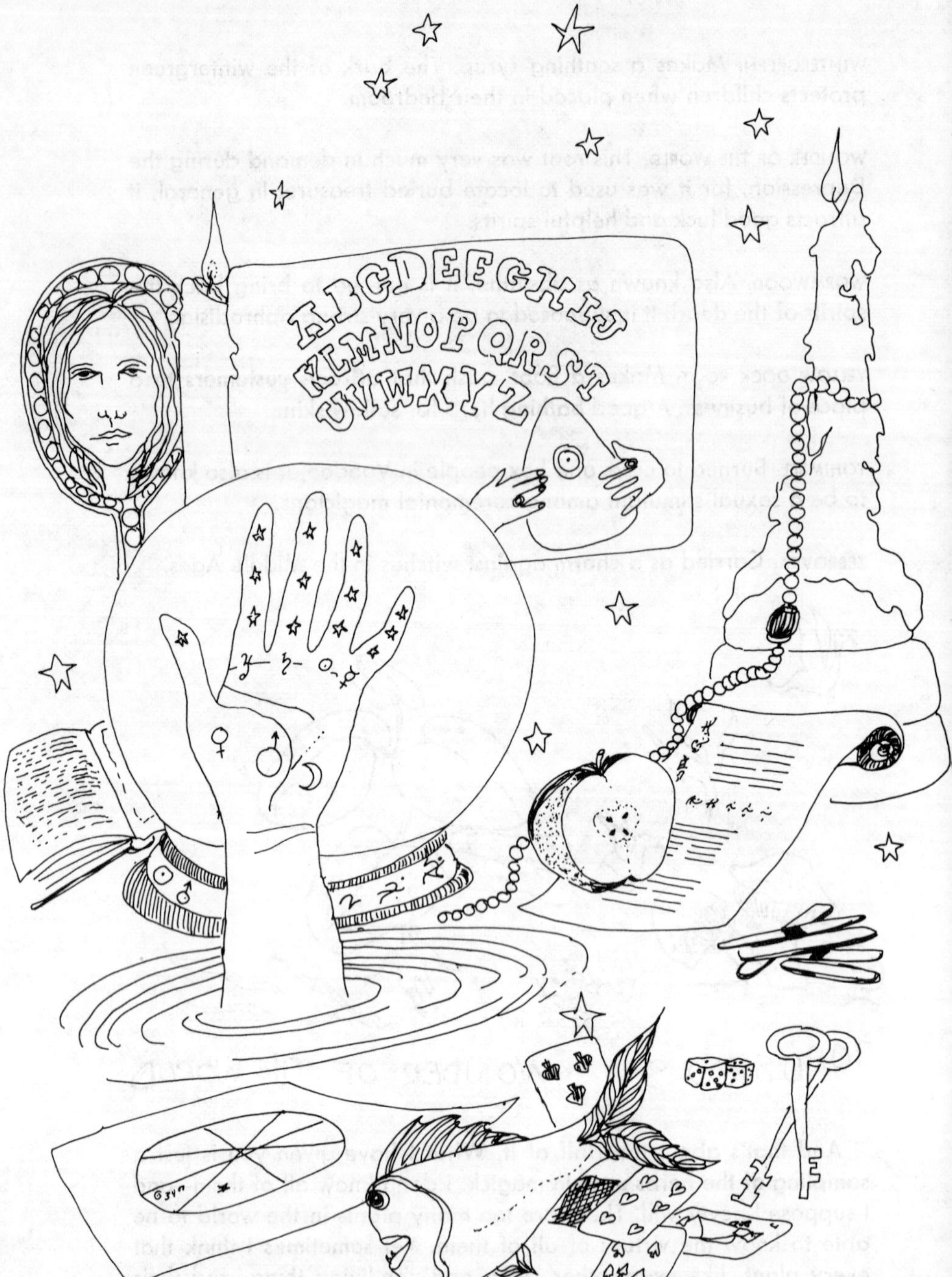

3
DIVINATION—HEXAGRAMS AND STARS

I wish to find out what the sybils have in store for me; you have got to know how to tread these days.
LA DUCHESSE DE BOUILLON

It's a pretty dull gathering where there isn't at least one wild-eyed individual running around asking for your sign or grabbing your hand and telling you the lines in your hand indicate you have a sensual nature.

Divination has always been a popular part of civilization, even when it has fallen into disrepute as the work of the devil or the work of superstitious minds that believe in the devil. The county-fair Gypsy predicting tall dark men and long voyages by sea is as much a part of our folklore as team sports and superheroes. It takes a very uncurious person to pass up a glimpse at his horoscope in the daily paper.

The whole Aquarian revival of interest in magick started with divination. Remember the Age of Aquarius, where magick, science, and religion were all going to harmonize the world? All those stoned-out kids wandering through the late Sixties really brought the occult back into its own. With an odd mixture of drug clairvoyance and the sudden interest of science in the power of the occult, a spark was lit from a dying ember.

Acid has become a bummer and Jesus is more popular than the Beatles, but the new interest in fortunetelling goes on and on to the point where department stores are offering courses in astrology and palmistry with the same selling lines they used to use for those charm schools back in the Fifties.

Divination means "finding the will of the gods." And it is the most basic magickal art. Divining the "will of the gods" is probably the best place to start learning about the occult. The ceremony, the ritual, and the mystery are all there—the same lures that drew Agrippa, Faust, Nostradamus, and Albertus Magus into their lifelong avocations as students of the powers that be.

Divination is the art of *seeing* the past, present, and future. It is the transcendence of that nebulous concept we call time. There are very few people who really understand time. Only a handful of people in the world have a total comprehension of Einstein's theory of time–space relativity. The rest of us just blunder along, looking at our watches and counting our birthdays ... as if our lives depended on it. We roll and tumble like dice, helpless pawns in the hands of a deity we call fate, scattered into an unknown future.

This unknown future makes man a very insecure animal. He can grasp a perspective on the past, feel his way through the present, and *hope* the future falls into place as planned. To give you some idea of what I mean, as I write these sentences the present has become the past, the future has become the present, and maybe the past is lining up out there in the future.

Many diviners see the art in this way. Somewhere in the heart of the cosmos, what we call time has no relevance. The past, present, and future are merely words there. Some part of everyone's brain is tuned into this cosmos, although we are not consciously aware of it. Subconsciously, of course, we are aware of it, and this motivates our actions (the beginning of *karma*). In order to activate the latent non-time mind one uses a tool. This medium may be the Ouija board, cards, book, candle, peyote, the crystal ball, dice, whatever helps us filter out the future in a code we can understand ... offspring of Jung.

Try to think of this non-time mind as the mandala, where a series of concentrics spin around within one another, or the symbol of the great serpent abides—a snake devouring its tail. Around and around and around. Fate is the mandala and the great serpent.

Divination is the means to unseal Fate's lips and seek her ear. This, supposedly the best of all possible worlds, is the Land of IF. It is a delicately balanced, uneasily poised world where goblins lurk in every corner. With divination, one can see that the emperor has no clothes ... VOILA!

So we run to the astrologer, our Tarot decks, and our Bibles to find The Answer ...

Although most religious dogma proclaims that the universe is laid out in a divine plan and one should not question the preordination of events, men, like the Magi, have always looked for "signs" of the future. The Chinese studied the footprint of an infant to determine his future; the Romans burned fragrant herbs to summon the gods and watched the flights of birds. The Druids picked over the entrails of their sacrifices and the Sybil sat on her tripod and muttered stoned enigmas to be unraveled by her clients. Arabian sorcerers cast their fortunes with cards and dice.

Diviners, soothsayers, and Dionysian madmen have advised kings and milkmaids alike. It would be a rare pharaoh who did not surround himself with soothsayers. The Hebrews looked upon their prophets as holy men with a special link to Jehovah. Hitler and Churchill were both guided by astrologers. The Empress Josephine was a palmistry freak. Abraham Lincoln attended seances to hear the spirit of Henry Clay. Queen Elizabeth I regularly consulted with two of the most powerful magicians and astrologers of her time—Drs. Dee and Kelley. She trusted Dee so much that she sent him to the Continent many times to do a little spying in his role as a master magician and "worker of divers miracles." King Saul passed a law against magick, but when he was in doubt, he ran to the Witch of Endor to consult with the ghost of Samuel.

Thus countless soothsayers, diviners, and prophets have passed through history. Some will be nameless, forever forgotten. Others, like Nostradamus, continue to haunt the world. Nostradamus's prophecies, written around 1555, covered events from the death of his sovereign to the end of the world in 2033. Among other things he predicted were several wars, the airplane, and the steam engine, all in cryptic blank verse.

But I have always loved the fortuneteller and the wise woman—the lady who lives in the woods in her little shanty, picking herbs in the light of the moon and talking to the spirits that less sensitive humans cannot see; the old woman to whom small children are brought to be cured of whooping cough and diphtheria with her magic herbs; the woman who can look into the crystal and see the future for those who ask . . .

Crystal gazing is another ancient art that seems to need an inborn talent. Aside from all those Maria Ouspenskya ladies in junk jewelry muttering dire things over fishbowls, scrying has always been a Gypsy art. It is the gift of *second sight* that enables the scryer to actually see visions in the translucent crystal, and the art is taught by the seer to an apprentice. The apprentice is taken to a dimly lit room at the same time each day and made to sit in front of the crystal presented to her by her teacher. The crystal is placed on a velvet cloth, shaded from direct light. The student gazes at the crystal for a certain length of time each day. It may take weeks, even months, before she will see anything, if she ever does at all. The apprentice can expect the crystal to cloud from within, and grow dark. After a

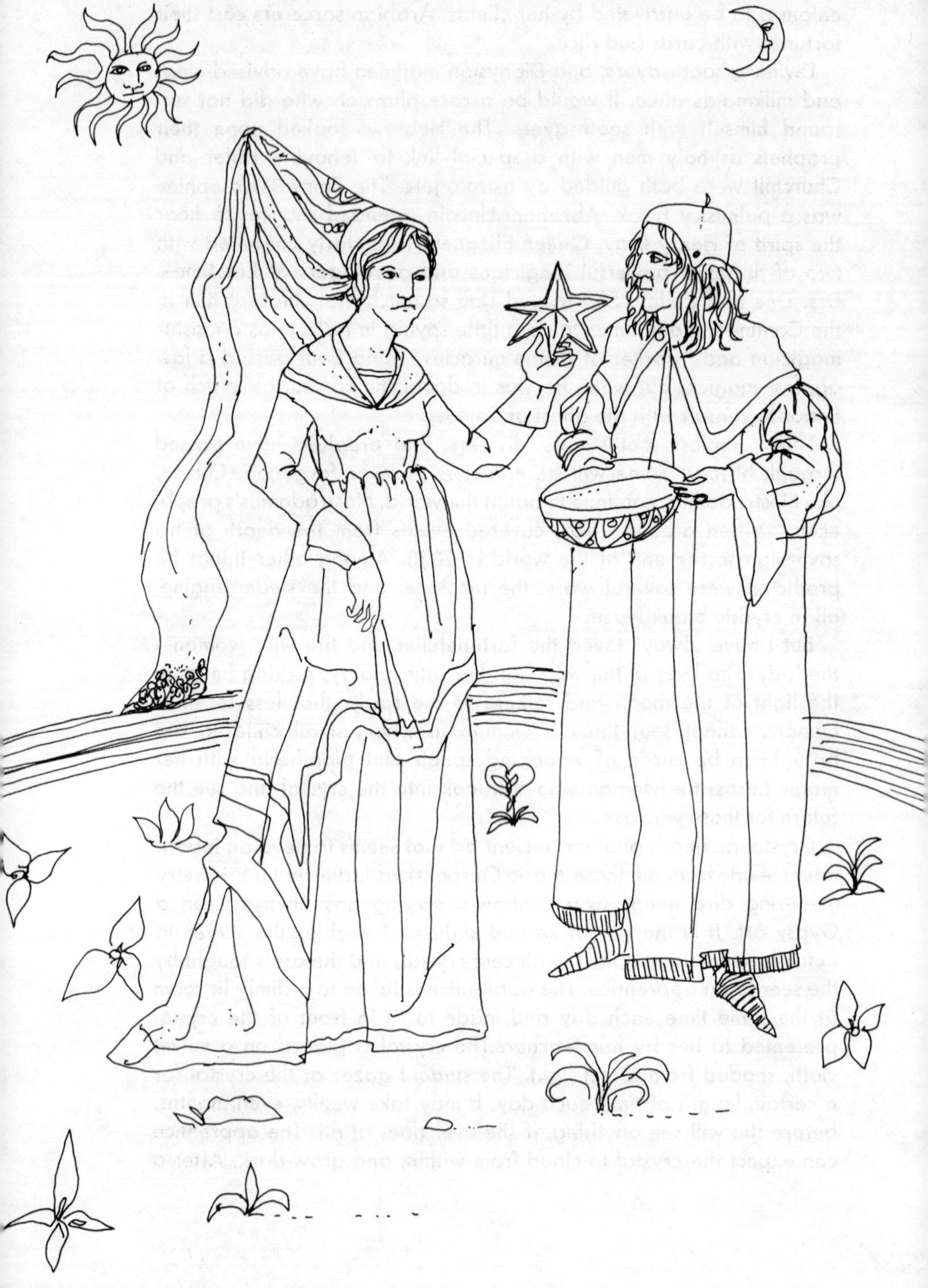

time, the cloud will part to reveal scenes and objects that must be interpreted by the scryer. No one should touch the crystal but the scryer. If she is giving the reading for another person, that person may be present in the room, must make no attempt to prod or harass the scryer, and must not touch the crystal. Crystals are not hard to come by, although the best-quality ones are expensive. A small crystal ball I purchased as a gift for a potentially psychic friend cost me about twenty-five dollars. Just looking at it made me feel very odd—it was so perfectly round and clear . . .

Some people can see visions in mirrors, or train themselves on crystal wine glasses filled with water. Ceremonial magicians in the Renaissance thought they got great results from virgins. The magicians would perform the ceremony and the child would do the scrying. There are many tales of magicians using children as their divinatory eyes. Children are natural clairvoyants and hence open to supernatural communications. Since the initiation into sex is considered a magickal rite in itself, the virgin's purity possesses the clarity and innocence of true visions.

A Victorian who revived an ancient art was Evangeline Adams. She shocked her prim and pedigreed Boston family right down into the ancestors when she abandoned the life of a proper debutante and took up the practice of astrology. What had started as a parlor pastime became Evangeline's raison d'être, and on the advice of her own chart, she packed up her trunks and moved to New York City. Even in those days more tolerant and open to the avant garde, New York welcomed Ms. Adams, and soon she was drawing up charts and giving readings in her Carnegie Hall studio for the likes of J. P. Morgan, Isadora Duncan, King Edward VII, Eugene O'Neill, and Carrie Chapman Catt. It was really Ms. Adams who revamped the concept of astrology. She trained many of the better-known astrologers working today, including Caroll Righter, whose horoscope blurbs in the daily paper first made a small child in Pennsylvania aware of the art.

But astrology goes centuries back into time. Long before Ms. Adams's ancestors stopped fighting with the tribe over the next hill, the Mesopotamians were looking up at the stars and making their calculations.

A subculture of Babylonians, the Chaldeans, were the first people to seriously develop and define astrology from their observations of the movement of the stars. They developed a calendar divided into twelve segments, each one named after a particular season or event in the natural cycle. Hence, the signs of the zodiac. The time of Taurus, the bull, for instance, was the rutting season of domesticated animals—an important event for an agrarian culture that worshipped the strength and fertility of animals. The sign of Sagittarius, the archer, would coincide with the hunting season. In their time-marking observations, they noted that certain patterns produced certain effects in the affairs of men. Astrology spread through Egypt, Greece, and Rome. A competent astrologer was as valued as a doctor or a priest and kings would surround themselves with a barrage of them at all times and even the poorest family would have a newborn's chart cast.

The Mongols and Turks spread the art into the East, where it has changed considerably from the form used in Europe. In the East, charts are cast from the year rather than month of birth. A person born in 1936, regardless of time, place, and month, would be a Rat person; someone born in 1900 would be a Horse person, and so on. There are twelve signs to the Oriental zodiac—a cycle of twelve years. The great Eastern cultures still retain their interest in astrology.

The Mayans and Aztecs had also developed an even more accurate calendar than the Mesopotamians and a sophisticated astrology. Unfortunately, the Spanish conquests of Cortés and Pizarro successfully managed to obliterate most of the pre-Columbian culture, and these cultures' astrology methods are lost to us.

Astrology has had a nebulous vogue in the West. Frequently, however, it has been the esoteric plaything of the literate classes. People with the time and money to study the science have been very few in the past, and of course, it was forbidden by witchcraft laws for many centuries. In the Renaissance it enjoyed a fashionable prestige with Catherine de Medici and Louis XIV. The Age of Reason sent all the occult sciences into popular disrepute and there they have remained until very recently under the heading of "all that occult garbage."

But astrologers are getting militant too. They claim that astrology is a science, and their batting average seems to prove them out. Scientists have been taking another look at astrology also. In their comprehensive book on the Soviet studies of ESP and other heretofore "occult garbage," *Psychic Discoveries Behind the Iron Curtain*, Lynn Shroeder and Sheila Ostrander reported that a Czech doctor, Eugene Jonas, is experimenting with astrological birth control and planned parenthood methods. It may not be enough to make a woman go off the Pill yet, but the doctor's research center has had high success in preventing birth defects, choosing the child's sex,

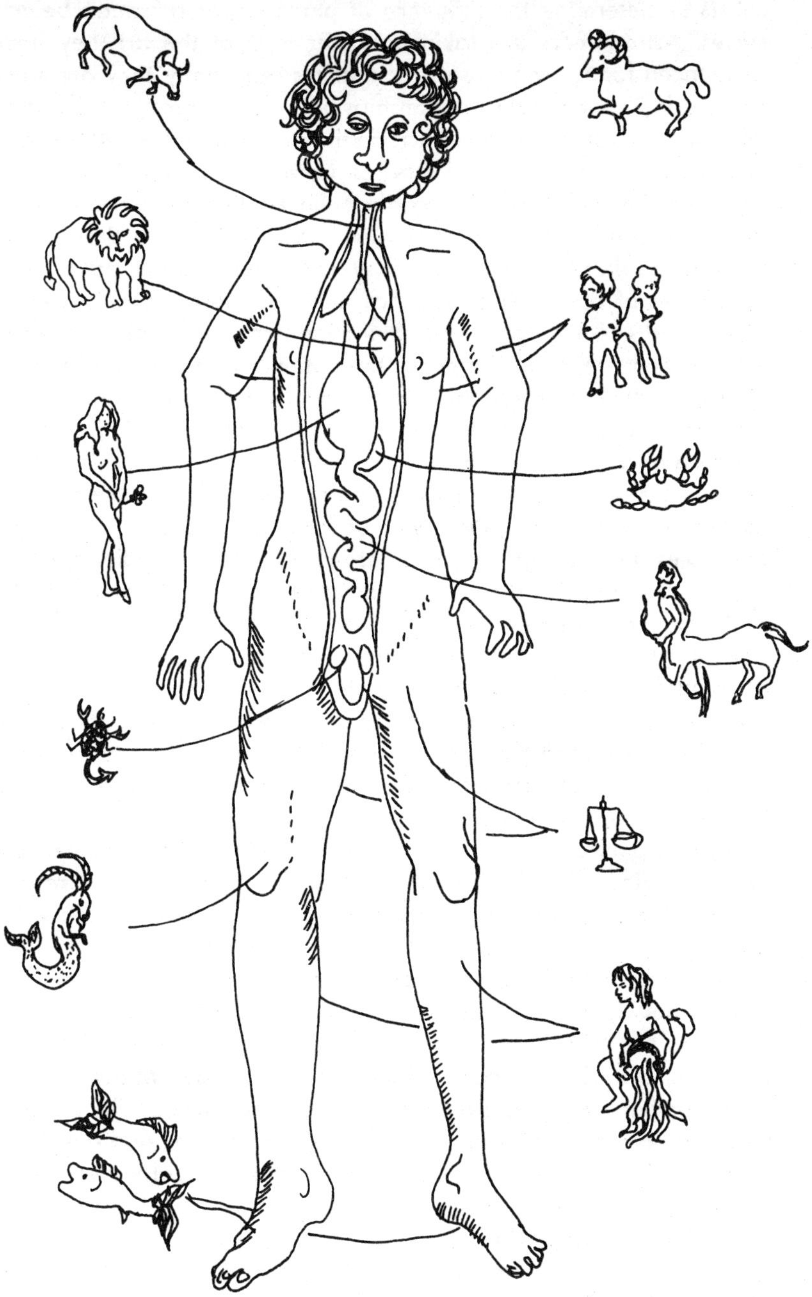

helping women conceive and not conceive by using the astrological charts to determine the influence of planets over a human being's cycles. Astronomers are taking another look at the art they have denounced for so many years. Sometimes reluctantly they are starting to admit that certain relationships between planets and the earth do tend to produce certain effects on the course of events. And everyone knows about the moon. Lunacy is derived from the Latin *luna*, the moon. In the Middle Ages, people believed that certain phases of the moon produced "moon madness." And any police department can tell you that they're always busy when there's a full moon . . .

In terms of data and experience, astrology may be the most exacting and accurate of all the divination arts. Anyone can learn to erect a chart, perhaps, if one has the patience and the mathematical ability to determine all the factors involved, but interpreting the influences requires a certain skill. I am terrible with mathematics, can't balance a checkbook, prepare a tax form, or add more than three two-digit numbers without using my fingers, so I have my own astrologer, a very competent woman named Pat Draut, who erects the tables and consults the stars for me. Pat is a professional astrologer and palmist who has what seems to me a very glamorous life style from her jobs as a reader in cafés and bistros.

If at all possible, I would suggest that one consult a competent astrologer in person. Have a natal chart drawn first, and then come back in a few weeks for a forecast chart. An astrologer should be chosen with as much care as a doctor. It's important to find someone who you feel a rapport with, someone whose instincts you trust. And I do not advise a computer!

My own personal prediction is that chieromancy will be the next art to gain serious attention from the scientific brotherhood. Already, Nat Freeland reports, doctors have found that an infant's palm print can show certain birth defects of the heart. And a Mongoloid's palm print is radically different from a normal person's.

Consider, too, that it was only in the last century that the Paris police found that every human being could be identified by his fingerprints, and such evidence is admissible in a court of law.

Just as fingerprints are individual, so are palmprints. The conception of a person's life being etched in the lines of the hand is at least as old as astrology. Once again, we must credit the Babylonians with the origin of palmistry, which traveled the same route as astrology, spreading east and west.

Another Victorian revived palmistry and left it with his name.

Chiero was born Count Louis Hamon. A sort of latter-day Caligistro, he was one of those fantasies that the Victorians loved, and he enjoyed as much popularity among the gentry as Evangeline Adams. His clients included Mark Twain, Nellie Melba, Sir Austin Chamberlain, the Infanta of Spain, and the Divine Sarah Bernhardt. Chiero himself was pretty amazing. He also worked in numerology, astrology, and color vibrations, and he served time as a war correspondent. Like most famous people of that era, he made several tours of the world, speaking before large audiences all the way. His books on palmistry are probably the best on the subject, despite a certain coyness typical of a Victorian writer. But such things as the handprint of Mata Hari and The Murderer's Thumb are quaint enough to make one fully recognize the charm of his work, and the man is a definitive writer on a subject that he spent most of his life studying.

Palmistry is more the science and art of character reading than divination. Most palmists regard the left hand as containing all the potential of heredity and environment, while the right hand maps out the progress of the life, and can change with age, emotion, and experience. Looking at my own palm right now, I have noticed that my devil's trident is growing clearer than it was the last time I looked ... But a palmist looks at more than the lines. The size and shape of the hand are considered. A person with long, slim hands, for instance, might fall into the type labeled artistic; flat square hands would indicate a strong personality. The length and shape of the fingers may tell a lot about your character. If there are gaps in your closed hand, it may indicate a generous nature. If the fingers are squared, with flat tips, it indicates a practical person who likes dealing with material things. The mounts of the hand are also studied. A firm, fleshy Mount of Venus (that's the ball of your hand) crossed with many lines means that the person is romantic with a strong imagination. The combinations and possibilities of lines and shape are many, and their indications can be fascinating. A friend of mine who really got into chieromancy used to find herself grabbing the hands of people she considered interesting and reeling off the stories of their lives until she realized that she was literally freaking them out because they were true.

When Alexander the Great was busily conquering his world, his armies ransacked and burned the great libraries of Egypt. The librarians and scholars who fled the chaos carried with them only a few manuscripts and the knowledge they could carry in their heads. Later, when they managed to get together, they decided to put all their knowledge together in the simplest manner, which could then be understood by everyone. In a time when few could read and write, they decided that a picture book would be the best possible way to leave the world a fraction of what it had lost. What they finally arrived at was a scroll of elaborate pictures, showing the development of the wise and spiritual mind. Their legacy was the Tarot. Each one pictured a story of arcane knowledge that would lead man from his animal nature to find his divinity. The Arabs took the cards and developed them into a divination game of individual pictures or cards. To this set of twenty-two pictures they added their own set of fifty-six cards responding to the fifty-two-card deck of numerological divination, but, later, bored harem ladies began to develop them into gambling tools to while away their empty hours.

The Moors brought the Tarot into Europe when they occupied

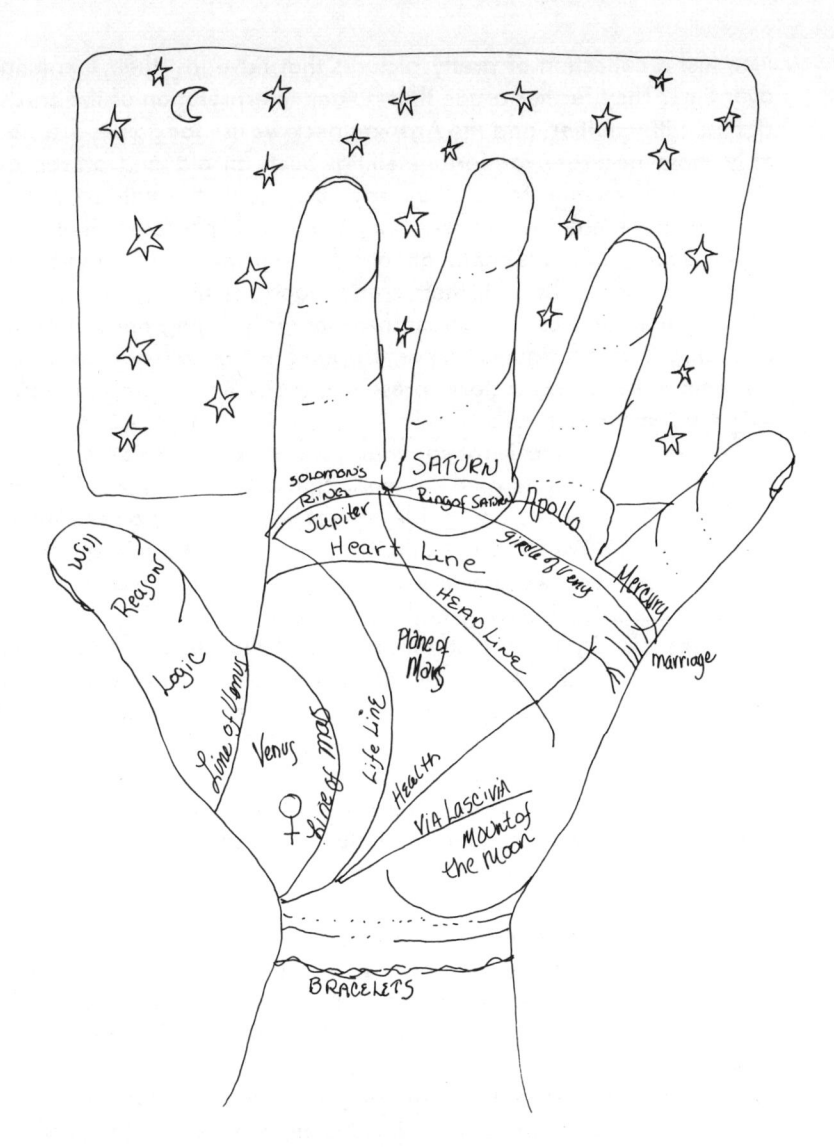

Spain, and the next we hear of them, Jacques Grendier, a sometime performer and dabbling magician, introduced them to the Court of Charles VI around the turn of the fifteenth century.

The Tarot became a fad among the French and Italian nobility for a while, and was picked up by the wandering Gypsies, who incorporated it into their act and carried it throughout the rest of Europe.

Many cartomancers (diviners with cards) say that the Tarot is useless, just a collection of pretty pictures that have lost their meaning over time. They further argue that no one interpretation of the cards agrees with another, and the Arabian deck we use for games is probably more accurate for fortunetelling. Such an old and oft-reproduced deck as the Tarot, they say, has gone through so many changes that it has no more relevancy than an old photograph album.

The Tarot does resemble an old photograph album. Even the very, very old decks with their crude woodcuts have a stillness, a frozen, eerie, timelessness about them that is haunting and curiously charming. The stiff figures forever trapped in their allegorical poses do seem to be telling a story, presented many times before, always with the same moral.

People who use the Tarot say that it is accurate in divination, and the pictures are a good guide to mediation on the paths that lead to wisdom. Whatever, no one guide agrees with another on the interpretation of the cards, or even the way they are to be laid out for a reading. The deck we use today is the one we inherited from the Arabs. It consists of seventy-eight cards, divided into the Major Arcana, the old Egyptian picture cards, and the Minor Arcana, the playing deck of the Arabs. Major Arcana cards represent strong influences; Minor Arcana cards indicate lesser forces in action.

Numerically, the Major Arcana goes from 0 to 21. In twenty-two pictures, it tells the story of spiritual progress, from The Fool to The Universe. Each of the cards is very much like a mandala. There is a central figure, representing the influence of the card, surrounded by symbols relative to the situation pictured on the card. Take any card from the set at random—The Hermit, for instance. In his aspect he represents the search for wisdom through introspection; in divination he is generally meant to represent caution, prudence, and second thoughts on the inquirer's questions. The central figure is an old man wrapped in a cloak, looking rather like an Old Testament prophet. His face is half hidden under his hood, his profile disguised by a long white beard. He is standing an a mountaintop, from the summit of which he can survey all sides of the situation. In his hand he holds a lantern or a torch, the light of knowledge that illuminates the darkness of ignorance surrounding him. Diogenes looking for an honest man, lighting the darkness with his knowledge and power.

The Lesser Arcana is like a playing deck. It is divided into four suits, from the deuce to the Ace, including a knave, a knight, the queen, and the king. The suits' symbols are like the Arabian deck. Wands, the sign of air elements, corresponds to diamonds; Cups,

representing the water element, goes to hearts; Swords, symbolizing fire, goes to spades; pentacles, the sign of earth, becomes clubs. To the ancients, the world was composed of only these four elements—earth, air, fire, and water. Of the twelve signs of the zodiac, three will be fire signs, three water signs, three earth signs, and three air signs. In divination by most popular methods, twelve cards are laid out, plus an indicator card representing the questioner, chosen from the court cards of the Minor Arcana. To choose your indicator card, you should use the one that corresponds to your astrological sign. If you are born in the sun signs Virgo, Taurus, or Capricorn, you would choose pentacles, representing earth. Libra, Gemini and Aquarius, swords, for air signs. Pisces, Cancer and Scorpio would choose cups, for water. A woman would always take the queen, no matter what her age, for a woman is always a woman (right on, sisters) while a man would choose either knights or kings depending on his age. A very young child of either sex would use the knave. The logic here is that young children really do not belong to either sex until they reach puberty. A very simple layout is the Celtic spread. There are more complex layouts, but they are really once a year or once a lifetime readings requiring a great deal of meditation and introspection for a good interpretation. I would recommend using either the Rider or Muller deck drawing your interpretations from Mathers and Crowe. If you really get into it and have the money, buy the very old pasteboards printed in France and Italy two hundred years ago. Their very age seems to render them more potent, even in the twelve-card layout.

What is the importance of numbers in astrology and the Tarot? Twelve was considered the perfect number, since the ancients used a base-twelve counting system. Thirteen, being one more than twelve, was the "joker's number," the number of "god," the unexpected guest at the banquet. It came to be very unlucky, for the custom was to seat a skeleton at the feast to remind revelers that life was very short indeed, that every moment was important. Six, two, three, and four are multiples of twelve, which leads to the idea they are important. Three is the sexual structure of the male genitals and four for the female. Three and four make seven, the number of creation, and all this leads us into numerology. Two is the number of unity; six is the number of sex.

Numbers have always had a connection with astrology and magick. Remember all those faery tales where three is the magick number? The ideal coven is composed of twelve people. Three on a match? See, you can have a lot of fun with numbers. Astrologers have assigned fortunate and unlucky numbers to each sign, and Cabalists and ceremonial magicians have spent a great deal of time assigning numerical values to every letter of the alphabet in order to determine the magickal potency of certain words.

Everyone is supposed to vibrate to a number, or several numbers. Odd numbers are harmonious to other odd numbers, and even numbers agree with other even numbers.

Although I know at least five different ways of divining with numbers, I am basically an anti-number person who feels that mathematics is the servant that became the master. So I am going to show you the simplest numerology divination, using only the numbers one through nine.

As I have said before, everyone has a number or a series of numbers they are influenced by. You have a zip code, a street or box number, a telephone number and social security, of course, but these make up simply a group of identifying numbers—they touch your outgoing life but not your soul. Once you have learned this system, you could even play around with them. If you are incompatible with your zip code, though, I really wouldn't tell you to move.

To determine your number and its attributes to your character and fortune, take the number of digits that make up your birthday and your name (your middle name, too, if you have one; use your maiden name if you've changed it after marriage) and add them together. Let's say your name is Susan McDonnall and you were born March 15, 1936. There are 5 letters in Susan, 9 in McDonnall. 5 + 9 are 14. Leave that for a moment and take your birthdate. March—the 3rd month of the Georgian calendar; 15th day; 1936th year A.D. Add 3 + 1 + 5 + 1 + 9 + 3 + 6 to the earlier numbers broken down (1 + 4). That makes 33. Since this method requires us to split numbers into single digits, we then add this 3 and 3 to get six. (Using the 9-base system, 11 reduces to 2, 12 to 3 . . . see?) Susan is a 6 person. Not only is that one of her lucky numbers, but it is also an interesting way to read her character. The number six is ruled by Venus, so Susan will be inclined to love others deeply, to be kind and generous in her dealings with others, although her Venus vanity will make her a little hard on herself. Six is a balance of both yin and and yang, which should make her a pretty stable person, not given to sudden impulses of shirking responsibilities she feels are hers. She might have a touch of the earth mother about her, or if six were a man, a kind of benevolent paternalism. A six could be overcautious, too secure in her environment to want to be able to deal with changes, and her Venus vanity could incline her to gossip and a bit of backstabbing when she thinks it would do her good.

Every number from one to nine has a character all its own, and each is ruled by a planet. Each has a value and personality as unique as its character. Let's briefly look at the logical and traditional attributes of each number.

One is ruled by the Sun. It may be the loneliest number, as the song goes, but it is the number of a person who is used to making decisions, a person who is active, who can seize a situation and take control of it. One people have a knack for organizing things, and they are basically loners. Negatively, one people can go into an eclipse, just like the Sun. Just by their own aloofness, they can make life extremely complicated for themselves. They must realize that they canot handle the world alone; nor should they let their pride stand in the way of asking for help or even extending a hand in friendship.

Twos are ruled by the Moon. Two people get along well with almost anyone, for they are harmonious and diplomatic. They are imaginative people with a streak of the mystic in them. Their intuition is rarely wrong, but they do not always listen to it. This can make them thin-skinned and hypersensitive to all kinds of real or imagined slights, and in their desire to avoid any kind of confusion, they will bend too far in their compromises with that wonderful intuition.

Three is an outgoing number, ruled by Mars. Three people are great actors and dancers, very much attuned to their bodies and physical expression. They have a very strong self-will; they are the kind of people who can stick to a diet or a decision with a fierceness that may startle others. Unfortunately, they are ruled by Mars, the God of War, and they can be belligerent if they're crossed. They are great people for a debate, and a very negative three will disagree with you just for the love of an argument.

Fours are ruled by Mercury, and like the messenger of the gods, they are fast thinkers and good correspondents. It's a good number for anyone involved in writing or any of the media. Four people are surprisingly loyal and patient. Their honesty can sometimes be painful if you ask for an opinion. Four people are used to fast-moving but their native caution usually keeps them from making faulty decisions. On the sinister side, fours count every penny and do tend to mooch a bit here and there. They're great ones for a free meal. More creative people may find their lack of imagination very dull, and their contrary natures exasperating. Sadly, some fours can get very hung up in petty details and forget the over-all picture.

Five people are really Gypsy folk, ruled by Jupiter. Like ones, they value their individuality, but it's the freedom of movement they want, the thrill of the hunt that gets them going. They have an enormous amount of curiosity, and a five could be involved in almost anything that requires research and travel. They like status and prestige, and there are few scruples involved in gaining that promotion. They have a tendency to lose interest in things as fast as they learn them, so watch your five lover very carefully. It's appearances they're interested in, and if they get restless, you can see the facade fall to reveal a very shallow bad five.

Sixes we've discussed, so let's move on to the sevens. Seven people are ruled by Saturn's influence. Saturn was the Ruler of the Dead, remember, but that doesn't mean every seven you meet will be an undertaker or a necromancer, although they may have a leaning toward the magick arts or any sort of mysterious undertaking. They are secretive people with a deep natural inclination for meditation and religion. A seven person might have a mind that juggles fact and fantasy and never know which one is real. Their interior and exterior realities tend to get confused with each other. Their particular gift is their philosophic outlook on life, which enables them to survive almost any disaster. A reverse seven can have a rather morbid, fatalistic personality. He is a constant complainer with a streak of melancholia so dramatic that it can be felt halfway across the room.

Eights are Uranus influenced. They're extroverted people who like to seize life and wring every ounce of experience out of it they can. They are persons with a lot of courage, who aren't afraid to take risks. Half the time they have some inside information that assures them of success anyway. Eights are very efficient. When they set themselves to a task, they finish it well no matter what the cost. They are masters of any situation, and they do love luxury. Unfortunately, sometimes they can turn this direction against other people to get what they want. A negative eight is pigheaded and conniving to the point of ruthlessness.

Nines are Neptune ruled, and like the sea they can be bountiful, loving people who will sacrifice much for the people they love. Nine people have a deep sense of the mystery of the universe. They move in their own mysterious ways, usually very careful to evaluate every aspect of a situation before coming to a decision. Their sense of values is based on some deep personal code of honor. They usually have very good judgment in matters related to peacemaking and treaties, but they like to surprise. Sometimes it's hard to tell if they're funny or profound. A negative aspect of nine can be like a storm at sea. When they finally do become angry, there is no restraint. If their sense of inner peace is threatened, or someone tries to block their special esoteric courses, nines can go into a manic-depressive hysteria that almost touches insanity.

Like numbers, words have an equally fascinating sense of occult power behind them. We all tend to believe, even for just a split second, what we read. The awe with which we treat language is drilled into us from the day we're born. In school, the first thing we are taught is the alphabet and a healthy respect for "good grammar." "Word power" is not just a catch phrase; it's a powerful tool for shaping our attitudes. Take a word as simple as "magic." My immediate image of that symbol is a man in a black cape pulling rabbits out of a hat. If I read "magick," the archaic spelling for the art we are dealing with here, I get an entirely different picture. Words are nothing but clusters of symbols put together to form a picture-symbol in the mind.

Until Gutenberg started printing Bibles, reading was a sort of magickal, mysterious activity practiced by the clergy, the bureaucracy, and that highly disreputable crew, the students and writers. And even up to the last century, only about one tenth of the world's population could read and write. Books were for the select few with time and money to study them. Literacy is now widespread, however, and despite McLuhan's prophecies, we continue to think in words as well as pictures. And this is where I introduce bibliomancy, divination by books.

A bell to summon the spirits, a book to read their words, and a candle to shed the light of wisdom on the prophecy. Basic bibliomancy is taking a sacred book (the Talmud, Bible, Koran, I Ching, PDR), opening it at random, choosing arbitrarily the first word or set of words that the eye falls on, and interpreting their relevance to the question you've posed. This has been used so many times as a dramatic device in Gothic novels that it's almost corny, but it does provide a basis for arbitrary decision-making. Traditionally, the best books for divination are sacred books of one kind or another, but I think you could use almost any book that has a special meaning for you—and the interpretation is entirely up to you. You can do the same thing with Tarot cards. The best way is to separate the Major Arcana, shuffle them, and choose one at random. If it doesn't answer your question, it might give you the card's opinion of the situation.

I was first introduced to the I Ching by an early hard-core acid freak who carried his Wilhelm edition wrapped in a while silk cloth and cast his hexagrams with a special set of inlaid ivory sticks. Verree heavy . . .

The I Ching is not to be laughed at, however; the Book of Changes is an ancient Chinese work, and a true oracle. Confucius is often quoted as saying that if he were given an extra hundred years, he would devote at least fifty of them to the study of the I Ching, so my brief, Western-minded explanation cannot begin to truly explore every aspect of this work. Like the Tarot, the I Ching explores many facets of the human condition and is certainly an excellent tool for meditation and rumination on the attributes and aspects of fate, mankind, and the cosmos. It is a tool, not a toy, and should be treated as such.

The I Ching is composed of sixty-four hexagrams. A hexagram is a vertical series of six horizontal lines, or two trigrams. The lines are either yang, unbroken, like so —— or yin, broken like so – –. Each of the sixty-four hexagrams tells a story, and each line has a meaning. In a weird allegorical way, the hexagram unravels a question by presenting a situation that nine times out of ten *does* resemble the situation inquired after.

Because the book is an oracle, one does not select a random passage (although I have done this when I feel lazy or desperate) but casts either coins or yarrow stalks to find the proper hexagram. Perhaps this bit of ceremony is yet another occult trapping, but it does seem to produce more meaningful results. As a ceremony, it enhances the consciousness of the questioner and gives him a moment of complete concentration on the ceremony he is acting in.

Occultists say to really understand the I Ching, one should learn Chinese, for the translations really do not communicate the fullness of the original. But the I Ching is the most important of all the sacred books in divination. I use it only when I want to ask a really important question, one with a lot of emotional weight behind it. It is not a device to ask what color of shirt you should wear tomorrow. It is a book to ask whether or not you should go to California, get married, commit suicide, sue your landlord, or anything that is really important to your life. The I Ching only advises in its own way; it's up to you to interpret what it is telling you, and yet the "I" is almost always uncannily correct in aligning its allegorical situations to the matter inquired about.

All of these classic arts are almost incestuously intertwined. You can learn much about divination by studying each of them in relationship to the others, and studying divination's relationship to the whole art of magick. Crowley's definition of magick as "the art and science of causing change to occur in conformity with will," really has meaning with divination. Before you start any major spell, it's a good idea to divine if all the aspects are good for a successful outcome at that time. If you can use these arts as tools to gauge the place you're standing on, as signposts for your perspective, you are being your own sybil. Divination should be used as a guide and adviser in your actions, but it should never be the master. You are your own teacher, and the only way to learn is through experience.

Before you wrap a scarf around your head and hang out your shingle as a fortuneteller, there are a few things you should know about divining.

If you are reading for someone, it is always a good idea to check yourself and see if you're in the mood. If you're tired, or you feel no sympathy with the person, don't waste your time trying to get answers for them.

My particular chose is reading the Tarot, so I will base my observations for you on that. It's interesting to read for strangers because it's a challenge to my ability, so before I even drag out cards I talk to them for a while, and let myself become a bit player in their movie. I try to judge them by the way they talk, the way they dress, and their body language. As much as I can, I try to push me into the back of my mind and let my impressions and observations of the inquirer take over. That's a little bit of psychology, a little trickery, and a lot of intuition. Suppose I am reading for a friend of a friend, someone I have just met . . . I have formed some kind of subjective opinion about the person, which will subconsciously influence my interpretation of the cards, but I try to keep my conscious mind as clear as possible. After the mood strikes me, I will get out the cards and ask the inquirer to select one of the court cards of the Lesser Arcana that he feels suits him. That is a key to his personality right there. Suppose he chooses the Knight of Swords. The Knight of Swords is a young man—he considers himself a boy, not a man, and it is a card of action and aggressive movement. So, my inquirer's self-attitude is defined—even if he is not aware of it.

I have already prepped him, asking him quite honestly what he does, what his sign is, and if there's any particular question he has in mind. So, he's a filmmaker, a Scorpio, and he wants to know if a proposed movie deal he has will be successful or not. From there, it's all a matter of interpretation. Using the Celtic spread, I see that he is covered by the King of Wands, crossed by the Six of Cups. That's his immediate situation, the factors he is dealing with on a conscious level. The King of Wands is a man of fair complexion, perhaps a sort of country squire type. The attribute of the card is specialized knowledge, refined wisdom. I ask him if that has any meaning for him. Yes, it describes the man whom he wants to finance the film. Six of Cups is the future. The financier is thinking about the potential success of the film. I feel he has come to no decision yet. Below, the past and subconscious position holds the Four Pentacles, reversed. Obstacles, delays . . . something has stood in the way of completing the mission? Yes, a lack of money. The card beside, conscious factors, forces in operation, is The Magician. That is manual skill, cleverness, juggling. Is he having to go through a lot of social-professional games to try and get the money for the film? Then it would be wise to play their games. He is crowned by the Ace of Swords. A card of power, direct movement, victorious action. What he should do is take the situation in hand and demand an answer from the guy. The subject of his film is timely, and if he has to wait any longer, it will lose its strength. In the position of fears, Temperance. This one is hard to interpret. It means combining of forces, moderation between extremes. Perhaps he is afraid that he will compromise his film in order to make it. In the position of Other's Opinions is Death. Those who care about my inquirer don't think he's dead—they just feel that he has gone through some bad changes over this project. The next card is in the position of his hopes. Eight of Wands reversed. That means fights and chaos. What kind of discord is he wishing for? Is he bored and wants excitement? No, he wants a showdown with the producer, to get a yes or no answer. Ah. . . . The last card symbolizes the Outcome. It's the Sun, reversed. Well, the Sun is material gain and happiness. Upside down, it is modified. Yes, I would say that the producer will come through with the money, but it won't be as much as he wants. Arbitrarily, I shuffle all the cards back together and ask him to choose two—the death pack, for those who don't expect it. This is a little bonus. Well! The Wheel of Fortune and the Seven of Cups reversed. The Wheel of Fortune is good luck, and the Seven of Cups down is resolution. He thinks too negatively, and is hurting himself by bringing back bad things—his chances will be improved if he tries to put himself into a receiving frame of mind, banishes the doubts from the back of his mind.

Usually, a reading will leave me tired out. The more exhausted I am, the more I know that I have been putting out a lot of psychic energy. My inquirer is happy, or at least a little less insecure about his future, and a little less skeptical about women who read Tarot cards. Right now, he's in Los Angeles shooting his film on a shoestring. It just may be a sleeper.

The worlds we inhabit in our dreams are our very own, as special and private as the little hiding places we had as children. Sometimes the dream world is just like real life with the same cast of characters; sometimes it's a Fellini film of surreal close-ups and fade-outs (the maestro admits he gets many ideas from his dreams) and sometimes our dreams are a journey into our own private hells. But only the subconscious knows, and it's not telling. It is leaving you with a set of images that you must interpret yourself, for your dreams are as unique as your fingerprints and far freer than your thoughts.

The Lucky Horseshoe Four Star Dream Book may be a lot of fun, but a little basic reading in psychology will take you further into understanding yourself and the messages your mind is trying to get through than all the occult books in the world. Because Jung was so sympathetic to symbolism and occultism in general, I would recommend a little reading of his basic works, especially *Man and His Symbols*. It's a comprehensive work designed for the layman's understanding of Jung's teachings and it's a great book for anyone interested in magick. If you intend to use your mind, to expand its possibilities, then you should understand a little of its workings.

My own way of dealing with my dreams is to keep a notebook. I record the date, my state of mind, what I can remember of the plot of the dream and its major happenings. If it really puzzles me, I try to find the universal meaning of the major symbols in the dream, weigh them against my own private symbols, make some kind of conclusion, and then go to the dreambooks and psychology texts for an interpretation of the omens. So far, my dreams have not prophesied anything really extraordinary, or any events I was not expecting or hoping for or dreading, but I intend to keep the record for several years to see if I can gain any clues that would prove my dreams to be portents of the future. The best thing to do is trust your intuitions. And don't eat pizza before bed!

The divination arts I have covered here are only the classics. You can divine in hundreds of different ways, using everything from dice to the entrails of sacrificed animals—including your fellow humans, which I do not recommend: it gives you bad karma and it's messy. And the best thing you can do with dice is shoot craps. But I think it is best to find a method you like, using a method that feels comfortable, using your tools as maps, not crutches. Divination is to be used as an ally, an adviser to your actions, but it should never be the master. You are the total of your experience, past, present, and future, and it is through this experience that you develop your intuitions.

It's very hard to divine for yourself. So much of your emotion is tied up with the answers that it's very easy to misinterpret your own readings. So, always think twice, try to see every angle, negative and positive, take your time, and trust your intuitions. If you're determined that something is going to happen, inevitably it will. But sometimes wishes have a sticky habit of backfiring, and so do interpretations of divination.

The important point is to weigh the nuances of your work, trying to be as objective as possible in weighing the pros and cons of the situation. Consider several methods you like and develop your abilities with them. Don't worry about perfecting your divination. There's no reason in the world why you cannot learn. Laughter, light, and love are as much a part of magick as smoky mysteries. The Irish are a marvelously psychic people, remember, who have their share of troubles and sorrow. Yet they have a saying that all those who would peer into the future should hold: "The longer you run away from a ghost, the larger it becomes. When you stand and face it, the ghost disappears."

Think about it . . .

DIVINATION SPELLS or What to do on a Slow Saturday Night

The Dumb Supper is an Old Elizabethan custom that still survives in parts of the rural South. Two unmarried girls select a night when they can be alone in the house. Without speaking, they must prepare a meal without salt and set the table for four with four purple candles. At a few minutes before midnight, they should light the candles and lay the food on the table. As the clock strikes midnight, the phantoms of their future husbands will come in and silently join them in the meal. If the girls speak so much as a whisper, the spell will be broken and they will never marry. It's a good idea to smoke a little or have a glass of white wine while preparing the meal.

DACTYLOMANCY—The Ring and the String

Dactylomancy is divination by rings. The following is probably the most popular ritual, and it is quite simple. Take a ring that has a special value for you—an heirloom or a gift is best, although a birthstone ring or even a bangle bracelet can be used. Take a piece of red string about as long as the distance between your elbow to your arm. Tie nine knots in it, and secure the last one to the ring. Prop your elbow on a table and allow the ring to hang suspended about two inches above its surface. You may now ask it questions that require a "yes" or "no" answer. Preface each question with "Mother Mary, tell me true . . ." If the answer is "yes," the ring will turn on the string in a circle. If the answer is "no," it will swing back and forth.

THE NEW YEAR'S EVE'S RUN

If you live in the city, I think you'd better pass this one by. The legend has it that if a person can take off all his clothes and run around the house three times on New Year's Eve without being seen, the next year will be bountiful. His wishes will come true, he will gain stature in his work, luck in love, and will not fall ill nor lose a loved one by death or argument. But he might get pneumonia.

WEDDING CAKE WISH

In German weddings, it is the custom to give each guest a slice of the cake, wrapped up, when he leaves the reception. Don't take it home and eat it. Keep it in the freezer until you have a plan you want to know the outcome of. Then take the cake out, defrost it, and wrap it in a white linen napkin. Put it under your pillow. If you dream of flowers, your project will turn out well. If you dream of animals, it is best to abandon the whole project. For a person considering marriage, if the loved one appears in the dream it's a good sign.

THE WAX BALLS

When you're scraping the candle wax off the furniture from your last spell, don't throw it away. Save it against the day you decide to divine the occupation of your future mate. Melt the wax in an old pot and pour a healthy slug into a bowl of cold water. Whatever shape the wax takes will be the tools of your future mate's trade. A sailor would be an anchor, for example, a writer might be a book, a sanitation engineer, a trashcan. Use your imagination . . .

RED HAIR SPELL

Those with red hair have always been credited with special powers. A redhead could be burned at the stake in the Middle Ages just for being born with the wrong color of hair. On your birthday, find a redhaired friend and ask him or her for a piece of bread and butter. If the redhead gives it to you generously and freely, without asking why (no prompting), you must eat it without thanking them to gain a year that will be better than the last. If the redhead refuses, you can expect a year without anything exciting happening to you. There won't be any terrible disasters or anything; it just won't be an outstanding year.

CASSANDRA SPELL

Albertus Magus, one of the medieval grimoire authors writes that if one puts a celonites—you know, that stone you find in the head of a snail—under one's tongue, one will have the power to see the future. Some people use a topaz. I call it a Cassandra spell because sometimes there are things in the future that are better left unseen.

TALKING TO THE DEAD

This, I believe, is German. I learned it from a Pennsylvania Dutch friend. If someone you loved very much as a child died before you reached puberty, you can summon that person back to help you. The idea that love transcends even death is common throughout the world. But this is somewhat risky, I think, because if you don't handle it correctly, it can hurt you. On the anniversary of the loved one's death, light three purple candles and one black cat (shape) candle. Arrange them around a table and sit down with a mirror so you can see your own face. The only illumination in the room should be the candlelight, and you must be alone. You must call out the dead person's name, as if you were chanting a mantra. If it's your grandmother, you would say "Granny, Granny, Granny," or whatever name you addressed her by. After a while you will see the specter of the person materialize behind you. If you lose your courage, you could put yourself up for a full-scale haunting. As you are chanting, you will hear the person speaking to you, as if it were a voice in your mind. When the person has said what he or she has to say, the specter will disappear. Then blow out the candles, thanking the specter out loud for coming. At the earliest opportunity, take a bunch of flowers to the grave to show your gratitude for disturbing the person's rest and to placate the spirit.

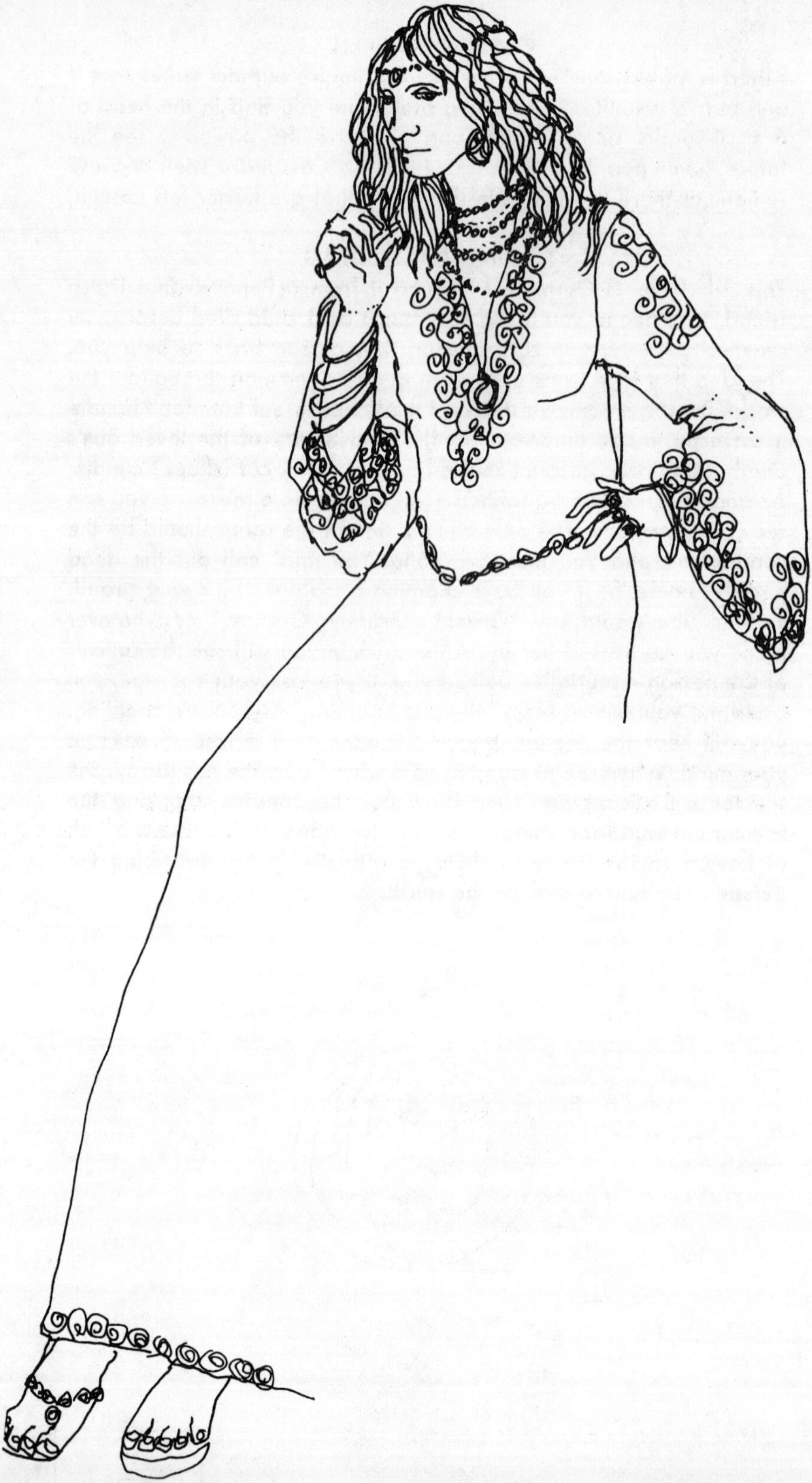

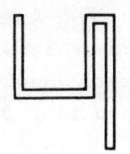

THE PERFECT OBJECT— AMULETS AND TALISMANS

... when you know everybody and everyone knows you, and you've got a rabbit's foot to keep away those old hoodoos ...
BESSIE SMITH

"I've found it . . . What does it mean?". I was browsing in an antique jewelry store with my friend Alice, a poet, who's also a bit of novice sorceress. While I was contemplating a pair of amber earrings, she had found a small silver ring. "What do you think?" she asked me, displaying a delicately made Egyptian hieroglyph on her finger. It snuggled there as if it belonged there, as if it had been sitting in the case for months, waiting for Alice . . . I grinned a little. It was obvious that Alice had found her Perfect Object.

"That's the Eye of Horus . . . it's a very powerful symbol; it means life force, creative power, and protection from the Evil Eye. Horus was the God of . . ."

Before I could wind into a long monologue on Horus, Alice closed her fingers and heaved a small sigh as she searched for her wallet. "I knew it was good," she said, and spent the rest of the day marveling over her lucky purchase.

From all reports that filter back, the Eye of Horus is doing its work. Alice has had some work published in the small quarterlies and has a new job at a drug therapy center that she loves. Alice has her Perfect Object.

On the other hand, those amber earrings were a disaster. Amber and I are just not compatible. They hung in my ears like lumps of lead and didn't do anything for me, spiritually or physically. I finally gave them to my astrologer, a bright woman whose affinity to amber charged them up with good feelings. The search for the perfect object is not always successful, even for the most avid collector of amulets and talismans.

People with an affinity for magick always seem to be collectors of objects. Maybe it's because we secretly still believe that we're going to find our fairytale version of the philosopher's stone, or maybe we just like the idea that certain things are magickal props from which we can draw raw animistic power. Some occultists and mystics argue that all those *things* are merely hindrances to really finding the source of power from within and a true Adept can work without them. But for me, it's just the love of beauty and vanity combined with a healthy respect for the protective charm against all those nasty evils lurking out there—including my own paranoia.

A collector collects for the love of the object rather than for its monetary or status-conferring value. Probably subconsciously, it's a security trip to own fifty-seven first editions of Proust or one hundred varieties of barbed wire, but security has always been one of the most elementary concerns of magick. It's a form of life insurance in its most primitive form. If you own your perfect object, then no real harm can befall you. By its virtues, your perfect object will protect you from everything from crop failure to being mugged in Bombay by a hunchbacked dwarf with six toes. The perfect object will keep you employed, loved, well fed, sheltered from the weather, un-depressed, and it may even help you win a lottery. When you find it, it finds you. It may be lying in the gutter or in a velvet box at Harry Winston's, but it picks you out and wants you. The perfect object finds you when you're least expecting it, believe me.

A lot of people wouldn't admit it, but they carry *something* as a lucky charm, even if it's just a small stone or a dried-up four-leaf clover. There is a story that a certain politician wore one tie through his entire campaign because he believed it brought him good luck. An editor I know has one dress that she believes brings her good luck whenever she wears it. I would rather be subjected to Alex's behavior therapy treatment in *A Clockwork Orange* with reruns of "Gomer Pyle" than part with the gold ring that belonged to my grandfather.

When I was a kid, we used to spend a lot of time poking through the clover patches in the yard looking for the mutant four-leaf. When you had one, you pressed it in a book because it was lucky. Only very recently, I learned that the four leaves have symbolic meaning. The first leaf stands for health, the second for wealth, the third for love, and the fourth for luck. What more could you ask?

Another popular charm is a rabbit's foot. But there's a catch. It has to be the left hind foot of a rabbit, shot with a silver arrowhead or bullet under a full moon. I know a gambler who went to a lot of trouble to obtain a rabbit's foot in just that manner. He kept it in his pocket with his stubs from the races at Brandywine, and holds on to it when the horses are running. I asked him once if he had any particular reason for a rabbit's foot and he just shrugged. Rabbits, according to English superstition, were supposed to be witches of the Satanic variety, of course, running home from the sabat. Apparently, the only way to kill such a were-rabbit was with a silver object, and, of course, the foot would be a symbol of the owner's courage and prowess as a hunter.

Horseshoes resemble a crescent moon, sacred to the lunar goddess who is in charge of fertility and abundance. Horseshoes make excellent house and barn charms when tacked up over the threshold, points UP, to catch and hold the luck. The best horseshoes, I am told, are the ones that have been thrown by a horse. Once the horse was a sacred animal and contact with the beast insures double protection and luck.

In America we regard black cats with some kind of horror. Ugh, a black cat just strolled across my path, bad luck. In England, black cats are considered lucky. An old English rhyme tells us ". . . as long as the cat of the house is black, the lasses for lovers never shall lack." Voodoos in America think that the bones and genitals of a black tom cat are a sure-fire way to restore sexual potency when worn around the neck in a flannel bag. Medieval sorceresses said there was a bone that could be found only in a black cat, and if you put the bone under your tongue, you would become invisible. Cats were a sacred animal to the Egyptians, who were great cat lovers, even going so far as to mummify them and put them in the tombs of their masters with the same elaborate care. A black cat is supposed to be the familiar of a witch and the devil's poker pal. The Chinese think a black cat around the house protects the premises from evil spirits. And a black cat charm worn around the neck is considered to be very lucky indeed by some people. One of the previous occupants of my apartment added a black cat knocker to my front door, probably as charm against burglars and vacuum cleaner salesmen.

Miniature animals are bric-a-brac fetishes for a lot of people I know. My friend Vivian found her perfect object in elephants. Within the space of a few weeks, she was gifted with elephant posters, an elephant charm, elephant stickers for her letters, and a shirt with pink baby elephants cavorting over the fabric. Since she is in the habit of checking out her astrological compatibility with men from me, she called one day to know what all those elephants coming at her from all directions *meant* for godssake. Elephants, I reassured her after a little research, are considered very lucky in India, where they are symbols of great strength and wisdom. The elephant god, Ganesha, supports the world on his shoulders. He in turn stands on the back of the giant tortoise. Ganesha removes obstacles and confers spiritual and physical strength on his worshipers. The elephant is one of the seven sacred animals of Buddhism, and white elephants are very, very lucky indeed. It's a very good totem for a woman who is going to school, holding down two jobs, and struggling to become successful in the New York art scene.

One should choose a totem animal for what it represents to its bearer. If you suddenly find yourself surrounded with giant tree sloth miniatures, pictures, and insignias, it may be a sign that there is some virtue in the giant tree sloth that you need.

Astrologically, I am a Taurus, but I have no particular fascination with bulls or cows; but if you like the emblem of your sign, there is good reason for you to wear it as an amulet. It reassures your identity, as a good amulet should, and gives you the assurance that the virtues of your sun sign are with you. Your sun sign is a form of personal totem fetish . . . a variation on a perfect object.

Luckily for me, another symbol for Taurus is the coiled serpent. I rather like snakes, so I have a Mexican snake ring. As I mentioned, the serpent biting its tail is a great symbol of the continuity and resurrection of all things from death to rebirth, a reminder of the balance of yin and yang. The snake is Damballah, the Lord of Life and Death in the Voodoo pantheon, an auspicious charm for anyone who practices Voodoo.

Religious symbols have always been considered lucky and protective. Both the cross and the Star of David go far beyond the nomadic Hebrew tribes. In the beginning, both were symbolic of sexual union—a very good fertility charm when set aside from their present religious significance. In this day, women hardly need fertility charms with the population exploding, but they are good for creative people who need fertile minds. As a symbol of faith, their magickal potency is doubled. Both are used to ward off vampires and other creatures of the night. Just be sure that you have the right symbol for the right vampire, as Roman Polanski pointed out in *Dance of the Vampires* when a Christian hero tries to fend off a Jewish vampire with a cross. "Wrong sign!" the vampire cheerfully remarks as he lunges toward his victim. The ankh, the Egyptian symbol of life, is another religious object with very lucky vibrations—especially if you're into Egyptian magick theory or the Tarot deck, or fascinated by the theories of the ancient civilizations. The Eye of

Horus, the particular charm of my friend Alice, is only one variation on the eye as an amulet. The concept of the evil eye is found almost universally. You've probably been subjected to it at one time or another in the most unwitting way. Usually it is women who are supposed to have it—another example of male chauvinism, one supposes, because I've had as much from men as women. Someone you barely know, or know all too well, will slither up beside you, usually the most obnoxious person in your class or office, and say something stupid or annoying in a smirking tone of voice that sounds like screeching chalk—and bingo, you're on a bummer all day. Or they compliment you on something in the same tone and you know they're jealous as hell. That's the evil eye in America. In other places, the "eye" isn't as subtle. I'd rather have someone give me the finger than the horned hand, although throwing someone the bird is about the same as the evil eye. Wearing the Eye of God, in any of its cultural variations, from the Eye of Horus to the yarn gods' eyes made by Indians, is a great charm against other people's nastiness. I've even seen a dude walking around with a rather bleary glass eye hung around his neck. Basically, the Eye of God watches out for you, deflecting jealousy and curses back on the generous donor. It's a good amulet for paranoid people, or those who have to work or live around someone who is genuinely malicious, for it not only deflects the evil eye, it also stops slandering and gossip about you.

Little replicas of the hand are popular charms in the Middle East and South America. Sometimes the hand is elaborately stylized, like the hand of Fatima worn by good Moslems. Fatima was the daughter of the prophet Mohammed. Because Islam forbids reproduction of anything in nature, this hand is carefully stylized and symmetrically designed. Sometimes a tiny eye-like ornament rests in the middle of the palm to throw the curse back doubly on its originator. The horned hand, a clenched fist with the index and pinkie extended, is worn by some Italians to repel the evil eye. I have seen beautiful miniature gold hands hung on the expensive watches of men involved with the Mafia. They *need* the protection, involved as they are in very high-risk jobs that sometimes erupt into violence. In Brazil and some other Latin American countries, macumbas wear a tiny hand with the thumb clenched between the second and third fingers, a variation at least as old as the Romans on the horned hand. This is figa, and it serves the dual function of being a good luck charm and a protective amulet.

The sun was the original Eye of God, watching the earth as it moved across the heavens every day. We consider the sun as a source of life-giving energy, and the sunburst symbol, with or without the face, is a very powerful amulet among the American Indians. Of course, the sun is especially good for people born under Leo, but anyone who wears a gold sunburst is assured of a long and prosperous life. The moon, done in silver or platinum, is good for people born under Cancer. Why there is a man in the moon, I couldn't tell you, for the moon is almost universally considered to be under the domination of a goddess. The crescent moon, worn with points to the left, or waxing side, is a good charm for people who feel the lunar vibes strongly, people like me, who sometimes feel loony when the moon is in the right (waxing) quarter and nourish secret fantasies of dancing under the moonlight. Stars, of both the six- and five-point variety, are lucky too. If you can afford it, a star set with diamond chips is a powerful amulet against being bewitched by magick seductions . . .

The star is also one of the great symbols of hope, a very good talisman for times when you're depressed or worried or feeling insecure. The early Christians, who had to hide their religion from persecutors sometimes, disguised their crosses as anchors. Anchors are a symbol of security and hope, especially good for sailors and fishermen, whose lives depend on the unpredictable moods of the sea. Wearing an anchor in combination with a cross and heart provides a triple charm. Three is a magick number; the symbols represent the three great virtues of faith, hope, and charity, and separately each one is a special amulet providing its wearer with belief, love, and security.

The swastika has not always had the evil vibrations of the Third Reich. It was an ancient symbol of the sun long before Hitler's occultists advised him to adapt it as the symbol for the Nazi party. When the spokes turn to the right, it is an auspicious symbol of life and creation. When they turn to the left, as they did on the Gestapo insignia, it symbolizes death and destruction. I suppose there are people who could wear the swastika and not think of it as having anything to do with the horror of war and brutality, but I don't think the unhealthy associations with the Nazis have completely vanished . . .

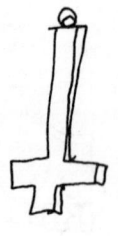

Another symbol with negative vibrations is the inverted cross. Worn as a crucifix by some Satanic cults who spend a large part of their time rejecting the Judeo-Christian religion (more time on that than on devil worship), it looks merely pathetic and a little sinister.

Saint Paul was crucified upside down, and that particular cross was his symbol. Since Paul took so many of Christ's teachings and distorted them into the kind of repression we still suffer from today, I really don't care much one way or the other for him or his inverted cross. If you're a Satanist, I think a better amulet might be the five-pointed star with the goat's head. The goat with his horns and rather grouchy expression is usually associated with Satanists of the Anton LaVey variety. In the aspect of the Great God Pan as lust, a goat might be a nice amulet for a Satanic Capricorn.

The pentagram, a five-pointed star set within a circle, is one of the emblems of witchcraft. The five-pointed star represents humanity —arms, legs, and head, protected by the goddess of the moon, to whom the circle is consecrated. It makes a very good amulet worn around the neck while working spells, particularly those of the European witch variety.

Fish and birds are good amulets for people who travel a lot, especially if you're traveling by sea or air. Fish are a symbol of sexual potency; if your lover isn't getting it on these days, present the dear one with one of those Saigon fish made in jointed layers of scales. But, don't tell your lover *why* that particular gift, or you might ruin the whole purpose of the charm by insulting him or her in a very sensitive part of the psyche. Conversely, if you're tired of sharing your bed and board with Harriet or Freddy, the sweet gift of a small mother-of-pearl bird charm should insure that the relationship has a graceful breaking off point, with no hard feelings on either side. The idea is of course that he or she will fly away as free as the bird. Little enameled bats have the same effect, but it will be a bit harsher, like a bat out of hell . . .

Necklaces of acorns are worn to insure that a current lover stays home. Acorn necklaces were worn by Norse women as a tribute to the mother goddess, Freya. The acorn is supposed to resemble the hairstyle of the goddess. A dried acorn kept around the house insures the faithfulness of a lover too.

The Voodoos are very big on all sorts of charms, most of them worn to attract good luck and keep away the bad. A favorite Voodoo charm of mine is the wanga, a small fabric pouch stuffed with herbs and various gris-gris. Usually the pouch is made of red flannel, worn around the neck or carried in the pocket. A client comes to the Voodooist and describes his particular problems, and like a doctor prescribing, the Voodooist will fill the bag with the appropriate herbs, black cats' bones, stones, teeth, or whatever is needed. I've been making these little bags for my friends for a couple of years, sometimes in the traditional red flannel, sometimes in linen or velvet, with some beadwork or embroidered designs. A friend of mine swears he feels as though he's wearing a tea bag around his neck, but I haven't heard him complain about having bad luck lately. Wangas are good for a certain length of time; gradually, you can feel the power draining out of them and you have to make new ones. If you wear your wanga until you feel its power draining out, give it to a friend whose vibrations will renew the power for himself. A wanga is particularly effective when you're working with Voodoo spells, or if you feel as though someone is working Voodoo against you ...

Scarabs are a good charm for Scorpio and Virgo people. The scarab beetle fascinated the Egyptians, always preoccupied with death and what lay beyond. These little hardshelled beetles hatched themselves in dung. To an observant and not very scientific Egyptian watching this process, it looked as if the beetle was magickally creating itself from merde. It was a miracle. Scarabs are a symbol of life everlasting. Cut from a semiprecious stone and worn about the person, they insure good health and a bountiful life.

In the search for the perfect object, never overlook your birthstone. The custom of giving a precious stone that falls under the domain of the sun sign is at least five hundred years old. According to the old occult philosophists, minerals, animals, and vegetables were governed by one of the planets and one of the houses of the zodiac. For instance, the topaz, with its clear, yellow glitter, is ruled by the sun and falls under the domain of Leo. A pearl, governed by the moon, falls under the domain of Cancer. In addition, the occultists wrote, each gem had special virtues and powers that were released when worn in harmony with the sun sign of the owner. Should you be threatened by any danger, the stone will change color; should you fail to notice that, it will fall from its setting. Every sign has at least three stones under its dominion, so if you hate diamonds and don't want to hock your TV to practice magick, choose a moonstone or an agate.

I'm totally hooked on body ornament just on its own beauty. I love the dangling, clinking earrings, necklaces, bracelets, anklets, nose rings, belts, and rings that are traditional costume among Eastern, African, and Indian people, not to mention the Gypsies. You could give me a handful of beads and I'd wear them—you could keep Manhattan Island.

But why would a person who must harvest rice or do other heavy labor burden himself with all that stuff? Certainly there is no reason for a status display in the field. Well, not true. The primal function of body ornament is to protect the invaluable person from the demons who cause disease and injury. Necklaces and headbands protect the precious head with the important circle, a universal mother symbol. Rings and bracelets guard the hands in their labors. Belts were originally hung below the waist above the genitals, the most important part of the body, the center of reproduction. Earrings must be large and dangly so that the noise and splendor will distract evil spirits from entering the ears. Anklets and toe rings protect and guide the feet away from harm.

Since demons are notoriously fond of entering the body through any orifice, each one must be sealed or protected by ornamentation. Hindu women wear kohl around their eyes not only to enhance the darkness of their pupils, but also to prevent evil spirits from causing them to go blind. Tattooing and cosmetic body painting discourage the demons from doing any harm. The bigger, brighter, and more elaborate the body ornaments, the more power and protection against harm.

Back in the Sixties, when some of us were running around with jingling bells and dangling fringes, carrying sticks of incense, we were unconsciously resurrecting the ideas of our ancestors who believed that loud, cheerful noises like bells frightened away little devils. The little devils we wanted to frighten away included the hostilities of straight society, most of all the law, and the Demon of Bad Trips. We knew we were different and open to all kinds of repercussions, and it was a primitive method of protecting ourselves from the consequences of our deviation from the norm.

Bells are almost universally rung over churches and temples and other places of worship to frighten away the bad spirits and attract the good. When David speaks of making a joyful noise unto the Lord, he is instructing worshipers to set up a sound that will attract the ear of God and repulse the ear of Satan.

In the Middle East, where the fear of the evil eye is a much more serious business than it is here, fringes and tassels are considered very lucky. Evil spirits become entangled in dangling things, growing so confused that they leave the person alone. Several years ago, a friend presented me with an Arabian amulet. A piece of carnelian was cut into the shape of a stylized leaf and engraved with ninety-nine of the names of Allah. The stone was set into a brass and silver decoration cast in circular patterns and suspended on a heavy silver chain hung with eight silver tassels. Including the pendant, that is nine tassels, a lucky number. The original wearer was meant to be protected by the power of Allah's name from the evil eye. Like some things you receive and don't understand, I had some bad feelings about this amulet originally; at one point, I even tried to give it away, but it wanted me and so I retrieved it and it's been a good amulet to me ever since.

Ornamental borders on clothing, especially around the neck and hem, are also protectors of the person. Demons love any opening, and these must be safeguarded against their entrance by the use of designs and colors, particularly in the East. If you look at an Indian shirt, you will notice the fine embroidery that rests around the collar like a necklace, protecting the all-important head. The tiny mirrors sewn into fabric are also demon repellent, for the little buggers, like Count Dracula, are deathly afraid of the flashing lights and reflections of mirrors. The more prominent a person is in the status of the community, the more protection he needs from jealous humans and injurious demons, ideas that have survived unconsciously into the twentieth century.

When you start your career as a sorcerer, picking and choosing spells from whatever culture suits your needs, a little of that sense of drama begins to creep into your tastes. You start dressing, furnishing, and feeling a little mystical. Very subtly, you want to create a magick ambiance around yourself.

The eclectic sorcerer is usually a born collector of the strange object and the odd information. Your friends have to drag you, kicking and screaming, away from every junkstore, bookshop, antique emporium, and import store, not to mention tattoo parlors and street scenes in your path. You may be standing in the unemployment line every week, but you'll sell your foodstamps for a book or a concert ticket. It's the experience. The experience of having something, not for how much it costs, but the joy of it all, the feelings it gives you, the experience of beauty and pleasure.

Good!—because your tools of the art are going to be the most important talismans and amulets of your spellcasting.

Whether you're making a Voodoo doll or conjuring up the Grand Demon of the Seventh Pentacle of Thoth, there are certain things that you're going to need.

The first thing to think about is a place for your spellcasting. Oh, there'll be times when you're outdoors, scraping moss off a tombstone or laying out shells and candles by the river, but most of the time, especially if you live in a cold climate, you're going to be inside with the door locked. And that means you're going to need a place of your own where you can set up your shop. Most people don't have a room they can dedicate completely to their art, even when you live alone in a seven-room apartment. Mothers come to visit, friends drop in, and Habondia help us, what if you decide to sublet for a summer in Haiti? Suppose you share a room with a sibling, spouse, or roommate? Try. I know a warlock who lived on a commune in Vermont and kept his occult practices a complete secret from everyone, including his ladyfriend, for years. And, on a commune, it's pretty hard to keep anything a secret. But he was really powerful and had a pretty high ratio of success. He simply arranged his time around everyone else's. If anyone pressed him, he'd say he had to meditate and lock the door. Amazingly enough, it worked. But, as I say, he was powerful to begin with. If you have any choice in the matter whatsoever, even if it's for a four-by-four spot in the attic where you can go while Mumsy and Daddy are nodding out over telly, I know you'll find a way.

When you've got your space, the next thing you'll want is a workbench for spellcasting. An altar. I recommend a low table where you can squat or sit for your rituals. The advantages of this arrangement are pretty obvious. For maximum concentration, it is best to be comfortable. If you have to stand for four or five hours, you begin to forget what you're working on and start thinking about how your back and feet are killing you, and that really does your spell in. If you have to work in your bedroom, living room, or any other place where the friends and family are trucking through asking a lot of questions. it's a wise idea to make everything very portable. A coffee table or low chest can double as an altar and a workbench. After your friends leave, you can throw the back issues of *Rolling Stone* in the corner and spread out your cloth. These covers can be as expensive and complex as hand-embroidered fifteenth-century altar cloths from a church, or as simple as a piece of clean, white sheet. It should be new and, like the other tools you're going to have to collect, bought or made for the purpose of covering your altar. When you disassemble the altar, the cloth can be washed to remove any trace of the spell's vibrations and folded away until the next time. It's easier to start out very simply and make the big investments later, when you're sure of what you want and how it fits in with your magicks. If you want to really invest some time and effort in the

BASIC ALTAR

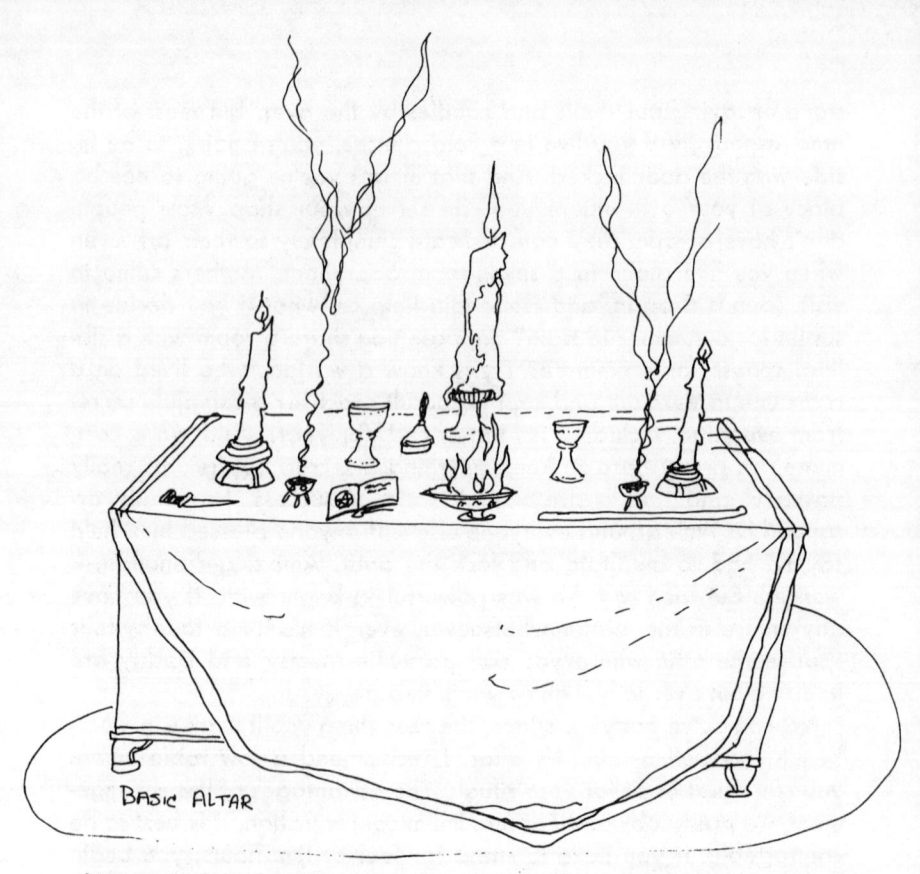

thing, you should make your own, or even a set of them, embroidered with the appropriate symbols in different fabrics and colors.

Candlelight, rather than artificial electric bulbs, not only make a much more dramatic setting, they are also an absolute necessity in creating the right vibrations in the room. If you can set up in front of a fireplace, all the better. But you will need candlesticks—at least four of them. The only requirement for your first candlesticks is that they be sturdy. They can be as elaborate or as simple as you like, as long as they have the right magickal vibrations on them. If you see a pair in an antique store, pick them up and handle them for a while, trying to see what sort of feeling you get from them. Be practical. Make sure that you can squeeze your candles into them. How you feel is the important thing.

You should also have at least four goblets or bowls. Anything, once again, from wooden salad bowls to gold chalices, as long as they don't leak and will hold water, earth, or herbs. Choose them by your feeling toward them. Incense, like candlelight, is an absolute necessity. So you will need an incense burner. You can get these really cheap little Indian brass things in any five and ten or you can go totally berserk and buy an antique censer from a religious supply store for as much as two thousand dollars. It's also a good idea to purchase a metal chalice or stand that you can burn larger things in, like image candles, or for those truly dramatic occasions when you want to impress the fools, a handful of musk crystals. A brazier is a good idea because it's fireproof—and you don't want the house to burn down, do you?

To complete your setting, you'll want to bring in your secondary amulets. The bric-a-brac of magick. Ceramic frogs, a skull, seashells, bead strings, crescent moons, agate hearts, statues, whatever. Your talismans and amulets that you don't wear.

Some people prefer to cast all their ritual spells in the nude, taking the idea from witches that the human body gives off more power when unencumbered by clothes. Just a few rings, beads, bracelets, belts, whatever. Some sorcerers say that even those ornaments interfere with the current of magick. I don't think I would want to cast a spell without my own special magickal amulets to protect me from any adverse vibrations that might arise. But keeping a robe around just for wearing during spellcastings is a good idea. You can make a simple caftan if you're handy with a needle, or you can buy something exotic and foreign with lots of embroidery and mirrors. I have several, in different colors and designs, which can be slipped off easily at the last minute, but my favorite is a heavy, green brocade dolman lined in red silk that came from . . . well, never mind, I'm not telling all my secrets. It's just a very potent garment for spellcast wearings.

These are basic tools, variations of the perfect object. Just because they are tools does not diminish their magickal protective power. When you're casting a spell, you are very, very open indeed; and it is then that you need the best allies you can summon. This is why it is so important that you choose your tools with so much care and love and feeling for the object. Each one is a treasure. The more you use them, the more power they have. As you pick and discard your tools of the art, each time the vibrations should become a little stronger. But don't be afraid to experiment at first. Simple spells deserve simple equipment, so don't be afraid that a pair of forty-nine-cent candleholders are going to blow your scene. The important thing is that you and your tools have a rapport. I've seen Voodoos in New Orleans working with some of the most pathetic-looking stuff (to my then closed eyes) bringing their own glorious faith to the work. There have been times when all I've had to work with was a deck of regular playing cards and a despairing friend. It worked.

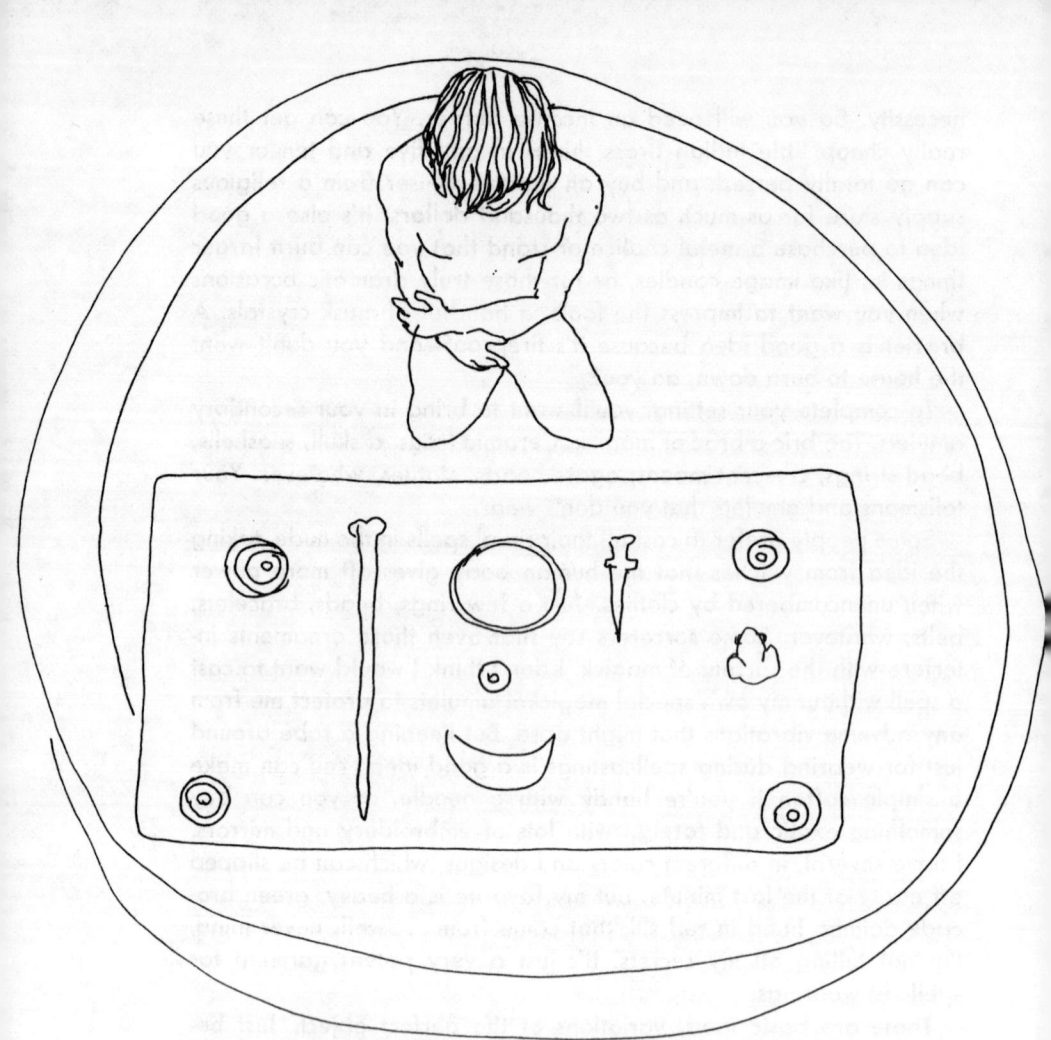

Your home base is a talisman in itself. The space where you set up your altar should be, like that of the old witches, easily disassembled and easily assembled. It is important that the curiosity of Mrs. Grundy is not aroused. Secrecy is often your best talisman, just as clever use of psychology is the charm at other times. Remember, you are a magician, a sorcerer, an adept of the art, and all the perfect objects in the world cannot stand alone. They are your accessories, lending you their inert occult virtues when you need them.

94

Which is why you should have a little black bag. Although you are operating from a home base, there are going to be times when you have to venture out on field trips among the mortals. You're going out and gathering herbs, or cutting locks of hair (Don't be silly, Andrea, it's juuuuust aaaa joooke—there. Took it from under the back. Doesn't even look as though I did it. Why? Well, you do have a birthday coming up, don't you? . . . you'll see. I want to match it with something . . .)

In fact, when the word gets around among your friends that you're into magick, you're going to get a lot of phone calls. Some people will be hostile, some indifferent, and some very curious. Most people will want you to tell them about their sign, or give them a card or palm reading, but there may come a time when you're jolted away from sitting there, minding your own business, by someone who is totally hysterical and has it fixed in his or her mind that you're not just a sorcerer but a witch doctor too. Depending on how charitable your nature is, or how much of a risk you're willing to take with other people's stupidity, superstition, or opinion of you, you'll either tell such callers to call a doctor, talk to them over the phone till they see how silly they're being, or go over and try to bail them out of the mess they've gotten themselves into. Usually, they just want someone to assure them that they aren't tripping out and seeing demons, that Freddy will/will not come back, or that you love them, they're good people, and there's no reason to be afraid. But sometimes, and I use that word to mean very rarely, they want some magick on house call. For those occasions—field trips—you will need a portable kit.

The contents of your kit vary from mission to mission, but a few basic items you might keep together in one place include:

A small pair of scissors (indispensable)
A penknife
A fountain pen or rapidograph
Two or three packets of black, red, green, and white
   embroidery yarn
A needle of the sewing variety
Two or three candle stubs (white, green, blue, red, or black)
Matches
A packet of all-purpose herbs

The rest can be improvised in an emergency, but think of the glory, not to mention the security, of being able to cope with almost any situation that can be dealt with by magick. A good sorcerer is always on the lookout for an opportunity to snatch up a piece of rare herb growing in the sidewalk or to duck into the bathroom to do some quick love magick at a loft party.

The longer you study the art, adepts say, the less you will need any kind of paraphernalia, including the amulets and tools. The highest adepts are able to perform spells requiring an enormous amount of concentration and strength just on their own will. But, to my direct knowledge, there are only about twenty people in the whole world, the true adepts, who have risen above the material plane so far that they don't need the day-to-day necessities of the rest of us. This doesn't mean that you should spend the next six months or sixty years walking around looking like a Christmas tree. Those who know, know. It's not only indescribably tacky to announce that you're a sorcerer to the world at large (Oh, there are people who do, believe me) when you're loaded down with beads, earrings, amulets, and an outfit that would make Kris Kristofferson look like the Pope; it also lays you in for some very hard times from more practiced magicians who aren't as tolerant as your mother or your dearest friends are of your little idiocyncrasies. Before you are a magician, you are a person. And that is probably the best amulet you can wear.

Amulets, you remember, are objects you choose or make because they feel lucky and protective. You wear them on your body and draw strength from them. They are charms to provide an all-purpose power. An amulet can be anything from a piece of red thread to the Curse of the Kohinoor Diamond. The choice is yours, for your perfect amulet is a subjective experience.

Talismans and amulets have a fuzzy boundary line. An object can be both an amulet and a talisman, but for the sake of clarity, talismans are objects usually manufactured or compounded for a specific magickal purpose.

Sometimes the making of the talisman is a little magickal ritual in itself; sometimes it is part of a larger ritual, in which the talisman is an essential piece of paraphernalia. This is particularly true of ceremonial magick.

The earliest talismans were magickal drawings, like the veve of the Voodooists and the hieroglyphs of the Egyptians, designs that were reproduced from the ceremony by the officiating priest. They were inscribed on the skin as a tattoo (very protective), engraved on metal, written on papyrus, scratched into pottery, worn about the person as a constant reminder of the power of the gods. Since gods are well known to travel under a lot of aliases, to draw veve for Ezili would be the same as engraving a talisman for Venus, or casting a pentacle for Habondia. To etch a seal for Jupiter would be the same as creating a veve for Legba or wearing a medal of Saint Peter. If you wish to invoke the services of a particular deity and charge your talisman with the power of that deity, then you would choose a day and hour of the week consecrated to that god and his planet. On that hour of that day, you make your talisman and consecrate it to your spell. If it is a long-term thing, like keeping a steady supply of money coming in, then you renew the spell once a month, at the particular quarter of the moon (for money, a new moon) that applies. Let's be really nasty and suppose that you are casting a very heavy-duty death spell. Reggie the Rat, your friendly neighborhood smack dealer, has been pushing bad skag and your brother is nodding out in a corner. Reggie deserves to die. You would cast the talisman of Saturn, Lord of the Underworld, or the Veve of Baron Samdei, or the seal of any death god from any magickal ceremony on the turn of the old moon at the hour of Saturn, on the day of Saturn. In the meantime, of course, you are working your other death spells, bringing your talisman to the ritual, touching it to the doll, or concentrating on it and what horrors lie in the future for Reggie the Rat. When the spells are completed, you either destroy the talisman with fire (the universal purifier), or if all else has failed, slip into Reggie's house or car and hide it there to complete its work.

Love talismans should be carried and created in the same way—created in the turn of the waxing moon, consecrated in the day and hour of Venus, and carried about whenever you expect to run into the Victim of your Art. Have the talisman present at all your love-inducing spellcasts.

For the traditional talismans of the grimoires (the medieval magick texts), which must be etched into specific metals, you have to be a silversmith or at least know someone who is discreet and cooperative enough to lend you his instruments and show you what to do. Failing that, both the grimoires and I advise that you get a jeweler to make up the seal. Since discretion is the better part of having jewelers make up odd-looking talismans, you can consecrate it at home and in your own way at the day and hour of the planet without having it lose any of its power. Any amulet or talisman you have made up to your own specifications by a craftsman rather than a practitioner of the art should be duly consecrated.

If you've found a great piece in a store, but you aren't really sure about its vibrations... it might have belonged to a Serbo-Croatian countess who spent her time making the lives of her people miserable, or a little old man who hung around in doorways in a black Robert Hall raincoat muttering obscenities at nine-year-old kids—those kind of vibrations you simply don't need—just holding on to something for a few days usually divests it of the former owner's vibrations, but some people are so awful or powerful that their aura clings to their possessions long after they've lost the need for them. Just to be sure that your perfect object is a perfect object, retaining all its inert virtues and none of the vibrations of an unknown former owner, it is best to perform the same consecration and exorcism ceremony that you perform over a freshly created talisman.

Assemble your usual paraphernalia on the altar as if you were going to cast a spell. Use white candles and a fresh incense of vervain, cloves, sandalwood, and rose buds. Fill your chalice with the Voodoo potpourri wash mentioned on page 40. This is one of those ceremonies where you should divest yourself of all your other ornaments and talismans so that their vibrations do not interfere with this very special magickal one. After you have gone through the processes of clearing your mind and drawing up the circle, present the object to the four cardinal points, repeating the incantation:

> To the North, hail! I present thee to the Gods.
> To the South, hail! I present thee to the Gods.
> To the East, hail! I present thee to the Gods.
> To the West, hail! I present thee to the Gods.

Having presented the perfect object to the gods, placate the spirits of the elements by passing it over the candles, saying: "I consecrate thee to my service by fire."

Then touch it to your chalice of earth and salt, saying: "I consecrate thee to my service by earth."

Then pass it over the empty chalice, saying: "I consecrate thee to my service by air."

Then pass it over the chalice of water, saying: "I consecrate thee to my service by water."

Last, anoint it with your potpourri wash and incant:

> By the spirits that command the air, by the spirits that command the earth, by the spirits that command the fire, by

the spirits that command the water, as here below so above. I consecrate this amulet to my power and protection, that its virtues may be my virtue, that my magicks may be strengthened, and the spirits commanded at their hour and day, do my bidding through their power.

Hold the amulet or talisman in your hand for a while and charge it with your very intense emotional vibrations. It is yours now, and all influences of other people have been driven away.

Ring the bell, shut the book, and blow out the candle. Wear your amulet for the rest of the day and sleep with it on your person. If you have nightmares, horrible things happening to you, and you haven't been eating lobster, it is better to discard the thing entirely. Nothing you can do is going to improve it. Better yet, give it to your worst enemy and let him catch all the horrors. Tell him it will change his luck. Probably he'll be thrilled as hell with your offer of friendship—unless he's into magick too. Nasty!!

In many cultures special prayers and spells are repeated as charms against everything from the evil eye to being an old maid. These incantations when written on something and carried about on the person are supposed to be extremely potent talismans. Even in cultures where only a very small percentage of the population can read, the symbols and letters that make up words are regarded with a great deal of awe. Anything that has your monogram on it—a pin or a shirt—might be a protective amulet. The Cabalists go so far as to assign a magickal significance to each letter of the Hebrew alphabet; particularly potent are the four letters that compose the secret name of God. The Chinese symbols for good luck are written on a strip of rice paper and carried as talismans to insure good fortune in all dealings; the many names of Allah for a Moslem are inscribed on charms and worn. The Pennsylvania Dutch copy passages from the Bible out in longhand and wear them tied into a scroll and hung on a string with three loops. Called *Himmel's-briefs* (literally translated, "Heaven's Notes"), they are Biblical passages combined with specific incantations from *The Long Lost Friend* to insure maximum protection from mad dogs, childbed death, bullets, crop failures, witches, hexeri, disease, and every other manner of evil. Particularly popular are passages from the first five books of the Old Testament and certain of the Psalms.

Voodoos sometimes follow the same practice, and carry in their wanga bags relevant passages from both the Old and New Testaments. They believe that anyone who can recite the forty-sixth psalm backwards is protected from the machinations of gris-gris.

It is interesting to note that some sects of Hasidic Jews have been carrying prayers around as a part of their costume for several centuries. The custom is known to the Gypsies, to the Arabs, the Hindus, and the Buddhists of Tibet, who ceaselessly spin their prayer wheels and meditate upon the passages inscribed upon them.

I have a written talisman, passed on to me long ago by a favorite teacher. On a small piece of rice paper she had carefully scripted the following charm against all evil that might befall an unwary traveler in the unknown world:

> Fire cannot burn me
> Earth cannot bury me
> Air cannot freeze me
> Water cannot drown me

I carry it in an old silver locket and recite it under my breath when I'm hitching or have to take the subway late at night. For double protection against perverts on the road, have it engraved on the back of a Saint Christopher medal. Saint Christopher may be off the official Catholic calendar but he's still pretty powerful in Voodoo circles.

Demons come in human and non-human forms. If you're threatened by some force or person, this talisman, inscribed on parchment in red ink, will protect you from any physical onslaught. It comes from Sanskrit text:

> Release me, evil power, release me, the unfortunate victim of your malice. Let me escape this evil thing and be happy again!

It's very effective for those day-ahead anxieties about such events as speeches, job interviews, and reunions with lovers, dealers, and parents.

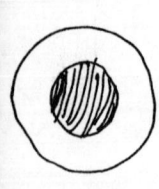

King Solomon was one of the greatest adepts in the history of magick. In the Middle Ages, several grimoires turned up bearing his name and purporting to be translations of his ancient works on magick. That Solomon was a writer we know from the two books of the Bible attributed to his pen. Whether or not he was the author of this charm to banish evil spirits, he sounds very mysterious; just pronouncing this formula should be enough to scare anything. Write it inside a circle and carry it about in your pocket.

        Lofaham
        Solomon
        Iyouel
           Inysenaoui

The last charm against evil spirits comes from Hebrew magick too. As the name of the Hebrew demon of illness diminishes, so will disease. Keep this on in a circle too.

        Ochnotinos
        Chnotinos
        Hnotinos
        Nofinos
        Otinos
        Tinos
        Inos
        Nos
        Os

If you want to deal with demons, and properly controlled they can be helpful little beasties if you don't turn your back on them, then carry this talisman with you. It should be written on black silk with the blood of a black hen, and stored in a black silk bag.

        Helix, Xileh, Helix, Xileh, Abarack O!

But what fun can you have from talismans that just protect you from demons? Suppose you'd like to attract someone to you who is quite undemoniacal in your eyes? Love charms are as popular as demon repellent spells in every culture. The following Japanese poem is written with brush and ink on rice paper and read three times while sitting by the river or ocean on a moonlit night.

        Waiting on Matsuo's shore
        This quiet evening
        For you who do not come
        I burn with longing
        Fierce as the fire of the salt pans.

The talisman below is written on a piece of red wet terra cotta and worn about the neck on a red ribbon. I picked it up from an Irish gypsy for about sixty cents. It wasn't much money for such a quaint charm to me, but to the woman who sold it to me, five shillings was a fortune. The charm may be switched around according to the sex of its bearer:

> He the cock, I the hen
> He the ax, and I the helve
> He the dog, and I the bitch
> This my will shall be.

It's a sad, sweet little charm that you can recite under breath. I honestly felt that I had been ripped off by a bit of impromptu charlatanism until I discovered the incantation is known in both Gypsy and English magick.

The third love charm was given to me by a sorceress in Long Island who swears it works. At least it worked for her. I'm truly hoping that my charms are stronger than hers, because I half promised I wouldn't tell it to anyone. But actually, I'm not breaking my promise—I'm writing it. You can write it inside a heart and wear it in a scroll. It's from a Sanskrit grimoire, the *Arthava Veda*. This one is for women.

> I am possessed by burning love for this man; and this love comes to me from Apsaras, who is ever Victorious. Let the man yearn for me; desire me, let his desire burn for me! Let him desire me as nothing has been desired before. I love him, want him; he must feel this same desire for me! O Martus, let him be filled with love. O spirit of the air, fill him with love! O agni, let him burn with love for ME!"

From the same Indian grimoire, a talisman for men, prepared in the same fashion:

> With the all powerful arrow of love do I pierce thy heart, O woman! Love, love that causes unease that shall overcome thee. Love for me! That arrow flying true and straight will cause in thee a burning desire! It has the head of my love—its shaft is my determination to possess thee! O Mitra! O Varuna! Strip her of her will, as she has stripped me of mine!

A medieval grimoire, *The Black Hen*, promises that by speaking the charm below, which, written on that legendary black cat bone and placed under the tongue, will make you invisible. Perfect for those embarrassing times when you say something stupid to Mick Jagger:

BENATIR CARACRAU DEDOS ETINARMI

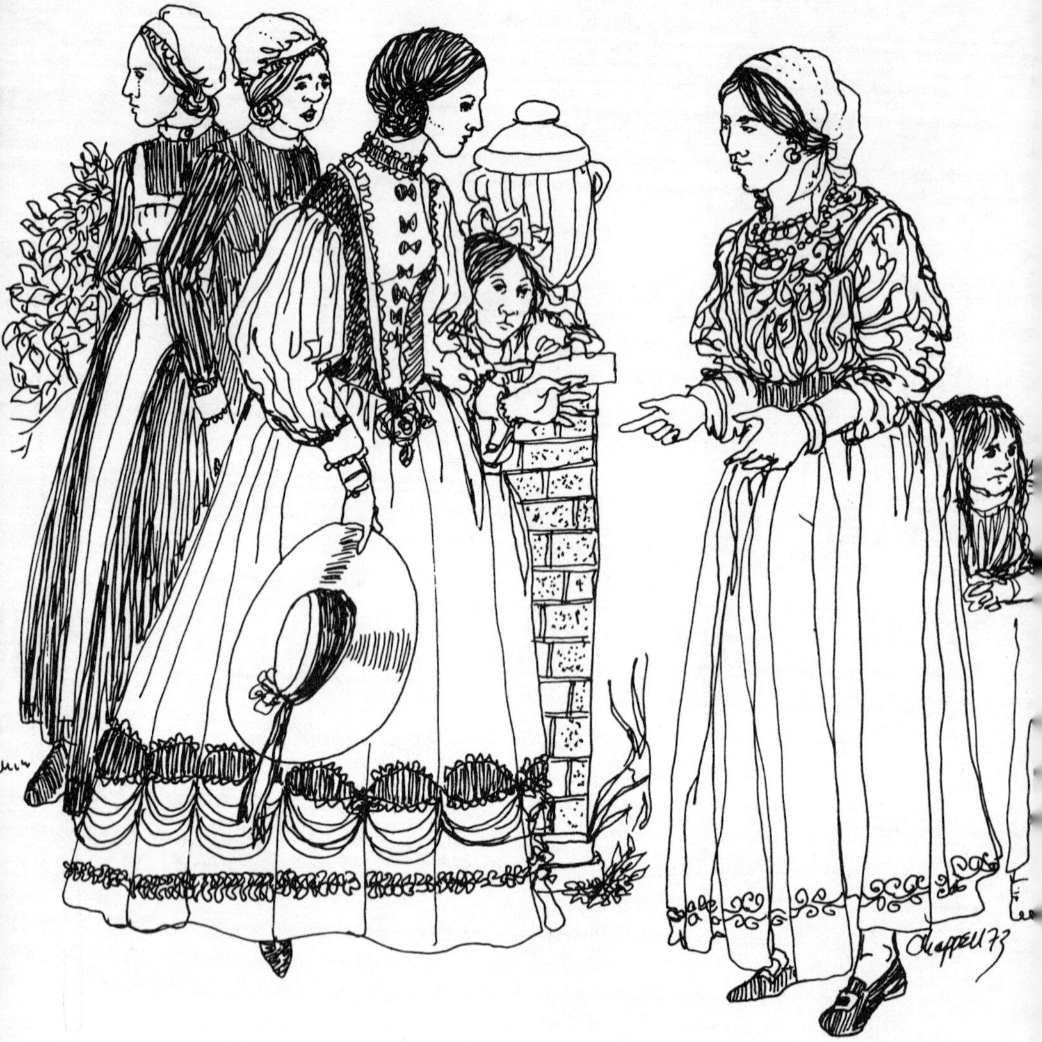

5

GYPSY MAGICK— PEOPLE OF EARTH AND STARS

Oh, to follow the wandering Gypsies, Oh.
OLD ENGLISH BALLAD

I don't suppose there is a person alive who hasn't at one time or another vowed to run away. To sea, to Aunt Amelia's house, or over the hills and far away with the Gypsies. Presumably, there are people who have managed to run away with the Gypsies, who have slept out under the stars, learned all the secrets of vagabond life and gone along with it quite happily. But in a world of indoor plumbing and television sets, the sacrifice of a comfortable camper with all its modern conveniences for a horse-drawn wagon or an old panel truck seems a lot to ask. The closest to the Gypsy life many of us will ever get is making the crossing from one coast to another in a VW van with a lot of other people. It is fun to play at being a Gypsy or at least the carefree music, palmreading, and traveling image we have of Gypsies, but even the hardiest flower child could not live happily for long under the circumstances of modern Gypsy life. For the Gypsies are unlike any other people on the face of the earth. Even today, when anthropologists seek them out and their privacy and freedom of movement are decreasing, the Gypsies have managed to retain their own secrets, their own beliefs and ways, changing with the times from horse-drawn caravans to panel trucks and winter homes, trading a certain amount of their own freedom for the ways of the gadje (non-Gypsy) respectability. Perhaps the comfort of civilization has finally gotten to many of them, at least in America, or perhaps, like any persecuted people, they have learned to go underground and outwardly conform to the ways of the world. But the people from whom the beat generation took the name Bohemians and tried to adapt a life style based on their image continue on.

Who are the Gypsies? Are they really the popular stereotype dark-haired, dark-eyed Romanies playing throbbing violins and dancing by the light of the campfire, dressed in richly colored clothes and covered with jangling jewelry? A people who have second sight and great magickal ability? Are they tramps and thieves who, as is still popularly believed in some parts of the world, steal everything from chick to child? Like any radical stereotype, the image has some basis in fact. The Hungarian tribes, who fit this stereotype most closely, still continue to dress and travel with flair, color, and music. But one can see a fashionably dressed fair Swedish Gypsy who works in an office and lives in a tasteful apartment with music and plants in the same way. Or an Irish tinker wrapped in tweeds, eating hedgehog stew on a bitter, cold fall afternoon. No . . . stereotypes do not always work, especially in the world of Gypsies. A fiercely clannish people, they themselves are sharp snobs about the divisions of tribes and occupations. A French Gypsy from the Basque country would have the greatest difficulty trying to speak his particular Romany dialect with a Russian Gypsy from the steppes. There are widely varied tribes and varieties of Gypsies. Some studies indicate certain basic patterns in all the tribes, but they indicate their differences too. For the Gypsies have always adapted to the ways of the people with whom they found themselves. Hungarian Gypsies dress in their own colorful versions of Hungarian peasant costume. American Gypsies shop at Sears Roebuck and yes, even keep bank accounts. Therefore, this discussion won't pin these people to any categories, for we are not really interested in affixing them to a type, time, or place. Admittedly, even Gypsiologists can't do that.

As far as can be determined, the Gypsies first appeared in Europe in the fifteenth century. A wandering band, traveling in wagons drawn by horses, some fifty men with wives and children appeared in a Balkan town with letters of passage from the prince of the territory. According to the records, they were metalworkers, performers, and fortunetellers. They also had an unfortunate tendency to take anything that wasn't nailed down. When the outraged town council demanded to know what the prince meant by giving these people a passport, he replied that he'd never even heard of them before. By that time, they were far away into the next country. Tribes of Gypsies continued to flow into Europe from the east. Their nomadic life outraged the more settled people of Europe, who alternately feared and hated, consulted and aided these strange bands of exotic people. They called themselves Roms, from which comes the word "Romany," also used to describe a person of Gypsy blood and language, or Dukes of Egypt, Egyptians. "Egyptians" was a word used in those days to describe any group of wanderers who performed for handouts both acts of magick and magic. The commonly accepted theory is that Egypt was regarded by people as a hotbed of every magickal art known to man. "Egyptians" becomes shortened to "Gypsy" in English, "Gitain," "Gitan," or "Gitano" in the Romance languages. The people we call Gypsies seemed content to accept this appellation. They in turn called their hosts "gadje," which seems closely related to the Yiddish "goyem," a non-person, a hick, a yokel, a person who doesn't know. The Gypsies regarded the gadje with as much indifference and dislike as the gadje regarded the Gypsies. They stole from them because, as it has been put, they had no particular sense of private property. And, too often, if someone is told that he is nasty, a no-good thief, charlatan, and liar, he is going to act that way.

Europe, working so hard to become settled and civilized, regarded Gypsies with a kind of horror accorded in America these days to hippies, Hell's Angels, and a Communist invasion. They were driven from localities only to return again, twice as many in number. However, if their habits seemed outrageous to the moral, they were valued for their abilities as craftsmen, horse traders, and performers. And fifteenth-century Europe was hardly a docile, law-abiding place in its own right. It was a time when many people were on the road, wandering from place to place in an effort to sustain life. There were runaway serfs, mercenary soldiers, homeless families, runaways of every sort vagabonding on the road in those days. Illiteracy, superstition, and bigotry were common to the day. The memories of the Tartar invasions, the driving of the Moors from Spain, and the Barbarians were still vivid enough to make people suspicious of anyone who was different and came from the East.

When the Inquisition was in full power, accusations of witchcraft and sorcery were death sentences. That the gypsies managed to survive this at all, to keep their own way of life, is a tribute to their tenacity. Perhaps it is this strong survival instinct that makes them keep their secrets so closely guarded even today, that gives them such contempt for the gadje. They wandered on, forever wandering, and no one really made too much of an attempt to exterminate them until Hitler. The Swedes tried to expel them with harsh punishments and death sentences, the French passed laws trying to regulate their activities and movements, but most countries seemed resigned to their presence, strange as it was.

And then the Third Reich: knowing Hitler's obsession with the occult, it is a terrible irony to note that over two hundred thousand Gypsies were known to have died in the concentration camps. They were of impure blood, like the Jews, it was said, and that was sufficient. But both peoples have always been persecuted and both peoples were commonly regarded as having strong magickal traditions. The oral traditions of the Gypsies seem to relate them closely to the Jews, and there may have existed between these two people, who have so much history in common, a mutual sense of protection and shelter in the times of terror. There is no data available on the fate of Gypsies in Communist countries, but one may safely guess that deculturalization, especially in Stalin's time, meant a Siberian camp. While there is much written on the treatment of Soviet Jews, the Gypsies as always remained a forgotten people in Russia.

Gypsies appear in literature about the time of Rousseau's interest in the "noble savage." The Romantic Age seized on them as a genuine species of homegrown natural man, romanticizing their lives and customs, but it took those good solid Victorians to actually start serious field research on their life style. One can see the would-be anthropologist down from his chair at Cambridge, sitting in a noisy, slovenly Gypsy camp with pen and paper, trying not to get frock coat dirty and scribbling away as some elder recited the legends of their being, beliefs, and customs. Disdainful and full of proper Victorian morality as these scholars were, one can read much of interest in their work, feeling only a faint annoyance at their bland assertions that all Gypsies steal, never take baths, and dance.

But a people with no written language, only a series of hieroglyphs like woodsmen's marks in a forest to mark the way for the next travelers, have a strong oral tradition. Their stories of their origins are evocative of the early Hebrews and other Mesopotamian people, the old legends of wicca, and strains of Hindu mythology. They have added to this some judicious Christian theology. There are three versions of their origins that are most interesting. The first states that they are the descendants of the smith who made the three nails that crucified Christ. For this sin, they are compelled to forever wander the earth, like the Wandering Jew, until the second coming, making their living as best they can. In another legend, they are the descendants of Cain, nomads driven by the same judgment, for the same eternity. In the third, the most ancient, the legend that corresponds closely with the traditions of witchcraft and Voodoo, they are the children of the incestuous relationship between the Sun and the Moon, paying for their parents' sins.

Scholars have transcribed these legends according to what was fashionable at the time. It was thought in the Middle Ages that they were one of the lost tribes of Israel. Later, it was seriously believed that they really were Egyptians who had been banished from the kingdom for some terrible sin. One exponent of the school saying that "Civilization and humanity came from another planet, and earth is just a forgotten colony of Venus" suspicions that Gypsies are extraterrestrials bent on their own mysterious purpose. But most serious scholars believe they were originally a caste of untouchables in India who made a living by traveling from place to place giving performances and performing skilled labor. To this day, there are still tribes of Gypsies in India.

As far as can be determined, Gypsies came to America from Turkey in the 1830s, although they may have come earlier. Most of them apparently didn't like the New World and went back to Turkey, but there is still a sizable Gypsy population in the United States, Canada, and South America. As recently as 1970, a group of over one hundred families obtained permission from the city of Reading, Pennsylvania, to hold a meeting and camp on the outskirts of that city. In this context, it is interesting to note that the magick of the Pennsylvania Dutch and the magick of the American Gypsies show some very similar spells and formulas. While I cannot definitely confirm it, I am fairly sure that there is a pretty substantial permanent group of Gypsies living in southeastern Pennsylvania, where there is a large concentration of German Americans popularly known as the Pennsylvania Dutch. To my direct knowledge, New York City, in addition to everyone else living there, also has its share of Gypsies. A friend who grew up in Brooklyn Heights recalls that in the early Fifties there were many Gypsies living in the neighborhood.

In general, a tribe of Gypsies is interrelated as much as possible. The more traditional groups tend to arrange marriages. Contrary to the opinion of the gadje, Gypsies are a moralistic people. Premarital sex is frowned upon, as are adultery and homosexuality. Elders are treated with much respect and deference. Children not only are a vital part of the community; they are also considered quite sacred. To mistreat a child is an unpardonable sin. Each tribe is presided over by its eldest member, usually male, although sometimes one hears of a female leader, and with the other elders—the council—this leader holds absolute power in all matters of policy and government. Gypsies prefer to handle their disputes within the tribe, and will never go to outsiders for legal help in settling their own disputes. In some tribes, the rule is inheritance of position, in some it is election to office. The second important person in the tribe is the Phuri Dai, or wise woman. This role comes closer to that of Gypsy Queen than any other. The Phuri Dai is the absolute mistress of all the magickal arts. She sits in council and is called upon for occult assistance in any matter. It is her duty to pass along her magickal knowledge to other women. Men are not traditionally associated with occult practices, although they may participate in the rituals.

The Phuri Dai is called to her profession as much as any cleric. She receives her knowledge from omens, ancestral spirits, and other symbols that present themselves to her. When she is sure that she has been called, she will announce her new role to the group and be properly initiated into the secrets and rituals. It would appear that Gypsies practice as much magick among themselves as they dispense to outsiders. But it is certain that there are those Gypsies who look upon these customs among their people as superstitious nonsense and reject it completely and with much embarrassment. It has been said that Gypsies have no real magick of their own, that all their arts were picked up from other cultures as they passed through in their travels, that Gypsy sorcery is an eclectic hodgepodge of spells and lore from India, Egypt, Persia, and Europe. While it is true that Gypsy magick reflects all these cultures, it is also true that Gypsies have their own original practices, and other cultures owe much to them. And like other good nomads, Gypsies would pick up an Indian art, like palmistry, and spread it as far as Ireland, at the same time picking up an Irish belief in omens. The Gypsies may have helped to keep the witchcraft tradition alive in Europe and they were probably the best purveyors of what we call folk magick, the half-forgotten rituals of a practical Paleolithic religion that combined theology, magick, and medicine.

By tradition, European Gypsies are Catholics, and like many other people who were pagans before they were Christians, they tend to combine Catholicism with their own set of beliefs. They have a great love for all the trappings of the Catholic Church. Icons are very much in evidence. Crucifixes and statues and brightly colored prints of the Holy Family and the Saints are popular ornaments. Like Voodoos, Gypsies not only accept the patronage of the recognized calendar of saints; they also have a few of their own. In Spain and France, thousands of Gypsies make an annual pilgrimage to the Shrine of Saintes Maries de la Mer to worship Saint Sara, the Black Virgin. Saint Sara is connected with the three Marys who arrived in France to preach the word of Christ. She is also associated with Abraham's second wife and the Hindu goddess Kali. Kali, who has such a bad reputation for Westerners because of her destructive aspect, is less popularly known to be the patron of women who wish children. She, like her other identity, Saint Sara, is probably a throwback to the old Moon Goddess—Earth Mother, an important deity to a people who regard barrenness as the worst fate to befall a couple.

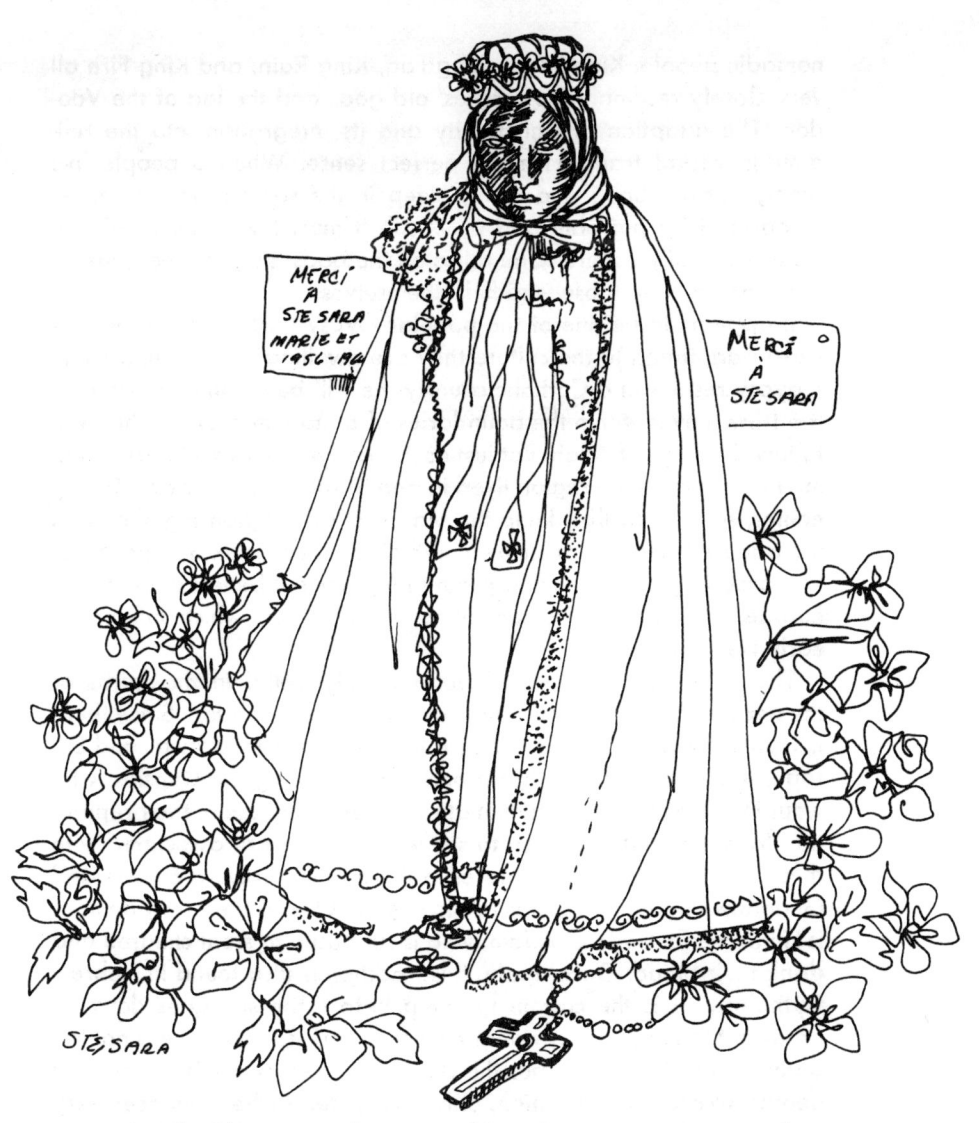

Until the last century, it would be easy to believe that Gypsies, like Voodoos, were pantheistic. The Father Sun, Cham, and the Mother Moon, Chion, were accompanied by other deities beloved by a nomadic people. King Wind, King Fog, King Rain, and King Fire all very closely resemble the witches' old gods and the loa of the Voodoo. The adaption of Christianity and its integration into the religious-magickal tradition make perfect sense. When a people live simply, move about, and rarely sleep in the same place twice, religion must be portable and practical. It must take care of all the aspects of daily culture. One relies on the gods, yes, but the gods, to paraphrase, help those who help themselves.

It appears to be one of the popular Gypsy traits to make an outward adaptation to the culture they are dwelling with, so that while a gypsy resides in a Catholic country, he will be nominally Catholic. If a tribe moves within the boundaries of a Moslem country, they will follow the ways of Allah. But just as it is a Gypsy custom to take common names from the region lived in and to still keep their own Gypsy names, so also do they keep the old practical religion together with the adopted religion. Their own mythology is complex and pantheistic, spreading out to touch a great many ancient beliefs of Asia and Europe, particularly the teachings of Zoroaster, which influenced early Hebrews.

The Gypsy mythology includes not only belief in the spirits of the dead, but belief in the vampire and the werewolf too. Since there is a strong werewolf and vampire tradition in Asia, Africa, and Europe, it is not surprising that it occurs also among the Gypsies, who would have a chance to study it at every turn. Because of their reputation for the occult, it is easy to see why Gypsies are associated with these two supernatural creatures in the parts of eastern Europe and Germany where the legends are strongest. One of their own demons is Lilith, the first wife of Adam, who is supposed to steal children and drink their blood. Once again, this tradition is also found in Hebrew mythology. It is the custom to camp before the sun goes down in order not to encounter a vampire on the road. The vampire is not the body of the dead man, but the doppleganger, or double, freed by death. According to tradition, only Gypsy dead who have been very evil in life will become mulo, or vampires.

With a contempt for the gadje that extends into death, Gypsies do not recognize or fear the spirits of the non-Gypsy, and since they keep no cemeteries of their own, they are not adverse to camping out in a gadje burial place. Perhaps they feel their own mulo will keep the gadje ghosts from annoying them. They believe that there is an afterlife, and that the spirit definitely goes somewhere else.

Gypsy mythology is also quite firm on the origins of disease. Just

as good health is caused by the beneficence of good spirits and good deities, so bad health is caused by a host of demons. A nomadic people who camp out in the open are naturally susceptible to all manners of pulmonary infections, and, of course, dental care was, and is, a rare luxury for them. With the heavy emphasis on bearing as many children as possible, attention must be paid to pregnancy, delivery, and childhood diseases. Most disfunctions are the result of a malignant demon at work. While this belief is by no means solely the property of the Gypsies, occurring as it does in almost every culture in the world, it is interesting to note that their hieroglyphs to represent these various demons could easily pass for a first-year biology student's worksheet with a microscope. Viruses, bacteria, and germs when magnified do tend to look like demons of the worst sort and, like viruses, demons are small and enter the body of the afflicted person by infection. These demons can be conquered with incantations, herb medicines, and other sympathetic remedies. While almost anyone can doctor, it is the drabrani, the specialist, who diagnoses and prescribes. The drabrani is primarily an herbalist, but she should have other charms and spells at her call. The names of the gods and saints are recited as charms, for a name is regarded as a word of power.

But the drabrani can be evil and, in revenge for some real or imagined slight, cause demons to enter the body too. The cohani, or black sorceress, is also greatly feared and dreaded.

This folk magick, eclectically gathered, is, for the most part, the classic sympathetic magick-religious ritual of a nature-worshipping people. Because the Gypsies have always been a people who live in close contact with the natural world, they have never lost that sixth sense of the movements of the earth and stars. Because they have lived outside the law of city dwellers for so long, they have adapted a sense that might be called psychic. A people whose lives depend on their ability to live by their wits cannot afford to be too secure. One must be able to make quick, accurate judgments and employ a primitive and effective form of psychology. These are the basic attributes of the true magician, and the Gypsies seem to be amply gifted with these qualities. Perhaps the Gypsies are more cynical about their art than their clients would know, but they have nonetheless been patronized by the curious and the faithful for hundreds of years, so they must be doing something right.

The gadje may think of the Gypsy sorceress only as a diviner, a teller of the future. While it is true that Gypsies are great fortune-tellers, using the cards, crystals, and palmistry (all of which are discussed in the Divination chapter), they also have at their command a great range of spells for every purpose.

To begin with, their charms for healing the maladies of humanity are fascinating, if not quite as simple as taking too much aspirin and going to bed. If someone came to the drabrani complaining of a migraine, for instance, she would catch several frogs and toads, gut them, collect the livers, and burn them to a powder, then adding to that ivy collected from the head of a statue and making the whole thing into a potion to be drunk by the sufferer. While the patient was imbibing this mixture, the sorceress would murmur an incantation over the person's head:

> Oh, pain in my head
> the father of all evil
> look upon me now.
> Thou hast tormented my head
> Remain not in me
> Go thou, go thou home,
> Whence thou, evil one, has struck,
> thither, thither hasten
> Who treads upon my shadow
> To him be the pain.

A simpler cure for a headache is to simply *bind* a strand of ivy taken from the head of a statue around one's own forehead. If you happen to be passing a statue with some ivy growing around the head, stop and gather a few tendrils for your collection. If you can keep the tendrils alive and rooted in water, a piece here and there is a good addition to many herbal concoctions. There you are at a garden party in your good silk dress and platform shoes pulling ivy off a statue's head . . . just tell people you want to garland your own head. They'll think either you're trying to emulate Zelda Fitzgerald or you're a devoted indoor gardener. But a good witch never worries about what people think . . .

The toothache is another common malady that the Gypsies have a most efficient cure for. While it may not take the place of a trip to the dentist, it might help at three A.M. on a Sunday morning. Write it down and carry it in a little bag around your neck as a charm until you can get to the dentist's office.

> Peter was sitting on a marble stone
> And Jesus walked by
> Peter said, my Lord, my tooth doth ache
> How my tooth aches!
> Jesus said, Peter, thou art whole
> And whosoever keeps these words for my sake
> Shall never have the toothache.

It may be small comfort in the night, but if you recite it over and over again, like a mantra, the pain seems to ease up a bit. A good

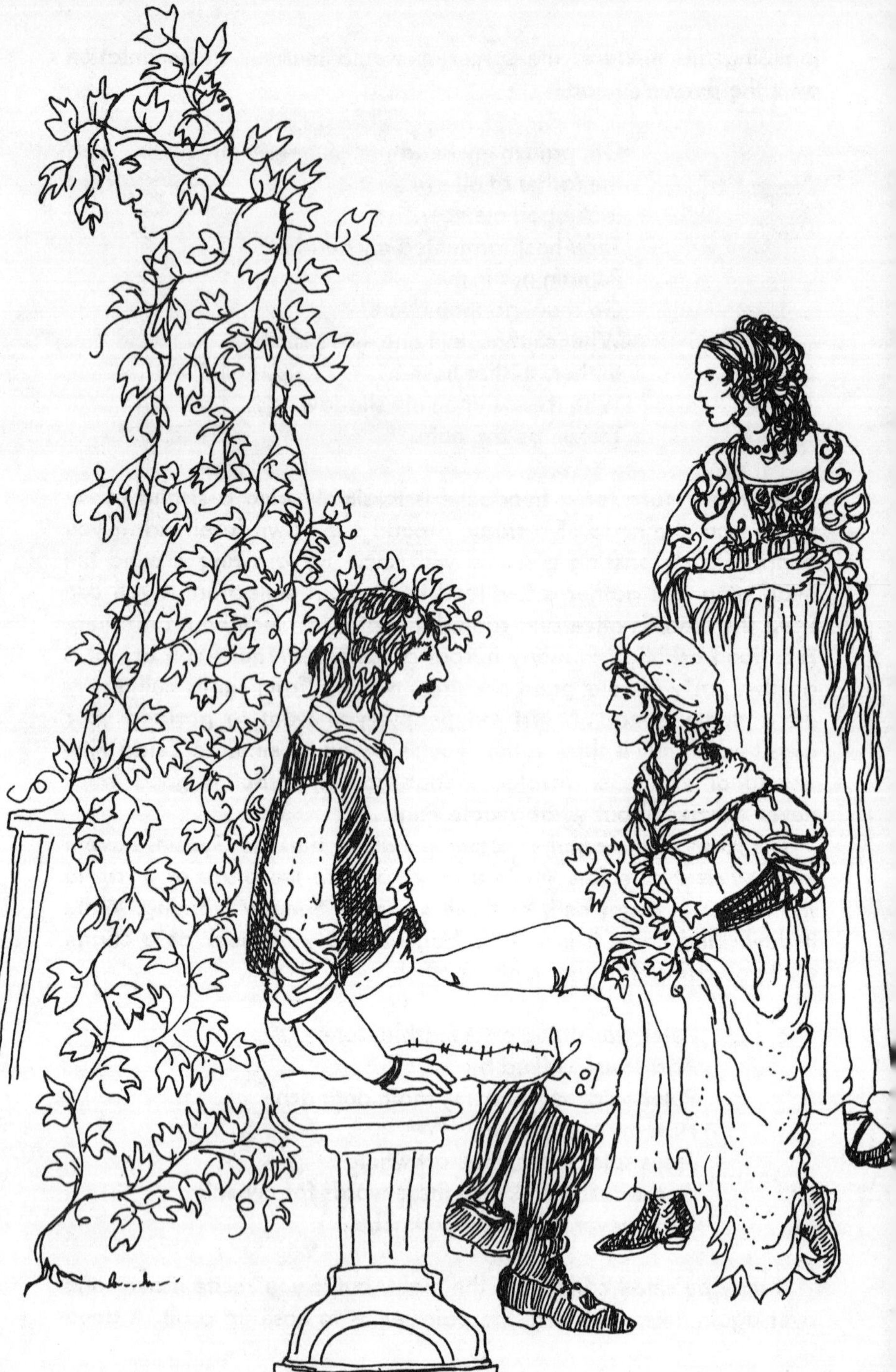

slug of whisky taken at the same time helps too. I have also seen this spell in books of Pennsylvania Dutch lore.

Gypsy sorcery is of the old animist school. The four elements of classical magick are regarded as great benefactors to humanity. Gypsies regard running streams and brooks as the dwelling places of spirits, and they will try to camp by running water as much as possible. When a woman goes into labor, she will try to deliver as close to a stream as possible in order that the spirits of the water will look with favor on her child, their foster sibling. At the same time, the midwives in attendance will build a huge fire of willow and ash wood to drive away any evil influence. Fire is the great purifier. In another ritual of healing, the afflicted person is tented outside of the camp by a running stream. The healer builds a great fire outside the tent flap, and sets several pots of herbs smoldering all around the person. The conjuration that takes place is recited thus:

> Great Fire,
> My healer and defender,
> Son of the Great Sun,
> That cleanses the earth of foulness,
> Deliver this name from sickness,
> That torments his night and day!

A similar formula is applied to snake bites, which are surely a common affliction of traveling Gypsies:

> When Babylon was young,
> The Great Mother sent a man
> from the mount of Shan (sic)
> Queen Volga may teach the serpent not to bite
> the Son of God (Dol)

Water gathered from a running spring is considered especially magickal, for the Gypsies have great faith in the spirits that dwell in creeks and brooks. A Gypsy woman who wants to bring on her menses will gather water from nine different places and break an egg on top of the pail. Then she will pour the water over her head while standing in a tenth place in the stream, letting the water run down her body. I personally would suggest birth control pills, but a roommate of mine who tried this spell said it worked. Although Gypsies are not particularly noted for either their extramarital adventuring (adultery is a severe taboo) or their own contraception methods, they have several prescriptions for magickal abortion or bringing down the menses, which they are glad to sell to the immoral gadje. A Gypsy woman would never dream, even in these days, of actually performing a straight D&C type of abortion, or of having an abortion, even though the method is ancient and well known as far back as the Egyptians. To "remove an egg" is yet another Gypsy taboo. They will sell herbal concoctions that are "guaranteed" to produce miscarriage or menses. The simplest one requires that a woman who thinks she is pregnant and definitely doesn't want to be go to the grave of a woman who died in childbirth and pick some grass from the top of the headstone. This should be cooked together with six red roses and strained through a woman's apron. The elixir produced from this mixture is then mixed with an egg and swallowed in one gulp.

The egg as a symbol of fertility plays an important part in many contraceptive charms. If a Gypsy couple decide they want a child and after several tries get no results, the husband will gather a fertile egg, pierce two holes in it, one at either end of the oval, and blow it like an Easter egg into his wife's mouth.

When the baby finally arrives, it is a cause for much celebration; but the newcomer must be protected from any jealous spirits by the simple effective charm of the Phuri Dai licking it all over and then touching the forehead, eyes, nose, mouth, heart, and genitals with salt. Salt is a universal panacea against evil, and this method is often employed to fend off the evil eye.

Speaking of which—like many other people, Gypsies have a fear of the evil eye—la malocchio. To be overlooked is a terrible thing to a Gypsy, and all sorts of measures are taken to prevent disaster. Not only do they employ all the standard gestures, but they also have a wide variety of amulets designed to ward off malevolent influences. Engraved charms are worn around the neck on a chain, even by the smallest child. Strings of beads, as well as elaborate necklaces of old gold and silver coins, are worn. They are not prized so much for their monetary value as for their magickal virtues. Cowrie shells are also highly prized charms. They resemble the vulva and the womb. As symbols of the beginning of creation, they are important, and their value lies in the belief in the Mother Goddess protection. Sometimes miniature animals are carried or worn, together with religious medals. The most popular are the pig and the frog. Pigs are popular because they are symbols of the well-fed life. Carved in wood or stone, they insure the wearer fecundity and prosperity.

It was noted in a witchcraft trial in Sweden that some Gypsy children kept frogs and toads as pets, much to the horror of those who associate the poor innocuous amphibian with the devil. Evil sorcerers are supposed to take the form of a toad in order to do their dirty work. Frogs and toads, while not excessively intelligent, are easily tamed and will follow someone around or return to a particularly unlikely spot over and over again if so inclined. They are the traditional symbols of love and lust. If you are so inclined, they do not make bad familiars.

The third amulet prized by Gypsies is the piece of parchment with a spell or a verse from the Bible written on it. Because Gypsies have no written language of their own, they place a great value on the literature of others. A verse or charm carried in a leather bag about the neck is considered quite powerful. As mentioned earlier, these particular charms are well known in Pennsylvania Dutch magick too as Himmel's-briefs.

While Gypsies prefer to settle their differences within the tribe, even if the case has been taken to a gadje court, they, despite their own reputation as thieves, are frequently called in to discover a theft. If, for instance, someone has stolen a horse or any other animal, perhaps the house cat, a Gypsy will gather some of its feces together and throw some to the east and west with the following incantation:

> Where the sun sees on thee
> Then thou shalt return to me.

A second way to get back stolen property is to find a willow tree growing by a stream. Pick two or three branches, wind them together, and throw them back into the stream, exclaiming:

> I tie up the thieves' luck
> That heart and liver and lungs
> That bowels and gut be bound
> Till my goods are returned to me.

If all that fails, then a vengeance curse is put upon the thief. Those who cross the Gypsy sorceress will find that a barrage of incantations and fetishes have been launched against them. Fire is invoked to punish the offender. A small pile of ash, linden, and hawthorn is burned together while the sorceress molds an image of the intended victim, concentrating all her hatred and lust for vengeance as she casts it into the fire, reciting the following spell:

> Fire, who punishes the evil-doer, fire who hates falsehood and deceit,
> Fire that scorches the impure, who destroys evil-doers;
> Devour (name) for he tells untruth, he thinks lies.

A second incantation is to take a fresh deck of playing cards, select the cards that represent the victim, plus the ace of spades, the three of clubs, the nine of spades, the eight of hearts, and put your left hand against the wall, incanting:

> I put five fingers on wall
> I conjure five devils
> Become five devils
> That you may enter the body and blood and soul of (name)
> And rend him helpless
> Tied and bound at the mercy of my terrible revenge.

Too many times the gadje represent the Gypsies as happy thieves. In the real world, they are used to being thrown from one place to another, used to the imprecations and threats hurled at them. Gypsy life is not all music and dancing and living off the land. But they *are* among the greatest romantics in the world. The rituals of courtship are followed by the whole tribe with indulgent eyes, and a wedding is one of the big events in Gypsy life. But should a Gypsy man decide he is no longer fond of a woman, she in turn may extract some revenge from the following spell:

She lights a black candle at midnight and pricks it with a pin three times, murmuring with all the vengeance she can muster: "Thrice the candle's pricked by me, Thrice thy heart shall broken be!" If he actually marries another, then she may secretly put a broken-up crabshell in his food at the wedding feast and hide one of his hairs in a bird's nest. The marriage will never be happy.

A more tactful way to get out of a relationship where love has departed on one side but not the other is to burn the hair and nails of the lover. This, I am assured, will destroy love without creating hatred.

If a man or woman should wish to acquire the love of another, there are many options available. In the first one, he should follow his beloved around until he can find a good clear footprint. This is dug up and buried under a willow tree with the following incantation recited over it:

> Many earths on earth there be
> Whom I love my own shall be
> Grow, grow willow tree
> Sorrow none unto me.

A second interesting love spell begins by catching, reflected in a mirror, two animals copulating. While watching this reflection, one recites this spell over it:

> He the ax, I the helve, (or "I the ax, she the helve . . .")
> He the dog, I the bitch,
> He the cock, I the hen,
> This be as my will.

The mirror is then presented to the object of one's affections in the hopes that the first time he gazes into it, he will be smitten with lust.

If that fails, steal a shoe from the beloved and stuff it with rue grass. If you sleep with it under the bed, your lover will come to you within a week.

One of the most universally popular and potent love charms in history comes from the Gypsies. Mix a little semen or menstrual blood into your loved one's food and he or she will never be able to resist anything you ask of him/her.

But what good is magick, even to a Gypsy, if you can't have any fun with it? Go to a barnyard and pick seven pieces of straw. On the first night of the full moon, set up a table by the window so the moonlight falls across it and recite the following spells:

> Pray to the moon when she is round
> Luck with you shall then abound
> What you seek shall then be found
> On the sea or solid ground.

And like *The Scarecrow*, those little pieces of straw will turn into little yellow people and dance before your eyes, or so I'm told.

The fate of the Gypsy culture cannot be determined. As more and more of the world is eaten up by freeways and housing developments, there are fewer and fewer places where a wandering Gypsy tribe can settle in for an evening. The days of the itinerant tinker are long gone. No self-respecting Gypsy would be caught dead camping by the Hollywood Freeway. Family by family they begin to settle down to live in one place and take a job in the pickle factory. The old way of life is unable to survive against the increase of population and progress, even in Europe. So, gradually, they stay in one place and with true Gypsy camouflage adapt to the ways of their neighbors. They go to the drive-in and eat at McDonald's. They buy television sets and put a down payment on a mortgage and they are no longer Gypsies but plain citizens of this country or that. No one has ever made a really good survey of the Gypsy life in the United States, and by the time some trained anthropologist gets around to doing it, all the real Gypsies will probably have blended into the housing developments.

One windy day in the late Sixties, I was hitchhiking across Ireland, from Connemara, trying to make Dublin by nightfall; I was alone, wet, and cold. My last ride had been a pig truck. I sat by the side of the road, smelling faintly of pigshit myself. A little girl was looking at me. I smiled. She did not. I offered her a chocolate bar. She took it without looking at it. The child was dark even for the Irish and much more poorly dressed than the most poverty-stricken Irish farmchild. Her face was dirty, but then, so was mine.

"Do you have a sixpence?" she asked.

"Why?" I asked.

"Mother said to ask if you had a sixpence for the baby, miss."

I glanced up the road. A green van was parked under the trees and a woman not too much older than I was was squatting by the campfire with a baby in her arms. I picked up my knapsack (Oh, they're all thieves and liars, the farmers had said) and walked over. We stared at each other blankly. I wondered if she hated me with my American boots and my knapsack, another stupid kid hitchhiking around the countryside, another gadje. I had three half crowns in my pocket and gave them to her. She took them and muttered some words of thanks. I asked if they were Gypsies. Yes. Where were they going? To Wexford, then. She looked at my Arab amulet hanging against my wet sweater. "Oh, you're one of them then," she said vaguely over the smoke. I nodded, not knowing what I was one of. "Are you all right?" I asked. "Is the baby okay?" "We get by," she said bitterly and turned away from me. I kept on walking down the

Gypsy Hieroglyphs

- ☦ : here they are hostile to us
- # : they give nothing
- ⊙ : generous
- ○ : very generous
- ⊖ : here we are thieves
- ⑄ : we have been here
- ≈ : they want a child
- △ : fortunetelling here
- ⊗ : A Death in the family
- ⚹ : MARRIAGE
- ⚲ : MISTRESS LIKES MEN
- ⚴ : Master likes women
- ⚺ : STAY AWAY
- ∆ : Hard bargainers

road to Dublin wishing that I had known some secret sign, some hidden gesture that would have made me more acceptable to her. But I was just a gadje!

> I've seen where you will never be
> And been where you will never see
> And yet within that very place
> You can be seen by me.
> For to tell what they do not know
> Is the art of the Romany.
>   C. G. Leland

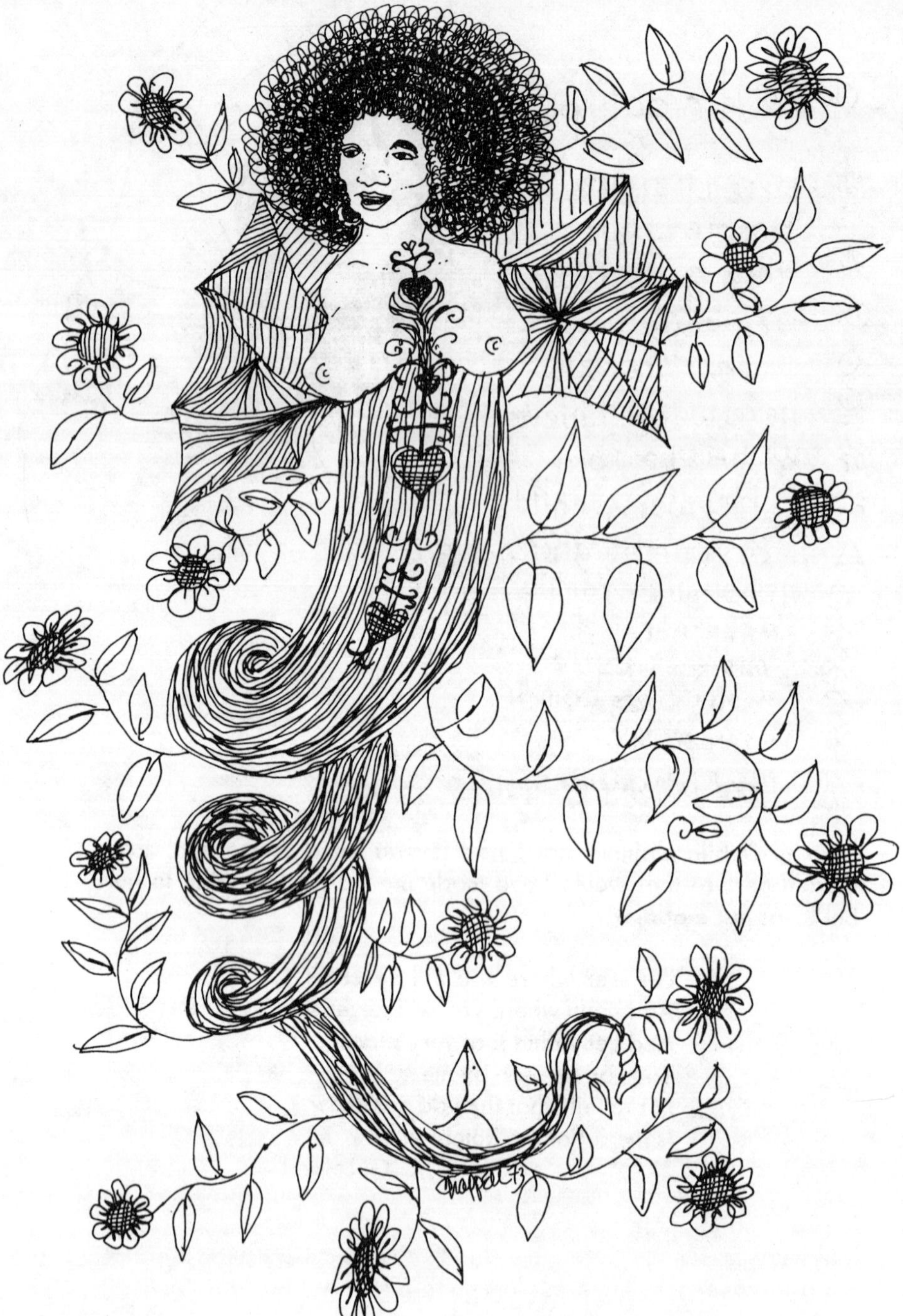

6

VOODOO—DAMBALLA AND LE GRAND ZOMBI

The believer in Voodoo—and there are millions of blacks
and some whites who practice it—centers hopes and
fears as strongly on it as does a follower of
Christianity, Judaism, Buddhism or Islam.
MILO RIGAUD

Marie, Marie, Marie Laveau,
She's the witch-queen of New Orleans.
RED BONE

VOODOO. The images it conjures up are dark and fearsome. Drums in steaming jungles. The dead who walk undead by night. Strange wasting dreams. The goat without horns. Pins jabbed in dolls. Little wax balls found in drawers. Even the most pragmatic people get the inside shakes when the word is out that someone is doing a Voodoo on them. Voodoo may be the original black magick.

Look at the word "Voodoo." It has been spelled Vodo, Veaudon, Veaux-deaux, Vaudoin, or Vaudon. Literally translated from the Fons dialect, VU signifies inward path—meditation, introspection, the secrets of the soul. DU indicates mysterious, hidden things, esoteric knowledge. Voodoo. The secrets of the soul. It is an old, old African religion based on a series of both simple and complex symbols and beliefs that came to the New World with the first slaves.

The slave trade is one of the worst disgraces of New World history, and the dark passage a horror within this disgrace. Thousands of Africans from different tribes, people who had never seen the sea or white men before, were chained together in dark, filthy holes of ships and sent across the sea to a life that could barely be called life at all.

With them, the Africans brought the beliefs and customs of their own religions and magicks. Among those slaves were the priests and priestesses of the many faiths, men and women who knew the secrets of strong magick.

Slavery under the European colonials was a particularly brutal and grotesque system. Blacks were regarded as subhumans, soulless, by people just barely out of the Middle Ages. No one really cared what the slaves believed in or thought at first and they were pretty much left alone to believe what they pleased.

In the revolts and uprisings that followed, however, the whites learned to develop a superstitious fear of their black captives' magick. By the time some attempt was made at Christian instruction, the shreds of the old African beliefs had already taken a firm root in the New World. The Christian gods were incorporated and merged with the old *loa*, the African gods and spirits. Already the white man had a healthy fear of Voodoo, for laws were passed forbidding the congregation of slaves for any purpose whatsoever. In New Orleans, the importation of blacks from Santo Domingo was outlawed because of their reputation as Voodooists. It was a good defense, perhaps the only defense against the white devil master the slave had. Like the Gypsies, the Africans learned to use their magicks to defend themselves through the power of psychology.

Today Voodoo in the New World can be divided into at least five related hybrids. It is spread over the Caribbean, South America, the Southern states, and most of the big cities in the West and North.

Voodoo in Haiti is probably closest to the ancient African beliefs. While Haiti is nominally a Catholic country, it is well known that *Vaudon*, to give it the French patois spelling, is the folk religion of most of the population in rural districts. Interestingly enough, Haiti was the first black nation in the New World to free itself from European domination and gain independence, giving it more of a chance to preserve its African heritage and beliefs. Vaudon is almost pure, but the traces of the white man's religion can still be found in some of its beliefs.

In Brazil, *Macumba* and *Umbanda* combine Catholicism, Vaudon, and spiritualism. *Quimbanda* also combines Vaudon and Satanism with faith healing and communication with the dead. My Brazilian friends tell me that this is very popular on all levels of Brazilian society and it is not uncommon for a wealthy, educated Brazilian to consult a Voodoo priest instead of a doctor.

In New York City, the *barrio* and other Puerto Rican sections of the city have *Espiritismo*, a kind of first cousin to Macumba that combines Voodoo, spiritualism, and a nod to the Church in passing. Yet it is completely different from either Macumba or Voodoo, practitioners tell me.

New Orleans has always been the traditional American home of Voodoo as a magickal art having little or no connection to any religion. Marie Laveau, the Voodoo Queen who made it a thriving business, lived and died in New Orleans, one of the most famous and powerful women in the history of the city. (See pages 132 to 136.) In the backwoods of the South, Voodoo is known to blacks and whites alike as conjuring.

Voodoo is also quite popular in New York, Philadelphia, Chicago, Boston, and Los Angeles, and now, I understand, it is taking hold in London, via the West Indies, where it is known as obeah or gris-gris.

Now, there is Vaudon, the religion that incorporates magick belief in animism and the spirits of the dead and there is Voodoo, the magickal practice, which also calls upon the spirits, employs many of the same ceremonies and rituals, and believes in the existence of the same gods. The difference is basic: Vaudon seeks to implore the spirits for help; Voodoo seeks to force their aid. If this sounds all very complicated, it is. Voodoo is like its practitioners—determinedly individualistic. To try and understand Voodoo, it's a good idea to look at Vaudon, the religion.

There are at least five hundred deities in the Vaudon pantheon, and at least two hundred different rituals used to summon these—the loa, or gods and spirits, that Vaudon bows to. The loa are important. These are the old African gods that often correspond to saints in the Christian pantheon. There are the spirits of nature, and there are the spirits of the dead—particularly the powerful dead.

In both Vaudon and Voodoo, there are several important loa who originated in the ancient African religions. There is Damballah, the snake loa, who is obviously a fertility god. His day is Thursday and his symbol is either a rainbow or a snake. Damballah rules rivers and streams. He is quite powerful, almost the Zeus of Voodoo. Damballah's wife, Aida Wedo, is the loa of childbirth and motherhood. Aida Wedo likes to create things. She restores peace and harmony, but she can punish unfaithful husbands. Pappa Legba is Saint Peter. He is the guardian of the doors between this visible world and the world that cannot be seen. Pappa Legba is very important to sorcerers often portrayed as an old sorcerer with a crutch. I have a small saint's picture of Saint George that is supposed to be Ogum, the Mars of the Voodoos. Ogum is a powerful loa of war and sexual potency. His female counterpart is Ezili, the Aphrodite of Voodoo. She is appealed to in matters of love and lust. Then there is the notorious Baron Samdei, the Lord of the Graveyard and patron of death magicks. Actually, he can be a lamb when he wants to be, and can cure frigidity and impotence for those who seek his help. Le

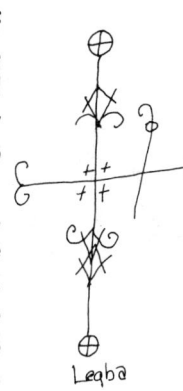

Legba

Ezili

Baron's friend is Guede, the loa of death and rebirth. He helps to find stolen or lost objects and can reveal all sorts of mysteries.

In Macumba, there are a few more loa who are both charming and helpful. My favorite is Yemanja, the lady of the sea. Yemanja is a mermaid goddess, corresponding vaguely to the Virgin in function and personality. There is Exu, the devil, who handles black magick and will also aid in gambling games. For each of the four elements of the sun signs, there is a specific loa: Yemanja is the patroness of those born in water signs; those born in earth signs can look to Oxossi, also known as Saint Sebastian; air sign people can look to Yorima, or Saint Cyprian, for aid; and fire sign people can depend on Oxala, or Jesus. These are very special patrons of the individual and it is wise to observe their feast days. Always feed your loa.

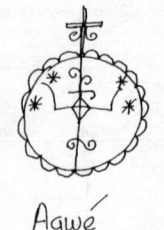

Like any good religion, Vaudon has a place of worship, a temple called a homfort. A homfort is built around a rada, or peristyle, from which the beams move outward like the rays of a stylized sun, from whence all life emanates. The Vaudon priest or priestess, a houngan or mambo (father or mother) lives in the homfort with the students and apprentices. It is the function of the houngan and mambo to interpret the will of the loa, to make sure they are appeased to serve as healers of bodies and souls and perform all the rites of passage between birth and death—and after. Vaudon is a large part of its followers' lives, for not only is it the ritual church, it also provides a place to get together and party at the end of the week. Consequently, there is much importance attached to food, drink and music and dancing.

The most interesting aspect of Vaudon is the manifestation of the loa in the worshipers. Where possession is dreaded by European-oriented people, believers in Vaudon welcome it, induce it, and consider it an honor to be so blessed by the gods. Possession—where the loa's personality superimposes the personality of the worshiper—is called riding horse. The Vaudon is the horse; he is ridden by the loa, the rider.

This phenomenon is interesting to watch. As the meeting gathers momentum through the use of drums, music, alcohol, smoke, and atmosphere, someone who has been sitting there very quietly tapping a foot in time to the drums will suddenly be seized by convulsions: the body jerks as if shaken by some enormous invisible hand; the eyes roll back into the head; and the voice makes some choking sounds. Suddenly one is watching an old woman's body going

Agwé

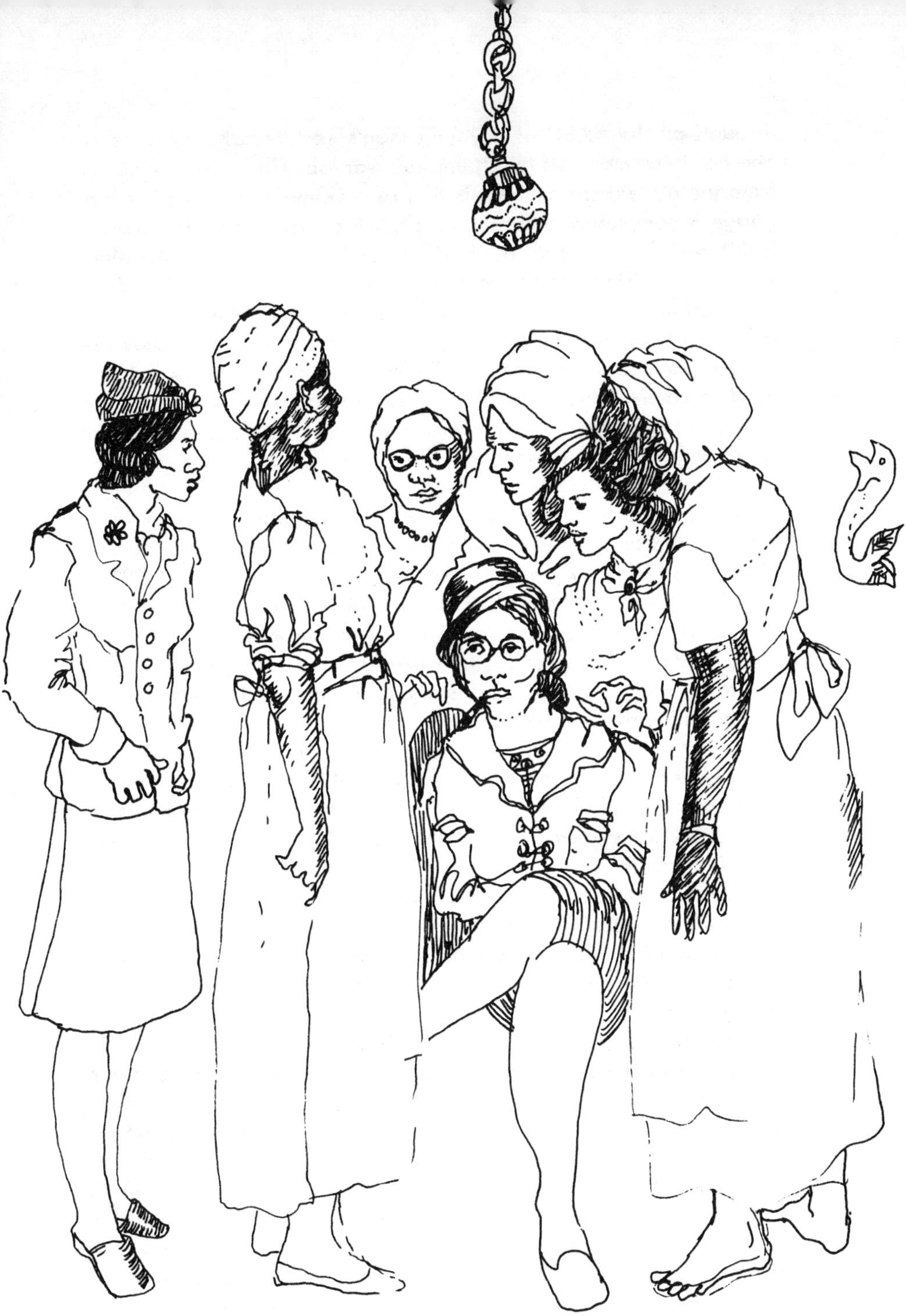

through all the rituals of a young man's gestures and movements. She has been mounted by Ogum, the war loa. The voice that comes from the old woman's mouth is that of a young man; even her language is completely different—it is much coarser and her phrasing is different. To all intents, her body is merely a vehicle for some other personality. When the loa mounts its horse, its function is to advise the Vaudons on both spiritual and material matters. Most people will, of course, seek to know the future; so the loa will predict. They are almost omnipotent in what they know, I am assured. When a loa is tired, it simply dispossesses the body, and suddenly there is an old woman sitting there in an old woman's body, blinking, demanding to know what has happened. The horse has no memory of the possession.

Vaudon has its darker side, where the houngan or mambo may be expected to deal with bokon. Bokon are sorcerers, practitioners of bad magick and a nasty lot they can be.

Bokon inhabit the world of the zombi and the loup-garou—the Haitian version of the werewolf. The bokon follow the lefthand path, invoking Pappa Legba as Maitre Carrefour and asking for the aid of Le Baron. Haiti has a law against trying to gain control over another human being through the use of drugs and/or other methods. There are several secret societies of bokon who are rumored to kidnap children for sacrifice, even in the streets of Port-au-Prince. It was a moot point whether or not this was a propaganda technique of Poppa Doc to keep everyone in line. Poppa Doc Duvalier's personal guard were known as ton-ton macute, which means, vaguely, a wandering herbal sorcerer. Duvalier was rumored to be a Vaudon priest of quite terrifying power. Whether he was, or simply used this image of himself to maintain his regime, is still under debate.

And then there is the zombi, so beloved by Hollywood, in search of a gimmick and the terror of those great bloody comic books of the Fifties. Zombi comes from the Congolese word *vumbi*, meaning a body without a soul. To a people who believe so firmly in the importance of the spirit and the soul, to have a dead friend or relation become a zombi is one of the worst things that can happen. A bokon will call up a zombi or two to provide himself with some cheap labor in the cane fields, or to enact an even darker revenge. To make a zombi, the bokon will approach his victim's house in the dead of night crawling on all fours backwards, carrying a reed straw. The sorcerer must suck the victim's soul out of the house by sticking the reed straw in a crevice, then withdrawing it and putting it into a

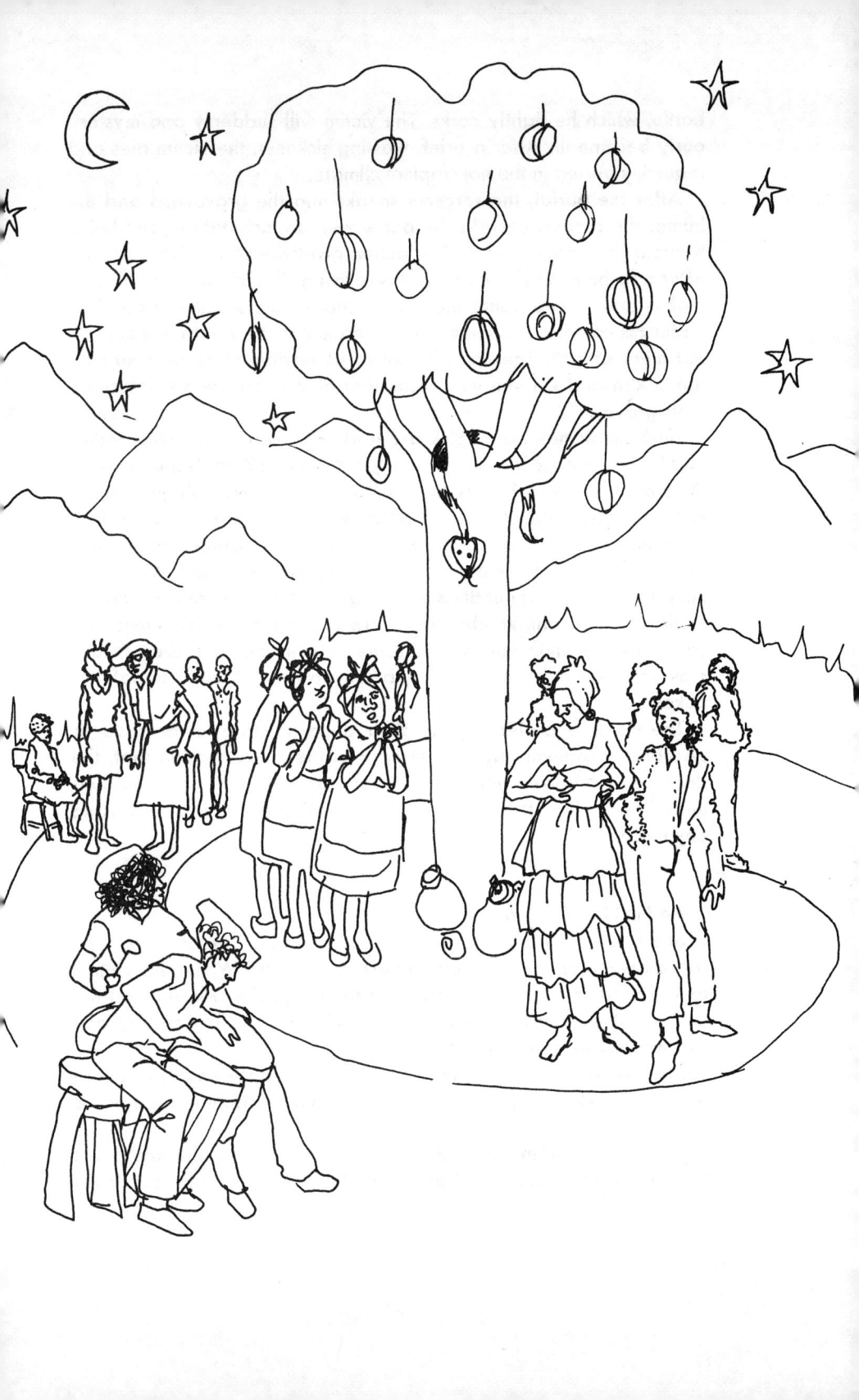

bottle, which he tightly corks. The victim will suddenly and mysteriously become ill. After a brief, wasting sickness, the victim dies and is quickly buried in the hot tropical climate.

After the burial, the sorcerer sneaks into the graveyard and exhumes the corpse, uncorks the bottle with an incantation, and holds it under the corpse's nose. This action gives the corpse back its life, after a fashion. While the corpse is reviving, the bokon gives it some herbs—and in two hours the zombi, the mindless walking dead, is under his control. This curse can be broken if the zombi happens to eat meat or salt. Then it will realize its terrible state and turn on the bokon and kill him with supernatural strength before returning to its grave.

Herb medicine and magick are fairly common in the West Indies and South America, where the many thousands of plants that grow in the mountains, rain forests, and dense jungles have only just begun to be classified and studied by botanists. It has been suggested that the bokon insures the "life" of his zombi by the prudent administration of a potent homemade tonic, giving his victim just enough to keep him a junkie, a mindless addict to the drug. If there is a rational explanation for the zombi—and there are too many eyewitness accounts for the myth not to have some basis in fact—the drug theory may be it. Some root or vine may be unknown to all but a handful of bokon . . .

The Haitians prefer to bury their dead as close to the road as possible, to prevent any tampering with the grave. Failing that, the deceased's relatives will stand guard night and day with shotguns until they are sure the corpse has deteriorated enough to be beyond any mortal use.

And in New Orleans . . .

She was called a saint and a miracle worker. One of her closest friends was the most popular priest in the city. When the yellow fever raged throughout the city, she tended to the sick, washed the corpses of the dead no one would touch. She was a welcome and constant visitor in the prisons.

She was called a devil and a pimp. They said she sold her soul to Satan and danced with a fish. Her Voodoo meetings were famous for their orgiastic abandon.

There was nothing that she couldn't accomplish. She could see the past and the future as if they were the present. The lowest slaves

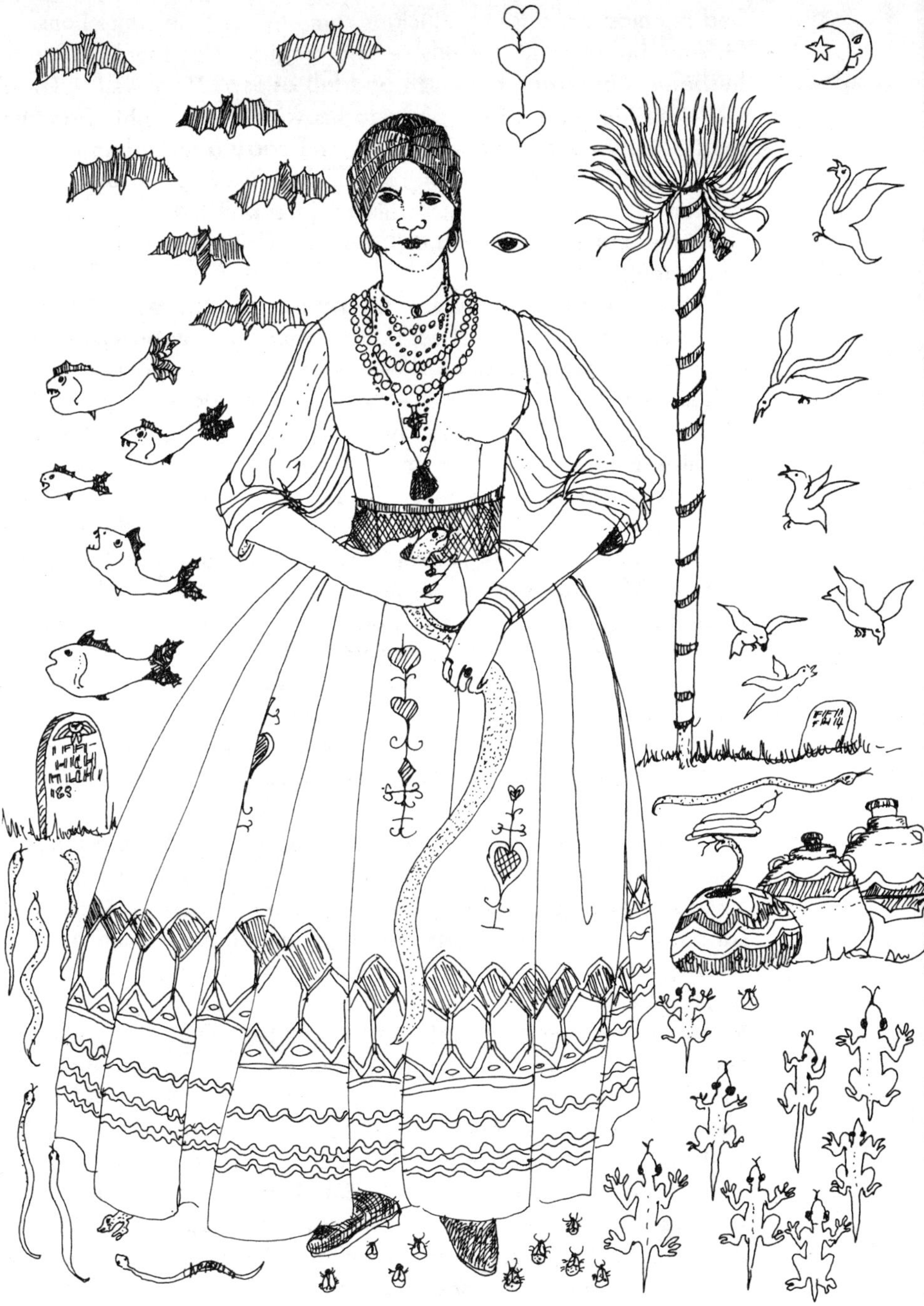

and the most important politicians came to her little white house on St. Ann, hat in hand, for advice and magick. Was there a tiresome husband, who drank too much and fell asleep? Very well, take this white powder and add a pinch to his wine every night. Gambling debts? Burn a green money candle and carry a lucky hand root. A sickly child? Cured with rabbit's liver and five-finger grass. A cruel master who beats you? Sew this conjure ball into his pillow and walk the streets a free man. It was even rumored that she could cheat death.

When her name appears in the parish records, Marie Laveau is listed as a "free woman of color," the nebulous antebellum designation for a black who is not a slave. The press of the day refers to her as the "Witch Queen" and the "Queen of Voodoos in this city." By all accounts, she was a handsome woman, a mixture of Creole, Spanish, Negro, and Indian blood. One old book says she was directly related to the Bourbons. She was tall, with magnificent black hair and piercing eyes that seemed to look deep into the soul. She loved clothes and jewels. It is said that she made a wonderful appearance walking down the street in her bright dresses, necklaces, and huge gold earrings. Everyone paid their respects to Marie Laveau, for she was one of the most powerful figures in a city of living myths.

The little white house on St. Ann has long been torn down, but less than a century ago it might have been crowded with heavily veiled ladies of the ton waiting with threadbare scullery maids and calico wilderness women for their turn at an audience with the great Marie Laveau.

For eighty years she was the Voodoo Queen, her legend complex. She professed to be a devout Catholic and yet she started the weekly Voodoo meetings in the bayous where the old gods of Africa were (and are) invited to appear. She was said to have been a skilled abortionist, yet she had fifteen children who grew up as models of respectability. Although there are rumors that one of her daughters took over her name and title on Marie's retirement. They said she kept a nine-foot snake in her back yard and danced with a fish, yet she always protested that she was a respectable Catholic widow and her ceremonies were open to the public, even to the police. They said she gathered her information and kept her power through a complex blackmailing of all the leading families, and yet she was attributed with miracles of magick that no blackmail could ever produce. Marie Laveau made Voodoo a business and a powerful magick. She took what she knew and added a certain satisfying touch of the mysterious. There was no one quite like her before and there will never be anyone quite like her again. Perhaps Marie Laveau's legend is larger than the woman herself, but she carried her secrets and her power to the vault where she lies.

Even that is in dispute. Some say that Marie Laveau is buried in Louis I, the old cemetery, in an open vault that only the faithful know. Others say she is buried in Louis II in the handsome tomb that bears her name and epitaph.

Walking through the Quarter in New Orleans, one gets the feeling that very little has changed in that city, and that its character will survive, despite the erosions of tourists, even time. Even if it were not the home of Marie Laveau, I would still love it, for it has a special magick all its own. New Orleans is a Scorpio city, a place of red beans and rice, and pinball, where faceless buildings open into little courtyards of paradise. Just walking around in the peace that follows Mardi Gras, I understood Marie Laveau, and I could begin to understand Voodoo, New Orleans style. But it wasn't so much for the Mardi Gras that I came to New Orleans; I came in the same spirit with which a Moslem goes to Mecca.

It was a hot afternoon, the kind of day when dogs lie on the sidewalk and sleep, where kids get a nickel for a popsicle and mad sorceresses pay their respects to a Voodoo queen.

When I finally found the tomb in the old cemetery, it was late in the afternoon, and there were two other girls standing there reading the inscription.

> Famille Vve Paris
>   née Laveau
> Ci-Gît
> Marie Philome Glampion
> décédée le 11 Juin 1897
> Agée de soixante-deux ans Elle fut
> bonne mère bonne amie et
> regrettée par tous ceux qui l'ont
> connue Passant priez pour elle

I decided to take it as an omen that one of the girls was a great-granddaughter of Marie Laveau, who had come to see her famous ancestress's tomb. A good omen!

It is the custom to make a chalk mark on the tomb and make a wish on Marie, then to leave her a nickel or a penny in return. Her great-granddaughter solemnly did this, then returned to her own normal life.

I wanted to linger a while longer in the past, to pay my respects with candles and coins before making my chalk mark on the tomb and returning to the twentieth century. Great sorcerers, sorceresses, and magicians should be respected, for death means very little to their legends. I lit my candles and said my piece, then left without looking back.

As you pass, pray for her!

Perhaps nothing solves the riddle of Voodoo better than a pamphlet I picked up in New Orleans. It gives no credit to an author or even a publisher, and for two dollars a bunch of paper stapled together must be very special. It is called, in its entirety:

> BLACK AND WHITE MAGIC ATTRIBUTED TO MARIE LAVEAU
> Burning of Candles, Use of Roots and Oils, Powders and Incense—Significance of Cards
> HOROSCOPES with Lucky Days and Lucky Numbers
> Guide to Spiritualists, Mediums and Readers
> Published for the Trade

This pamphlet is a gold mine of Voodoo advice and magick for every occasion. In addition to advice on what color of candles to burn for what sort of spell vibrations, the dressing of churches, altars, and homes for a spiritualist ceremony, and some wise words on LUCK ("Your turn may come at any time"), its spells are quaintly phrased in little paragraphs, with such interesting titles as How to Promote Peace in the Home, The Person Who Wishes to Be Uncrossed, The Lady Whose Husband or Man Friend Has Left Home, etc., etc., as they used to say. I think my favorite example is called How to Attract Attention:

> My friend, sometimes it seems as though everything is against us and whatever we attempt to do turns out in the opposite direction. We find it very difficult to find the way to straighten things out. When we almost reach our goals, our desires disappear into nothing, leaving us in a state of want and despair.
>
> Here my child, take it with more calm and faith and

fill your heart with hope. Burn the Triple Action Candle every day anointed with Altar Oil for one hour, until you have burned seven candles; anoint your head with High Conquering Oil, apply Drawing Powder to your body every day, and pour one teaspoonful of the Dragon Blood Bath in your bath water. Use the Attraction Perfume as the regular perfume. God bless you. SO BE IT.

The Voodoo's world is full of these oils and powders, candles and incenses. Supposedly they are blended from the finest and most exotic ingredients on the market, and have great powers when used correctly. I know many Voodooists who swear by their application.

In every large city there are boutiques of Voodoo. They were there long before the occult became a fad, and they will continue to be there long after the mainstream has turned their interest to something else. In New York they are called *botanicas* in Spanish neighborhoods, and Botanical Gardens in black neighborhoods; they also go under such titles as Spiritual Shops, Religious Goods, or, bravely, Occult stores. You may stumble by accident into a store that sells Methodist hymnbooks and choir robes and ask for Flying Devil Oil, so be cautious.

A good way to find a shop that deals in Voodoo and occult paraphernalia is to look for a window filled with Sacred Hearts, Indian Guides, Blessed Mothers, Bleeding Christs, Black Saints, White Saints, crucifixes, and strange-looking lamps. These are good indications that inside there will be statues, incense, powders, herbs, exotic herbs, candles of every imaginable shape and color, and cases of strange little charms—everything from beads to dried bats. The best thing to do is to know what you want before you go in, and then browse out the vibes and tell the proprietor what your needs are. Since the law takes a dim view of these things, the phrase "sold as a curio only" is simply a device to keep the FDA away.

Browsing in these shops is an interesting way to spend a Saturday afternoon and five dollars. You can wander from store to store buying such things as a seven-knob wishing candle (make a wish, burn a knob each night), Boss Fix Powder, Lucky Hand Root, Come to Me Wash, Dove's Blood Ink, Cleopatra Oil, Lover's Powder, Commanding Incense, Attraction Oil, Come-to-Me Powder, Get-Together, Black Arts Oil, Chinese Floor Wash to get rid of your bad luck, a pair of lodestones, an Indian arrowhead, Mummy Dust, Dragon's Blood Powder. I like to buy them for the names. Of course, it is absolutely necessary to have, for raising power, image candles, male and female, and black cat candles; Holy Altar Candles for meditation; and a rabbit's foot to keep away evil spirits.

It's all a lot of fun, and it is also deadly serious. Why do you think Voodoo magick has such a powerful reputation? I think Voodoo is effective because it is a magick that deals with objects. The most successful magick is an act performed in imitation of nature, in rehearsal for an event that is anticipated. All these oils and powders add to the atmosphere; they trigger the psychic reaction that initiates the event. Objects are the medium through which we express our desires. If plants are sensitive to human thought, how much more sensitive are humans to each other's thoughts?

Like those famous dolls. Suppose a Voodooist wants to destroy an enemy. On the surface, the people are apparently good friends; the slights of the enemy are laughed off or ignored. No tension. Yet. So the Voodooist visits his victim's house. Maybe he pulls a few hairs from the brush lying on the bathroom sink and swipes a washcloth, or a shirt. Good old victim actually has the nerve to sit in the Voodooist's house and clip his dirty toenails all over the floor. After the victim packs up his toenail clipper and goes home (What do you mean, no one's ever clipped his toenails in your living room? What kind of life do you lead?), the Voodooist picks them up and saves them. Now, when the moon is waning, the black candle comes out and a doll is stitched together from the washcloth and stuffed with hair and the nail clippings. Our Voodooist has a good imagination. As he is making the doll, he pictures his enemy—the doll becomes his enemy. He sticks a needle into the doll's arm and imagines his victim getting a sharp pain. It helps if the victim hears this is going on, but it is not absolutely necessary.

Voodoo works because it employs these objects upon which some action is performed similar to what the Voodooist would like to do to his victim, patient, or lover. This is why Voodoo is so popular with so many people. It is easier to channel thoughts into an object than it is to deal with them in the abstract.

So, snap your fingers to conjure up the spirit of Marie Laveau. If her spirit appeared, she would laugh and tell you that you have the power—if you want to use it. And, laughing, she would disappear into the depths of time.

LEMON PEEL LOVE SPELLS

If books on magick are to be believed, the lemon, not the apple, is the forbidden fruit. If you want to get married, take a lemon peel anointed with Cleopatra Oil and carry it around in your pocket all day. You must peel the lemon in one long strip so that its skin never breaks, anoint it with the oil, and pray to Saint Expedite. At night, when you're ready to go to bed, rub the four posts of your bed with the peel and sleep with it under your pillow. The next day go to a bridge or take a ferry boat ride. When you've reached the middle of the river, mash the peel around a dime with the year of your birth on it and throw it into the water with another prayer to Saint Expedite. The prayer is quite simple. You snap your fingers twice and say, "Saint Expedite, do it now!" Don't forget to leave him a slice of pound cake in the church on your wedding day or your marriage will be unhappy.

CONJURE WOMAN'S SEX SPELL

A lot of people see no reason to get married today—it's a free world, after all, and the Pill and other contraceptives have strengthened our sexual freedom. Unfortunately, sometimes you can't always get the person you want, or if you're involved in a relationship it doesn't always seem equal. She stalks out in the middle of the night swearing that you're a rotten bastard and that she's never coming back, you can call her at her friend Lucy's when you've changed your ways. Try to get a pair of her (or his) underpants, stick nine pins in them, and bury them under the eaves, where the rain water will wash over them. This will ensure that she/he will always come back to you.

THOSE VOODOO DOLLS

You're on your own here. No one can make one for you, and no one must know what you're doing. You can make them from wax; you can sew them like rag dolls; you can put them together from straw, red string, or anything—as long as the doll has some part of the victim's essence in it. You should use hair or nail parings. Hair is probably easier to get, but, failing that, use an article of clothing or a photograph of the person to make the doll have the person's essence. All the time you are making the doll, you should set up the atmosphere. If you're making it to "destroy" or injure the person, burn black or brown candles and call upon Baron Samdei and Maitre Carrefour to assist you in your task. Really work yourself into a frenzy of hate, concentrating on all the nasty things your victim has done to you. If he wears a flannel shirt and jeans, dress or mold your doll so that it appears to be wearing the same. Make the doll as close to a miniature of your victim as possible. When you're done, baptize the doll with salt and water in the name of your victim. His full name, now. Then you should stick pins in it, burn it slowly over a fire, or, best of all, bury it or throw it into the water. As the doll rots, so will your enemy.

For love, the ritual is very different. Light pink and red candles, and while you're preparing the doll, pray to Ezili and Pappa Legba; talk to the doll as if it were the person, calling it by name and treating it gently as you would your lover. Use nine red pins—three to the head and three to the heart and three to the genitals. Warm it gently—don't burn it—over a red candle, imagining your lover burning with passion for you. Keep it wrapped in a piece of red silk or velvet under your bed.

GOOFER DUST

If you feel as though you're too old to play with dolls, try playing around with this spell. Go to the butcher and buy a whole tongue. Get some red pepper and some black peppercorns, nine black pins, and a clean piece of paper. On the paper write the name of your enemy in dove's blood ink and pack up the whole kit for a midnight trip to the nearest graveyard. Find the newest grave, and with your hands dig a little trough about nine inches to a foot deep in the dirt. Open the tongue with your knife (don't you carry a pocketknife?) and spread the pepper around inside. Then nail the paper with your enemy's name into the hole with those pins, calling on the spirit of the dead and Baron Samdei to wreak havoc on your enemy's life so that he will waste away and be glad to join with the dead. Close up the tongue and bury it vertically in the earth so that it cannot speak out against you, and cover your deed with dirt. It's a good idea to take along a small jar and keep a handful of the dirt—goofer dust—with you (goofer dust should be a mixture of moss and dirt scraped from a fresh grave). As long as you're there, steal a flower from the grave and scrape a little moss off the tombstones for future spells. Don't forget to thank Le Baron, of course, as you are slinking away into the night. This spell is the most effective when worked under a waning moon.

CRISS-CROSS SPELL

If you have any reason to think someone is working magick against you, take one day off from work during the waxing or full moon. Spend that day cleaning your house from top to bottom, keeping a careful eye out for any gris-gris fetishes, of course. Rearrange your drawers and cabinets and as much of the furniture as you can. Clean every corner of the rooms carefully, and wash your sheets and clothes. Now draw a hot bath (you will probably feel as if you need one by this time) and light a blue candle in every room of the house. After you have stripped down, sprinkle a little van-van powder in every corner of the bathroom and a few drops in your bath water. Wash yourself carefully from your toenails to your hair, and rinse again when you're finished in a whole new tub of fresh water. As the second tub goes down the drain, so will your gris-gris.

POWER SPELL

To increase your power as a Voodoo, catch the first rain water of May in a glass container. On seven consecutive nights light seven white candles and drink the May water with one drop of your own blood. Call on the spirits of your ancestors to assist you in any magickal act you may have in mind. On the last night, get a white hen and cleave the head off with an ax. While the hen is still struggling, catch the blood, mix it with the May water and the goofer dust, and smear the mixture all over your body. If you've never killed a chicken before, it is going to seem pretty awful. Just remember to burn the entire chicken to ashes afterwards, apologizing to its spirit and praying to Pappa Legba that he look upon you kindly.

Note: Live chickens may be purchased at any poultry farm and even in large cities, but whatever you do don't tell them you want it for a ritual sacrifice. Chicken people get very weird about that kind of thing...

CANDLE SPELLS

Candle spells play a large part in common Voodoo practice. The seven-knob candle is for wishing on. You anoint it with a perfumed oil and burn a knob each night, making a wish on the flame. You may make a wish on each knob or the same wish on the entire candle. Adam and Eve candles are bought in pairs. Scratch your name into the one of the appropriate sex and your lover's name into the other. Anoint the candles with Attraction Oil and burn them between seven and eight o'clock in the evening, starting on a Friday night. Place them close together, facing each other, so that as they melt they will merge, hopefully, into one loving puddle of wax. As the candles melt, so will your lover's heart. If you want to curse someone, you should buy a skull candle. Take a few of your victim's hairs and plaster them into the cranium. Carry the candle to a cemetery at midnight and place it on the grave of a suicide, reciting the name of your victim three times before you light it. The black cat candle is burned for good luck.

THE VÉVÉ OF DAMBALLAH

The véve of Damballah is considered to be a very powerful charm against all evil in Vaudon. If you carry it about on your person, inscribed with dove's blood ink on a piece of clean paper, you are safe from all manner of evil. As you are inscribing the veve on the paper, recite this prayer to Damballah:

Ah, Monsieur Damballah-Wedo, Da Sa Lavayto paso!

GOOFER DUST SPELL

The goofer dust spell is one of the traditional spells. Make a mixture of moss scraped from tombstones and earth from a freshly dug grave. Sprinkled with a little holy water, the mixture should then be molded into a small image of a person who you want to gain control over. Burned over a fire of elmwood, the image is complete when the ashes are sprinkled in the path of the victim. Goofer dust is also powerful in itself: scattered over the doorstep of an enemy, it causes him to become ill.

MAY WATER

A favorite charm among Georgia conjure women (no mean Voodooists these ladies) is May water. Gather a jar of the first rain water of May and brew it into a tea of sassafras bark and pine needles to insure your good health all year long.

WART CURE

Another good Georgia Voodoo spell is the wart cure. Take a string and tie a knot in it for each wart. Hang the string under the eaves of the house so that the water running down the string will wash the warts away.

CONJURE BALL SPELL

A good way to obtain power in magick is to use the conjure ball spell. Take the wax melted from your other candle magicks and melt it down again into a lump. In the middle of the lump, put a red pepper, a drop of oil, and three hairs from your own body. Carried as an amulet, this conjure ball will supply you with unlimited Voodoo power. To keep it strong, light seven candles on the first night of every month, place them in a circle around the conjure ball, and let them burn all the way down.

LOVESICK CLIENTS

Marie Laveau had a favorite spell that she employed for lovesick clients. She would take a lemon peel and wrap two needles in it, eye to point, bind the whole thing with red thread, and sew it into a black silk pouch. This she would present to the lovesick one. If it was worn around the neck and the person encountered the beloved, this beloved would fall directly in love with him or her.

THE EZILI SPELL

Another old Voodoo love spell tells a girl who wants to get a man to take a piece of Friday's bread and a dime with her birthday year, knead them together, and carry them to church on Sunday; then go directly from the church to the ferry. Halfway across the river, throw the bread into the water and say, "Ezili, get me married," three times. The Ezili spell has been around for years. I first heard it from an old woman in Virginia many years ago.

Vévé Ezili

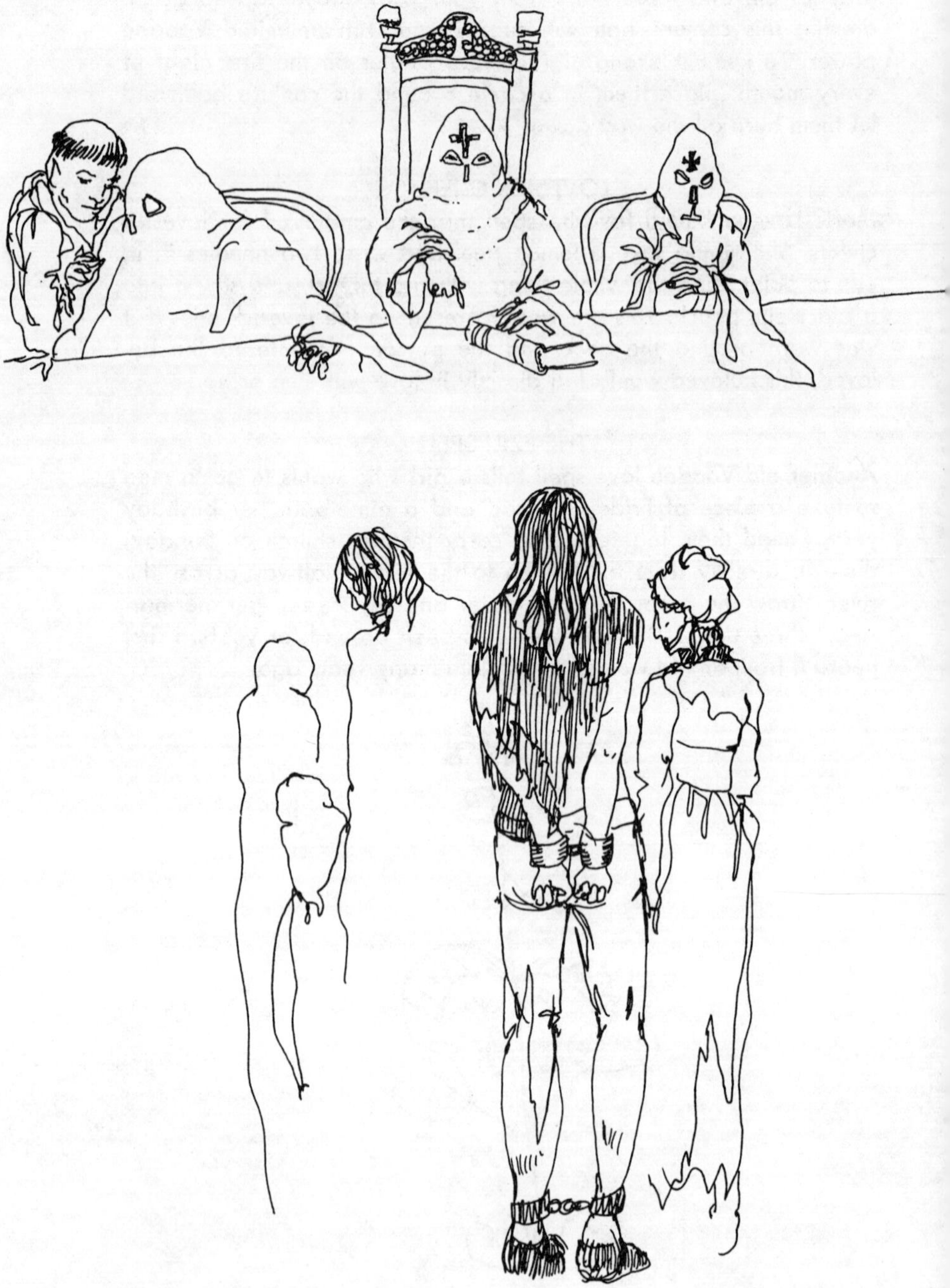

7

WICCA—THE LADY AND THE HORNED GOD

A witch; and one so strong she could control the moon...
WILLIAM SHAKESPEARE,
The Tempest

Ah, witches! Little old ladies in long black capes, cackling over braised toad livers and bat-wing stew. For the power to blast a hearth or curdle milk, they sold their souls to Satan.

Ah, witches! A few hysterical old women, victims of the medieval religious mania, tortured into absurd confessions and burned alive at the stake. Innocents, destroyed by glinty-eyed fanatics.

Ah, witches! Acid crazies, helterskeltering in the night, the bloody reality of Hollywood nightmares comes true.

Witches.

Housewives in Honolulu, medieval scholars in Toronto, insurance salesmen from Iowa, art students in Chicago, practitioners of the Old Religion.

The beginnings of witchcraft are rooted in the beginnings of time. When Paleolithic man stood up and looked around his primordial world he saw spirits dwelling in every animal and plant. Existing closely with the earth, he recognized his dependence on the natural cycles and his own spirit responded. He watched the seasons change from winter into summer, the plants and animals living and dying, the sun and moon moving across the heavens. The thunder rolled across the mountains and man trembled in fear. The game was killed and he rejoiced. When he plucked the nuts from the trees he was happy. In the winter he shivered near the fire in his hut, watching the bare branches covered with snow. His survival depended on forces he could not control. Obviously, it lay within the power of these spirits to bring the spring and the plenty of his world back.

To assure himself that the spirits dominating the world would maintain the precarious status quo, he tried to influence them by bribing them with awe and worship and sacrifice.

These are the beginnings of witchcraft, the Old Religion. With time and civilization, the craft and arts of the religion were defined. The first magicks in England evolved under the name "wicca." In Old English the word means wise. In Middle English the spelling changes to "witch." It was a religion of nature and fertility, regarding the sun as the Great Father and the moon as the Great Mother. Man was their spiritual child, for whom they created earth, from whom they demanded worship. In return, the sun and moon continued the cycles of nature, keeping an eye on the welfare of their earthbound children. The spirits that dwelt in the animals, plants, and mountains became a pantheon known as the Old Ones, gods who dwelt in the back of the universe among the stars.

As a nature religion, wicca draws its magickal powers from the regeneration of the earth and the fertility of this god and goddess, the Great Mother and the Great Father, God of the Sun, Goddess of the Moon.

The goddess is the Lady, the female principal of creation. Her colors are green and silver, for the fertility of the earth and the drawing power of the lunar phases. She is in charge of the summer months, all the flora, love, healing, and the seas and waters of the world. Her symbol is the crescent moon, and she is worshiped under names like Diana, Habondia, Setha, Anis, Hecate, or Tanta.

The god is the Horned Man, lord of the winter, the harvesting. He rules the land of the dead, somewhere behind the sun. His empires are the earth and the sky. He controls the fauna of the earth, the mountains, and the powers of destruction and lust. Like the Lord of the Beasts, the god has stag's horns to symbolize his powers of death and regeneration. He has been called Pan, Lucifer, Herene, Janicot, Robin, and Apollo.

The Lady and the Horned God are both brother and sister and husband and wife. The legend of wicca has it that the Lady seduced her brother in the guise of his pet cat. From that union there was a daughter named Aradia. When she had come of age, her mother sent her to earth to teach mortals the craft of wicca. Aradia is regarded as the Messiah of the witches. Aradia brought the skills of magick to the witches. She instructed her followers in the formation of the coven and the election of a priest and priestess to represent the sun and the moon in their worship. She imparted the secrets of the universe and the rituals and ceremonies to engender their power. Aradia taught the art of healing and poisoning with herbs, divination, and soothsaying and all the magicks that give the witch her power.

Aradia gave the witch cult its tenets of belief.

For the witch, there is no reason to fear death; witches believe that the soul passes from the physical body to Twilight, that place of warm flowers and meadows ruled by the Horned God. There, Aradia said, the soul rests and greets old friends while awaiting rebirth in a new body. When the soul is reborn, it will remember loved ones from past lives. Eventually, the soul will no longer have to be reborn, but will travel forever through the mountains of Twilight.

Aradia cautioned the witches to think carefully before using their magicks for evil, for whatever one does in this life will be returned threefold by the god and goddess within the space of this life. The witches were given their powers, but they must use them wisely.

When Christianity spread into western Europe, it was at first the religion of the upper classes and the educated. In the Dark Ages following the fall of the Roman Empire, it grew in spiritual and temporal power, existing side by side with the old pagan ways. The first Christian missionaries were advised to incorporate into the faith as much of the old pagan traditions as possible so as to more easily convert the peasants. The two religions existed side by side for several hundred years as the Church grew in power.

It is hard to imagine the isolation and ignorance of the average human being in the Middle Ages. It was a time when thousands died from the black plague; when the most learned scholars could spend hours and years debating over how many angels could dance on the head of a pin. The devil was not an advertisement for Dr. Pepper; he was a very real demon walking among human beings on earth. And that horned god was none other than Satan, his evil self, and the Old Religion must be stomped out. The pagans were a threat to the Church's power. To the celibates who followed the teachings of Saint Paul, a cult that worshiped an openly sexual goddess and a horned god was worshiping Satan. So the Church misinterpreted to its own satisfaction, and set out to exterminate and suppress the old cults that had preceded it. It is sometimes hard for a more tolerant twentieth-century mind to understand the horror the good Church fathers felt about this pagan religion in which women played a dominant role. One need only remember that their fundamental translation of the Bible cautioned that one must "not suffer a witch to live"; this dictum shows what fear and loathing they felt against witches. Witches, they said, ate babies and killed cattle. They were the cause of the plagues that raged throughout Europe; they destroyed the innocent minds of the faithful. Witches were heretics along with Jews and other dissenting sects, and the Church felt they must be exterminated.

There is an interesting legend that the pagans sheltered the persecuted Jews from the wrath of the Church. Certainly there are some Cabalistic strains in the Old Religion that appear around the time of the Inquisition. It is nice to believe that the two sects did meet and exchange magicks, even if only for a brief time.

But in six hundred terrible years, what witches call the Burning Times, it has been estimated that six million men, women, and children were tortured, maimed, and horribly executed for the crime of witchcraft.

Doubtless there were covens whose ancient traditions were corrupted into the worship of Satan as the diametric opposite of God. It is probable that Satanism as a religion unto itself started around this time, as a bitter parody of the established Church. God, as he

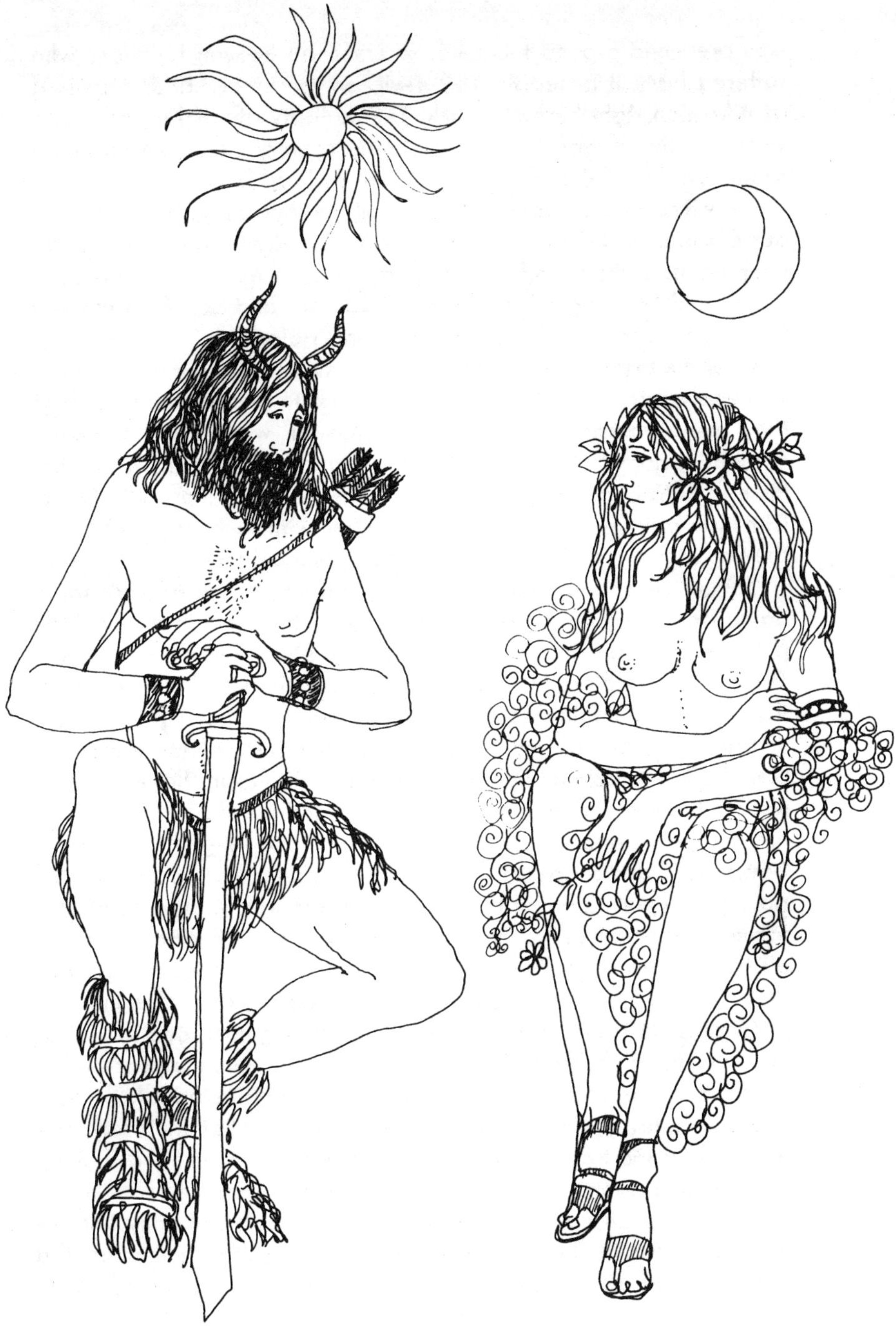

was preached around this time, reserved his heaven for those who suffered his will on earth. The devil, on the other hand, promised gratification right here on earth. The majority of witches, however, were not Satan worshipers, but simple country farmers who clung to the religion of their fathers and their fathers' fathers.

So, wicca quietly went underground; existing in pockets throughout Europe. And there it has stayed for hundreds of years, silently keeping its secrets and enduring the misconceptions of outsiders, desperately seeking to preserve its traditions and beliefs in esoteric form against the fear of persecution and ridicule.

After the last war, witches began to come out into the open again, cautiously saying only what has to be said to debunk the myth that they are Satanists and cannibals. Satanism, witches will patiently explain, is not what they practice. You have to believe in God to believe in Satan, and they believe in neither. Nor do they ridicule the Christian religion. Why need they bother with such practices, since they have nothing at all to do with the witch beliefs?

Covens are springing up like peyote buttons all over America these days. And it would probably be hard to find two that agree on procedure, leadership, rites, charms, spells, or even form of dress. The intramural bickering between witches is incredible. A coven on the West Coast might meet for magicking, thirteen in number, dressed in brocade robes embroidered with all the signs of the zodiac. A New York City coven might go through their rites in the nude using Middle English and worshiping the Lady and the Horned God without the use of any magick at all, performing a religious ceremony. Covens snip and snap at each other in a manner that borders on the ridiculous were it not for the many Satanists who walk around pronouncing themselves witches. There is a universe of differences, yet all true covens do believe in the god and the goddess and believe that those two have the power to control the outcome of events.

To become a member of a coven, or to organize one, is not as easy as one might think. First of all, you must renounce your beliefs in the religion you were brought up in—Christianity, Islam, Buddhism, whatever. One must consciously decide that the Lady and the Horned God do exist and are deities to be worshiped and respected and loved. That is a hard step for most people to make.

Contacting an established coven is even harder. Usually witches don't advertise in *The New York Times* for prospective members. If a person is interested in the Old Religion and decides to commit him-

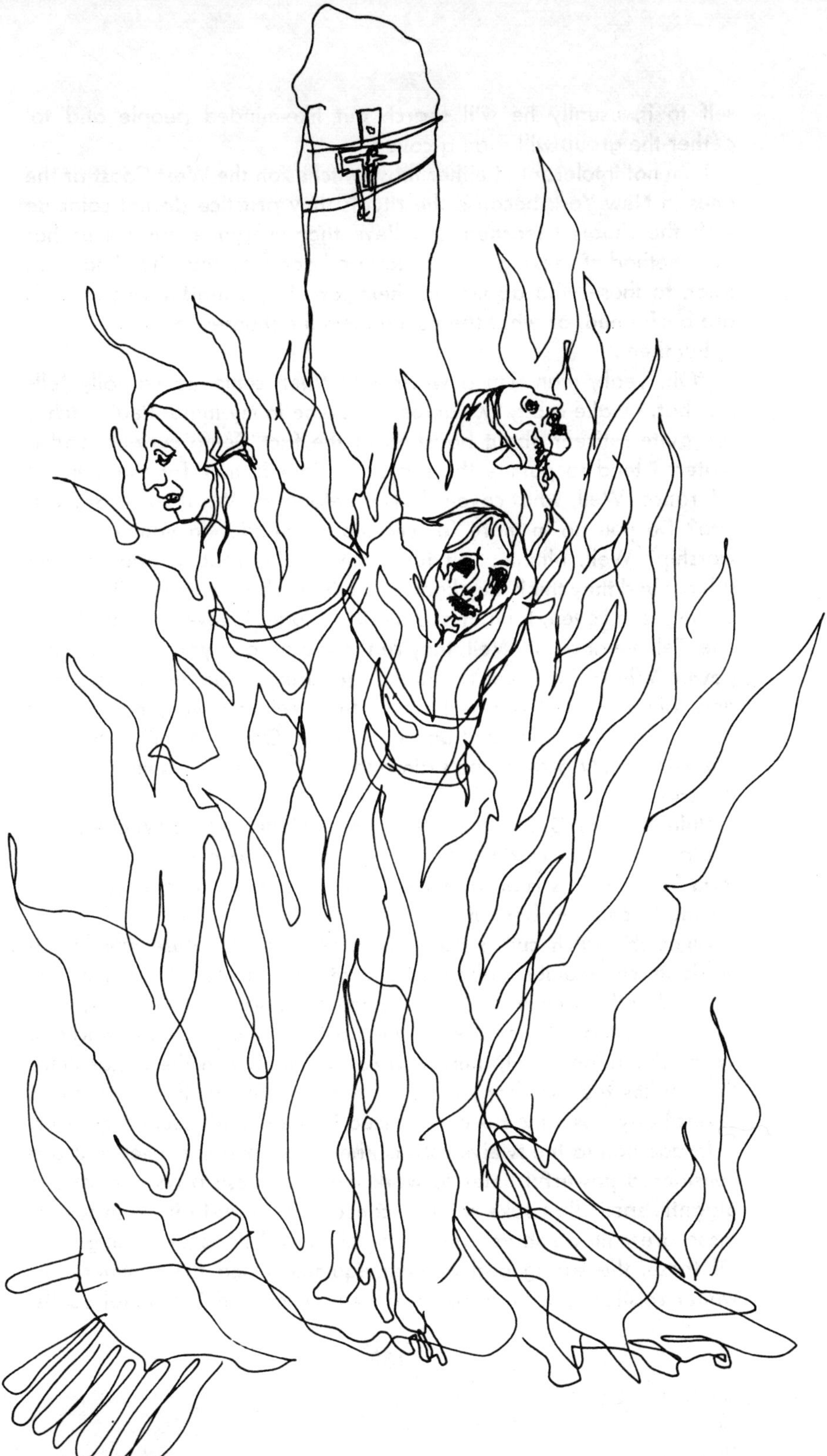

self to it, usually he will search out like-minded people and together the group will form a coven.

I am not intolerant of either those witches on the West Coast or the ones in New York because the rituals they practice do not coincide with the rituals I learned. I believe that everyone has his or her own method of seeking out the god and goddess, that they hear and listen to those who appeal to them for aid no matter what rituals are performed, or what the coven member chooses to wear.

But then . . .

"Oh, yeah, man, I'm a warlock." When someone casually tells me that, I make a big "X" across his name in my mind. Real witches are quite reticent about boasting of the fact. Being curious, and a writer, I tend to pursue the subject a little further for the sake of tolerance. Well, what coven do you belong to? What spells are you into? Do you go in more for ceremonial magick in your coven or worship? Well, uhhhh . . . it turns out they've read a book on the subject and they think they know something about magick. Uh, I don't belong to a coven, I, uh, make diodes. Diodes? Never heard of that one. Tell me about it. Well, they're these diagrams you make to raise power. What? Oh, I see. You mean (gesturing in the air) pentagrams and talismans and runes? No, diodes. Well, anyway, my brother does. He calls on the devil and everything. On the devil? I see. And one very firmly grasps one's gin and lime and moves away through the crowd.

Rule Number One in the International Codebook of Witches: You are a witch or a warlock only if you belong to a coven. Even the term "warlock" is regarded with some suspicion, most covens preferring to call members of both sexes witches.

Since the witch cult is basically a religion of nature worship, it holds its ceremonies, called esbats, at certain crucial times of the year. Usually a coven will meet once a month, under the first full moon. This night is considered the strongest time to work magicks. When the moon is full, there is a certain energy in the atmosphere that makes the air charged with strong vibrations. If a spell takes several days, usually it is commenced in the moon's second quarter.

In addition to the twelve esbats, there are six other times that are considered powerful times to work magick. These days are for the gigantic spells that take a lot of concentration and effort. In wicca, these are called sabats, and no witch would think of missing one. Of these, the spring and autumn equinoxes and the summer and winter solstices are times for new beginnings and individual spells.

The two High Days are Walpurgis, the first of May, and All Hallows, the last day of October. These are times when the entire coven gets together to really work magick.

Even non-witches should be aware of these days, when the forces of nature are most in tune with the vibrations of man.

If one decides to become a witch, what is entailed? You cannot go shopping for a coven in a supermarket. If you decide to join a coven, or form one, you will be initiated into the mysteries of wicca through a simple initiation rite. If the novice is a male, he will be initiated by the High Priestess, representing the goddess. A woman will be initiated by the High Priest, representing the god. You may or may not work nude—or skyclad, as the witches term it. Some covens prefer to work in the nude, believing that clothing short-circuits that astral current of the body. Others, for reasons of modesty or mystery, choose to wear robes of a uniform design for the rituals. It's all a matter of personal taste. The women of the coven will wear a string of heavy beads to symbolize the cycles of nature. These beads may be acorns or chunks of amber; it doesn't matter. But a woman who enters the Circle without her beads is as invisible as a barrister in a British court without his wig.

The High Priestess is the most important member of the coven. Without her, the coven cannot meet. Usually she is nominated to her office for her virtues of power, experience, and seniority. The High Priestess is in charge of arranging a meeting place for the coven, keeping the minutes of the meeting and the record of the spells and rituals called *The Red Book* or sometimes "The Book of Shadows." At Walpurgis, she assumes total leadership of the coven, her role as the goddess manifested. She presides over the coven meetings until All Hallows, when the High Priest, as the Lord of Winter, takes over. But she always has the final decision in any matters of coven policy.

The High Priest is usually the leader of the magickal aspects of the coven, preparing the spells and leading the invocations and chants. He is chosen on much the same basis as the High Priestess. The Priest is also in charge of the witchcraft tools, consecrating them to magickal use by passing them through air, fire, water, and earth, inscribing the witches' runes on them. The runes are an ancient alphabet whose squiggly lines correspond to letters in our own alphabet (see illustration on page 163). Most correspondence between witches is conducted through the runes.

If you are invited to attend a coven ceremony, an esbat, you will probably arrive at the Priestess's house about ten o'clock or so on

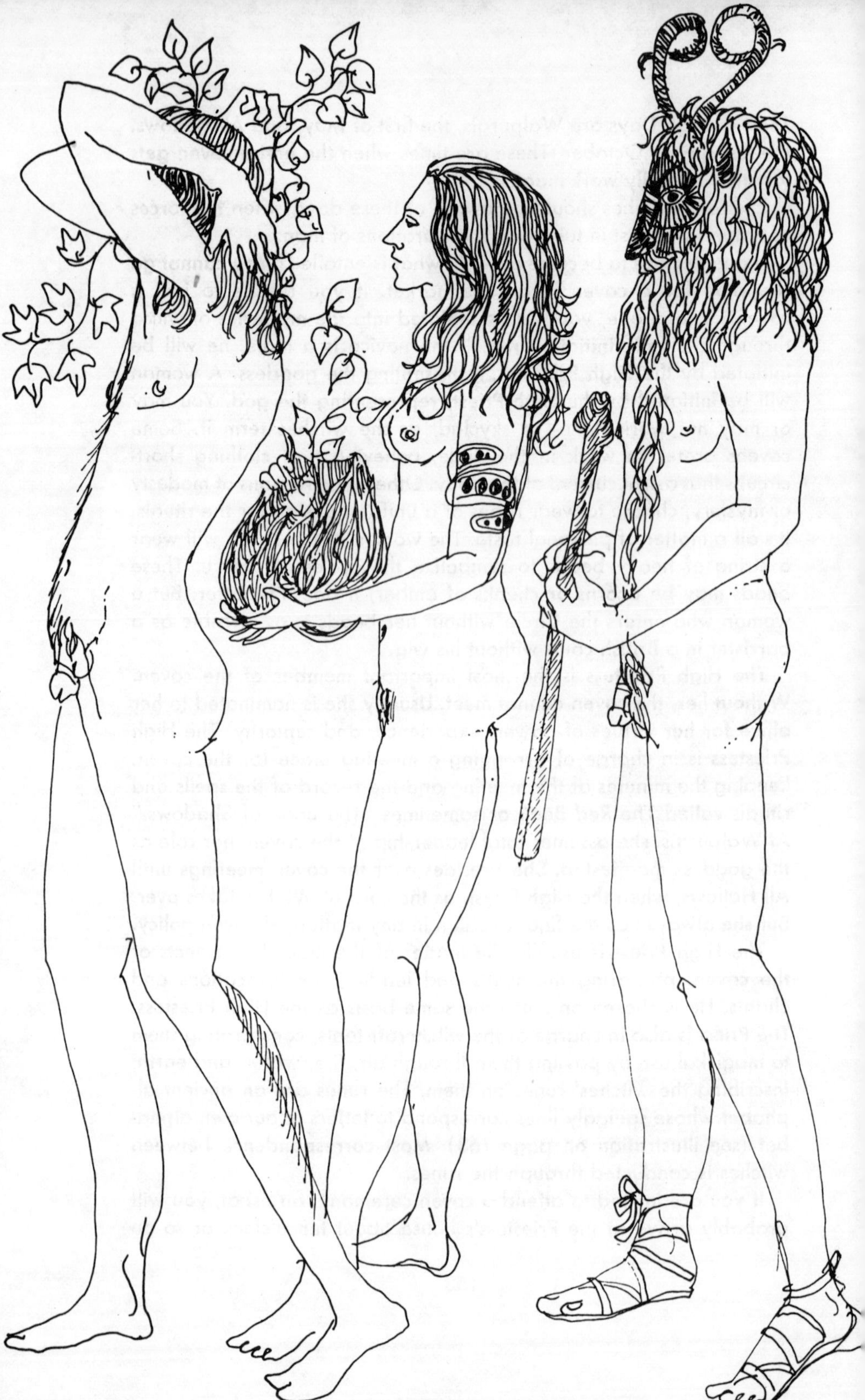

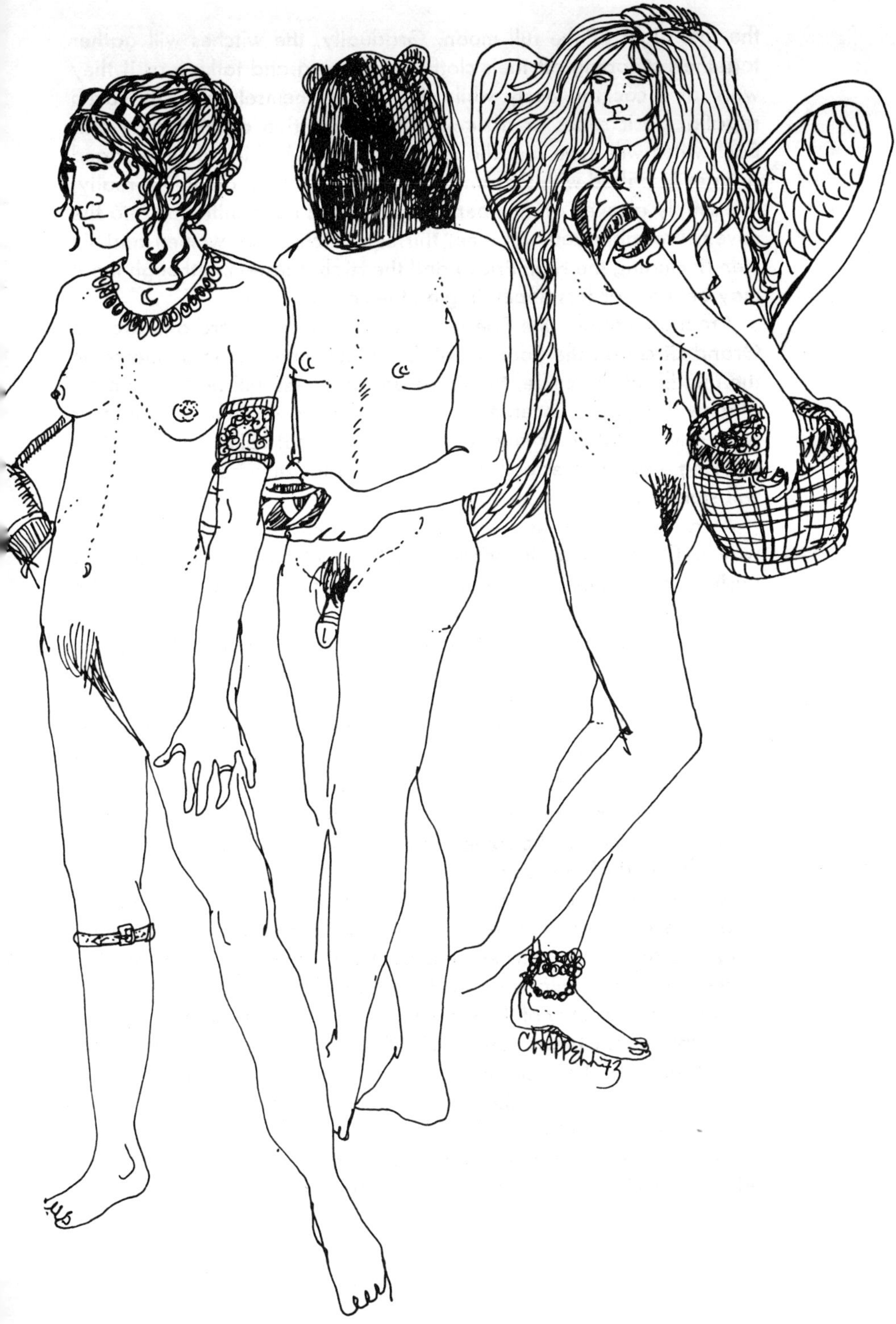
CHAPPELL 73

the first night of the full moon. Gradually, the witches will gather together, stripping off their clothes, gossiping and talking as if they were at a cocktail party while they array themselves in the coven regalia, be it robes or a simple silver cord tied around the waist. Each witch will have an athane, a very lethal-looking double-edged dagger inscribed with the runes. It is not used to cut anything, really; it is simply a token of membership presented upon initiation into the coven. Probably you will meet thirteen witches—six women and six men (including the High Priest) and the High Priestess, although there may be more or less depending on the coven.

Around midnight, the Priestess will take up her sword and draw a Grand Circle on the floor. It will be about nine feet in diameter. In the middle of the circle, the Priest and Priestess will have set up an altar with candles, incense, flowers of the season, and a chalice of wine and a platter of tiny pastries called sabat cakes. The Priestess will ring a small silver bell three times and the members of the coven will step inside the circle.

As a non-member you will be asked to sit outside the circle, and watch. There will be invocations to the god and goddess and the business of the meeting will be taken care of. If there is a spell to be performed, it will be done now.

After the spellcasting, there will probably be another chant, and then the witches' dance. Yes, they do cavort. It is a snake dance, with male and female partners intertwined, going around and around the circle, at first very slowly, working faster and faster as they go. At a signal from the Priestess, the Priest will pass his wand, symbol of air, over the platter and chalice. He will then sip from the chalice and pass it to the Priestess. She will in turn drink from it and pass it among the dancers. The same ritual is followed with the sabat cakes. This is the end of the esbat.

As the last member steps from the circle to give you the wine and cakes, he or she will quietly explain that the ritual was designed long ago to put the witches in contact with their gods and that the chant and dance help work up their magickal energies.

After the ceremony of the wine and cakes, there is a sort of covered dish supper that breaks the Circle. Everyone laughs and talks and eats. There may be rock music and dancing of a different sort. You circulate among the witches, who are chatting about the ceremony, the weather, gossip about other covens, life in general.

"You really get high just from the power you raise," one girl will tell you, eating potato salad from a plate. "We don't practice orgies here. Some covens do, you know, but we're more traditional. To us, sex is a very powerful thing—it's a lot of energy raised, but we direct it toward magick—I mean, if you want to gang bang, you should go to some of these orgies they have uptown. To *them*, it's just an excuse to get together and ball."

"I always feel very pure, very powerful after a sabat or, especially an esbat," a dude wearing nothing but a gold earring will tell you as he heaps your plate with dried apricots and chunks of fresh coconut. "I feel as if I've been cleaned inside and out. I was never really happy being a Catholic. There were just too many complications. But in wicca, I have this sense of unity with everyone here. I believe in what we do. It transcends magick, you know? It becames a spiritual thing."

The High Priestess, a woman in her middle thirties with a crescent moon pinned in her hair, speaks: "We tend to be paranoid, with outsiders"—she smiles an apology at you, like a blessing—"because we've been given such a bad name, even recently. We don't practice black magick or white magick. We're witches. Very rarely do we do something evil on someone. Only when the entire coven feels it is justified. We're pretty together here. There's a coven of homosexuals over on the East Side who get kicks from dressing up in these elaborate robes and beating each other with whips and things . . . that's not what the Old Religion is about. I feel rather sorry for them, having to use the craft as an excuse for that. Real magick is a lot of hard work, you know. Working within the coven, we raise a lot of energy, and we use it constructively. Being a witch makes you more aware of your environment, of yourself as an individual. *It's good!*"

After a bit, people begin to exit and return in their street clothes. There are hugs and exchanges of "call me this week" and the traditional wicca parting of "Blessed Be."

As you fumble and bumble back into your clothes to face the cold winter night, you reflect on what you have seen.

Witchcraft is not just another fanatic cult. It is a very deep philosophical and spiritual commitment. It means having to accept and live a life style and a belief. It cannot be picked up and put down like a toy. Witchcraft is a joyous reunion with the realities of life.

One needn't join a coven to work group magick. Obviously, if you have a few friends working magick with you the results are going to be much stronger than the forces of one individual practicing alone, especially when you are starting out. When I was in college, a few of us used to get together every once in a while and concentrate on a specific occurrence we wanted to happen. We would gather in someone's room, turn out the lights, sit in a circle, and stare at a candle placed in the middle of the floor, concentrating on what we wanted to accomplish. At the time, we were just goofing. If it did work, we were a little apprehensive—after all, the dormitory had once been a resort hotel; we thought it might be haunted. But we also felt good when a spell worked. One guy passed an exam he was sure he was going to fail. A girl found that we had made her boyfriend cut down on his almost daily use of acid—at least for a while. The mania for our sessions died out after a time when we found newer and better amusements. But I have found since then that working with another person does tend to increase the power flow.

It is not such a long way from the first witches gathering together in some dark cave to raise the sun and the moon to a group of sophisticated twentieth-century individuals meeting in a city apartment to communicate with the Lady and the Horned God. The outside trappings of civilization change from year to year and century to century, but the belief and the power remain the same. The forces that move the universe are there—and it is entirely within your power to use them.

The witches' spells and magicks have been handed down from generation to generation. You don't have to belong to a coven to practice magick or use these spells. Since a great part of working magick relies on mental concentration and channeling of will, the first wicca spell you should learn to use is *the raising of the cone of power*.

Actually, this spell is halfway between a ritual and mental exercise. Both yogis and magicians use it to keep in touch with the cosmic forces and to raise the subconscious energy from the back of the mind, like charging a battery. It's a good preliminary spell to use before going on to another magickal ritual. At first, you may find that instead of feeling powerful you feel very drowsy, but with continual practice you will see that your psychic energy is being raised to a high level.

Light a white candle and place it at the foot of your bed, sleeping bag, or any other place where you can stretch out on your back comfortably and keep the flame in view. Stare at the flame, repeating over and over to yourself: "As my will, so mote it be." Allow your body to relax. Let your lids droop over your eyes, breathing in and out deeply and slowly . . . in . . . out . . . in . . . out . . . ahhhh.

As your lids close, tense and relax each part of your body, starting with your big toe and working on up through your body to the top of your scalp. Complete relaxation.

Imagine your mind floating gently up from your body. Feel the spirit detaching itself from the shackles of the physical body, allowing your soul to float upward through the cosmos, charging itself from the energy reservoirs of the universe. Imagine yourself as an empty vessel being filled with the elixir of life. Feel almost magnetic, now, allowing the astral and physical bodies to merge and mesh back together. Allow yourself to surface, picturing your spell in your mind and the final results. Now, open your eyes and blow out the candle. You're charged and ready to go.

Working this spell could take you four hours, or five minutes. The more you do it, the easier it becomes. Try at first to do it at the same time every day. Gradually it will become easier and easier for you to slip in and out of the trance state.

A great love spell for beginners uses the poppet. Poppets are little dolls, but in witchcraft you don't stick pins in them (more about that later); rather, the poppet is used for good.

If at all possible, obtain a piece of your beloved's clothing. Beg, borrow, or bribe the laundryman for a shirt, a scarf, or a handkerchief belonging to your friend. If it's dirty, so much the better. Cut two matching human shapes from the fabric and sew them together with a binding stitch of red silk thread. Leave the top open and fill the doll with aphrodisiac herbs. Make a potpourri of lovage root, mistletoe, bay laurel, coriander, thyme, and dried rose petals. Now close up the head with red silk thread. Dress the doll in the same style of clothes that your lover wears. If he wears jeans and a leather jacket, get a scrap of denim and a bit of leather and make the poppet denim pants and a leather jacket. If she wears a black silk dress and pearls, make a miniature black silk dress and a little pearl necklace.

Name the doll for your beloved by passing it over a red candle and reciting:

> In the Name of Setha and Herne,
> I do name thee N. . . . N.

Repeat this three times. Now wrap the doll in red silk and sleep with it under your pillow for a week. Soon your beloved will start to take an interest in you. If you want to hasten the results of your spell, pass the poppet over the red candle every night for the week before the full moon, just enough to warm it up, all the while thinking about the person the doll represents. As the doll gets warm, so will the person's heart. When you're not using the doll, be careful to keep it wrapped in red silk.

In the Old World, lemons have always been a symbol of Aradia. Italian witches used to cast this particular spell to bring good luck. The spell of lemon and pins is best performed at midnight. Buy three fresh lemons and a box of those pins with colored heads.

Purchase three white candles. At the stroke of midnight, light the candles and stick the lemon with pins, reciting the following verse with each pin:

> Diana, I present to thee
> Queen of moon and stars!
> With each pin I cast a charm
> To keep my friend from all harm!

Given as a present, the lemon brings good luck, and it keeps evil away from the giver and the recipient.

Perhaps there is someone who has genuinely incurred your wrath—the girl who stole your boyfriend, the neighbor who is constantly complaining about nonexistent noise coming from your apartment, the man who got you fired from a great job because his daughter wants something to pass the time ... well, you don't want them to die, precisely, but you would like to have them see a run of really bad luck. The kind of times when phones go dead for no reason, cars break down, buttons pop off, trains get missed, acne breaks out, and deodorants fail. Maybe even a bad cold and a raise in rent.

Get a large head of garlic and nine black-headed pins. Light a black candle and stick the pins in the garlic, reciting with each pin:

> N. ... N. [full name], thus I curse thee!
> For the wrongs thou hast done me!
> As my will, so mote it be!

Mail the garlic to your enemy. The minute they open the package and touch the garlic, they've got your bad luck.

The new moon, of course, is the best time to work spells for increase. Especially when money is low. If you're really broke and welfare and food stamps seem to be the next step, you might try the moon spell.

Take a friend, three candles, a metal bowl of water, wine, and salt and go out into a meadow where the full moon shines directly down. Light the candles and sit down in the grass between them. Together you must say three times:

Aradia, Aradia, I thus implore thee
That thou wilt grant my wishes for me
As my will, so mote it be!

Together you must set the bowl between you so the moon's reflection is caught in the water. Gently run your hand across the surface as if you were skimming the moon off the top, capturing the silver in your hands. Before the water has a chance to settle again, empty the bowl into the earth and blow out the candles. While you are returning home, do not look at the moon or the spell will be ruined. Before the next full moon, you should have money from an unexpected source.

He left you, but why? Everything was going along so well, you thought. And then for no apparent reason, he just stopped calling. And if you call him, he makes excuses and hangs up. If you want him back, you're going to have to charm him. To witches, the seashell is a

THE TOOLS OF WITCHCRAFT

symbol of female receptivity. So go down to the beach and find one. Bring it home, and place it in your bath with lovage root, vervain, and rose petals. Burn a purple candle and take a leisurely soak, rubbing your entire body with the shell. Think of some pretext to drop in on him the next day. Very casually, hide the shell somewhere in his house—preferably under his bed, if you can manage it. He'll be drawn back to you more strongly than ever before.

There comes a time in every witch's life when he or she is faced with the ugly task of dealing with a hostile magician. And that's the kind of thing you've got to watch out for. So in the sorcerer's war, where paranoia and delusions are thrown around like juggler's balls, the protection amulet is good to have around.

Traditionally, iron is a powerful magickal amulet. If you carry an iron ring with you, no magick can ever hurt you.

As discussed earlier, the wicca runes are an important part of magick. Whenever a tool is consecrated to the art, the name of the user is inscribed on the object with a new pen and ink, and most correspondence between witches is conducted in these characters, shown below.

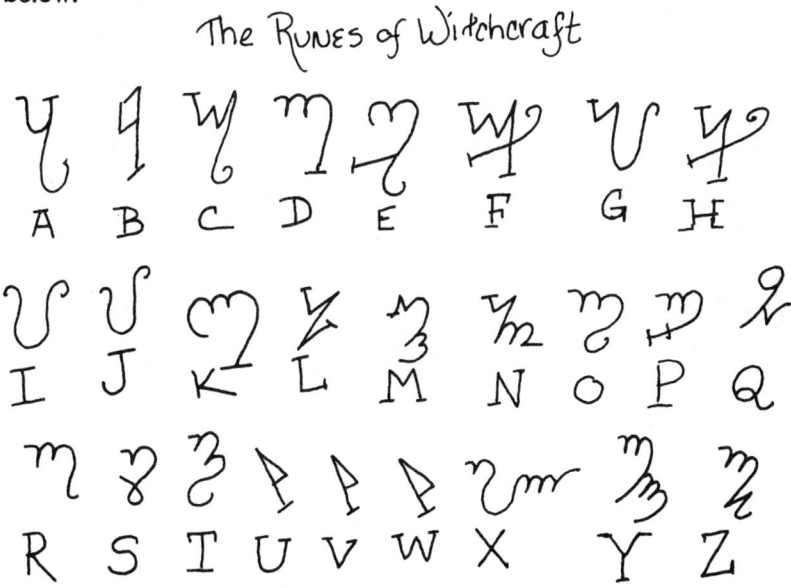

The Runes of Witchcraft

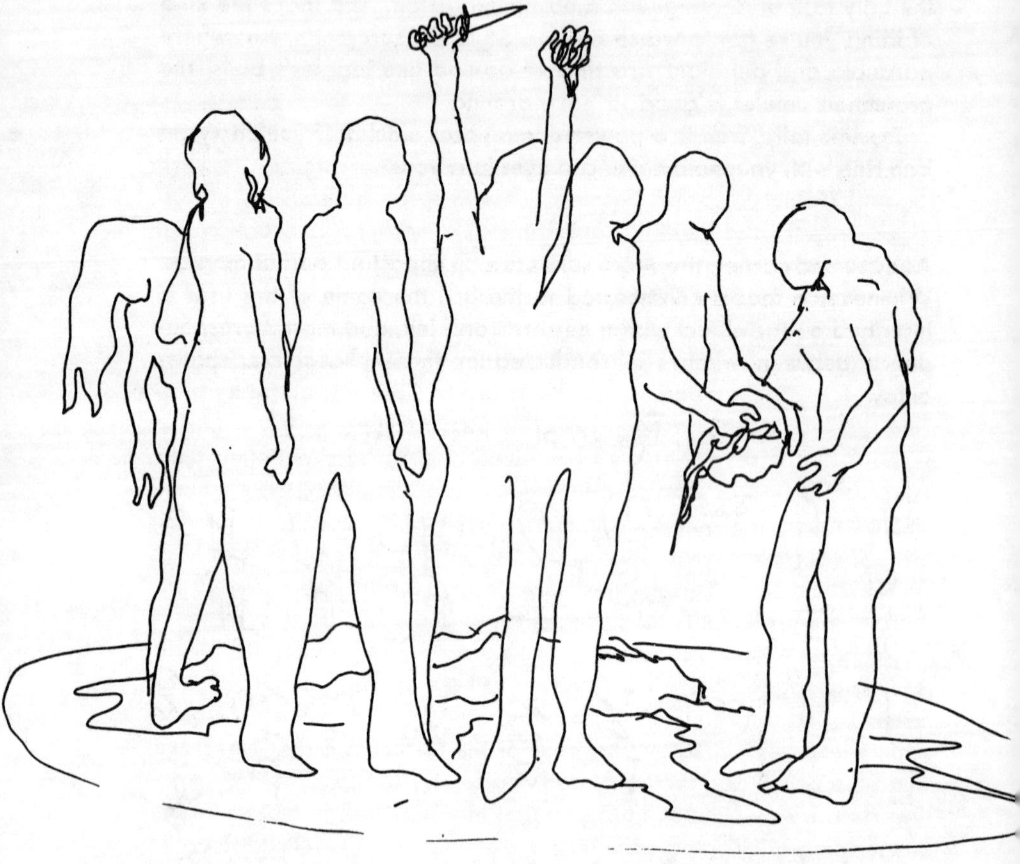

SATANISM—THE BLACK MASS AND THE DEVIL'S TUNE

> Please allow me to introduce myself
> I'm a man of wealth and taste...
> MICK JAGGER–KEITH RICHARD,
> "Sympathy for the Devil"
>
> ...and then again, maybe we're all dead and this is hell.
> JUDY BROWN

Satan has always been one of the fascinating characters in literature and folklore. Whether serving as the prosecuting attorney for hell against Daniel Webster, helping Faust to trade his soul for knowledge, power, and wealth, appearing at a Fiddlers' Convention (I'll bet you didn't know the devil is a great fiddler!), or making a guest appearance for Billy Graham, the devil is fascinating.

Is he the Dark Rider galloping hell-for-leather, the nameless eternal bad guy, The Master of the Lefthand Path, the lurker in the shadows of Dachau and Mylai, the Prince of Darkness eternally plotting the Armaggedon from the black fires of hell?

Or is he the revolutionary? The fallen angel who challenged God and lost? Is he the seed of discontent questioning the establishment in the cause of happiness of all men? Is he "that force which strives for evil yet causes the good"? *What* is the nature of his game?

We seem to have inherited the idea of Satan just as we've inherited the Protestant ethic, pay toilets, and the two-party system.

While the moral concepts of acceptable and nonacceptable in society change with each era, we are still caught between our animal instincts and our intellectual strivings.

Intellectually, we know that fear of the darkness is silly; yet if we push the switch and the lights don't go on, we feel a primitive nameless dread. Any child will tell you that monsters lurk in the darkness, just waiting to gobble up the unwary. We know all too well the darkness that dwells in our souls, and the monsters in our heads who are waiting to devour us from inside. Because we are afraid of the darkness, we gather together in groups. If we want to maintain our frail and sensitive connections with one another, we must suppress those instincts that would push us away if displayed. If we argued and I clubbed you over the head with a bookend, I would no longer be acceptable in society. I would be thrown back into the darkness, cast away from the tribe, forced to face the whims of nature by myself. So we argue and smile, in order to keep our positions safe and sound within the tribe.

No one wants to face nature all alone. Human beings have always been a little paranoid about their relationship to nature. In one mood we see nature as a miracle of beauty and harmony, and on the other hand we live in mortal terror of her caprices. Since nature does not have to worry about being thrown into darkness, she does what is necessary to continue her survival, and affronts us with her complete disregard for our darkness-fearing values. We simply cannot accept the idea that everything on this planet is food for something else. So we try to cut ourselves out from nature, living in our manmade environments where we can mitigate the effects of nature, even control her forces a little. And the more we cut ourselves off from our natural instincts, the more we yearn for nature's beauty and fear her power.

This kind of splitting off can drive people into analysis. The concept of an evil force working outside of man to make him violate all his taboos is a very old one. Unable to reconcile himself to his schizoid concept of good and evil, man found it necessary to create a scapegoat with enough power to create evil—not only humanity's capacity for evil, but the evils inflicted by nature.

Human beings have always created their gods in their own image, making them as fickle and capricious as those they were supposed to help. Even the evil ones who walk in the night and lurk in the wildernesses should be placated. O Yama, Lilith, Loki, Sathanas, Baron Samdei—even these must have their priests, their temples, and their worshipers.

The relationship between religion and magick has always been close. Perhaps the dark forces are more easily rendered to than those of light, for Set, the Egyptian version of Satan, was greatly appealed to by sorcerers, who believed that he had more power over the unknown—the darkness—than his brother, Osiris, the Lord of the Sun. Set was perhaps the earliest deity of evil incarnate—planned, plotted, and executed. Zoroaster expounded the idea that Ahriman, evil incarnate, was the brother of Ormazd, good incarnate, and the continual battle between the opposing forces is the raison d'être of the universe. Equal and opposing forces combine to form the divine, and

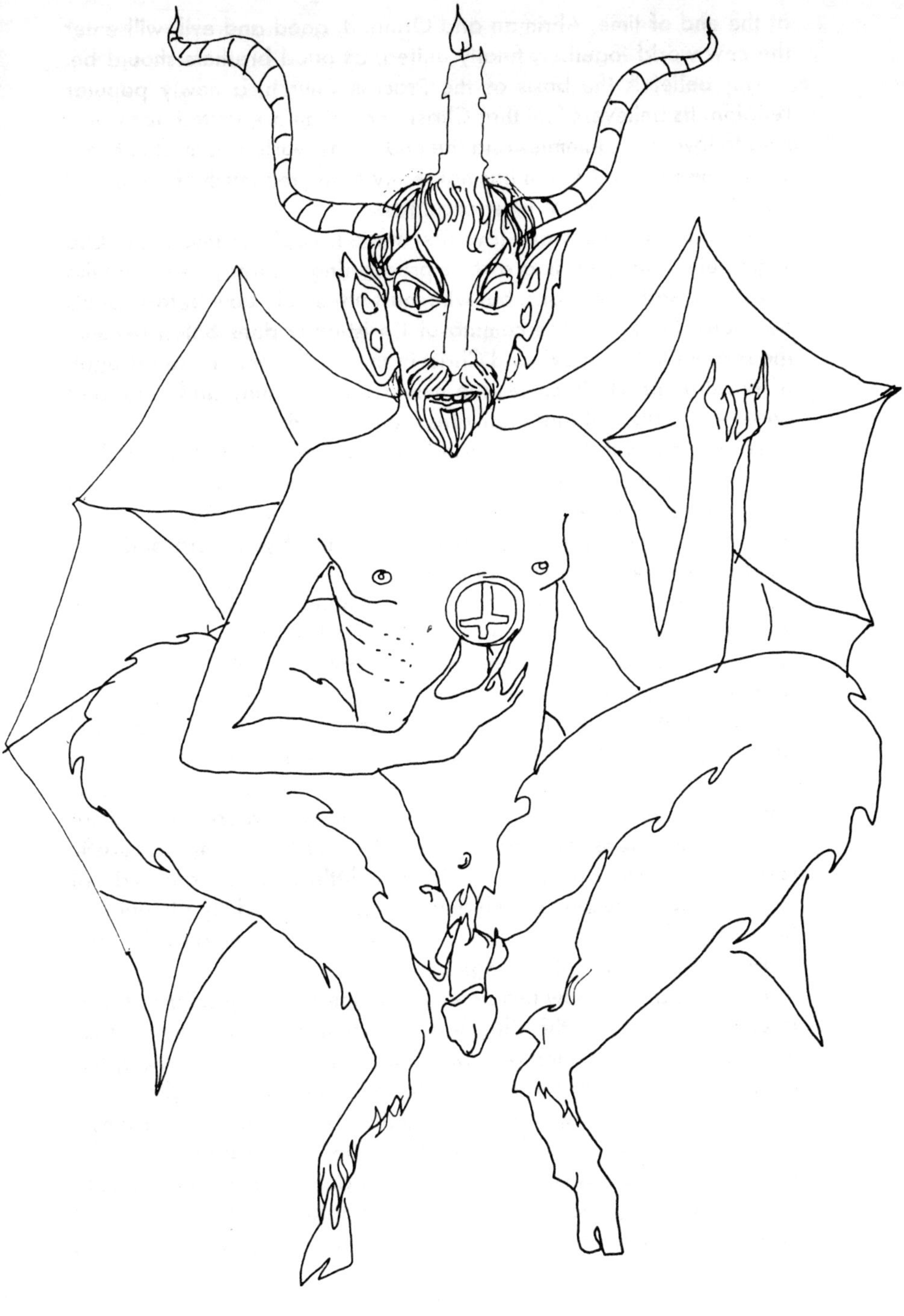

at the end of time, Ahriman and Ormazd, good and evil, will enter the new world together, finally united, as good brothers should be.

This belief is the basis of the Process Church, a newly popular religion. Its believers feel that Christ and Satan are united, for Christ said to love one's enemies and the end of the world is almost coming. So far the Process Church has not really made too much of an inroad into the basic beliefs of most occultists.

The Satan we know and love first made his appearance in the Old Testament, where he is a sort of prosecuting attorney, a cynic who questions God's decisions, but who must ultimately bow before God's decisions. Only with the coming of Christianity does Satan become the serpent to tempt Eve and Christ in the wilderness, the red dragon of Revelations. He becomes the nemesis of humanity and God, and once again, the evil that motivates the last battle.

Tradition has it that Satan tried to rebel against God and failed. For that transgression, Satan was thrown from heaven and set up camp in hell. Christians see hell as a place where sinners receive eternal torment in pits of fire and brimstone. If you were bad, you went to hell—no two ways about it.

Satanists say that hell is heaven and heaven is hell. For his followers' delight, Satan reserves a world of red velvet plush, rather like a Victorian bordello. The bars all serve double drinks in an eternal happy hour and the supermarkets stay open all night. A garden of earthy delights awaits the Satanist in the afterlife. Every whim shall be indulged and every inclination will be satisfied, I was informed. When I commented that it sounded like a lot like Los Angeles, I was told that there was a very special place in hell where hypocritical non-believers were tortured expressly for the benefit of voyeuristic sadists. Satanists, I decided, could be a little touchy. I decided not to pursue the discussion of hell any further but turned my attention to Satan and the occult. Why should the being represented as the anti-Christ be so prominent in magick?

The devil as we know him now, rose in the Dark Ages. Europe was in culture shock and the Christian Church was the only light at all left of the old Roman Empire. It became fashionable among the upper classes to profess Christianity, and to force their serfs to follow, and this emerging feudal system was condoned by the Church, which had become a political power in its own right. The Church and the nobility made up the repressive establishment before which the old religion of the god and goddess, the worship of nature must bow. It is not hard to see why a celibate and Paulistic clergy were horrified by the joy and fertility of the old deities. Sex played a natural and important role in the pagan rites and sex was just about the only thing that wasn't taxed by the nobility or tithed by the Church. But it could be repressed. People were told that the only reason sex should be performed was to produce more Christian babies. Anything that felt good must be sin. Rebellion was anti-establishment; since God was the establishment, and the Church was God, anyone who did not bow before the status quo was sinful. Be meek and accept your lot in this earth, said the Church, for you will be rewarded in heaven.

God was good; God was powerful. And the Church was the Voice of God upon Earth. Before the Church spread its tentacles into Europe, Satan had been a rather nebulous creature, sometimes supposed to look like a winged serpent. But when the old gods became the new devils, Satan became much more sinister and menacing. He was the God of the Witches, Herne, Pan, Lucifer. The Lightbearer had become the Prince of Darkness, and the purveyor of magick.

Some of the worshipers of the old gods saw the Christian devil as their Herne, and they were right. Lucifer represented lust and the fertility of life. If the rich worshiped the dead carpenter and became more and more powerful, while their serfs worshiped the old god and got poorer and poorer and more wretched, perhaps the devil as the Church saw him was the god to worship. For the old gods were dead and Satan, the living enemy of Christ, was triumphant. The rebel had won the first round.

This is where Satan and the occult really do come together. What had been Pan Lucifer became Evil Incarnate, an evil that could be directed against the oppressors. Worshipers of Satan implored the angry aspect of the old horned god to wreak revenge. It was a political thing.

Popular ideas of the devil in the Middle Ages are interesting. Unlike God or Christ, who lived in heaven and interceded from some lofty pinnacle on behalf of the righteous, Satan was everywhere. The devil is a master actor who has appeared in many roles. He was pictured at various times as being green, black, fleshtone, and, of course, the ever-popular red, the color of carnal desire. As master of disguise, he was assumed to be able to take on any form pleasing to his audience. At various times he was pictured as a large fly, a winged serpent, a vampire bat, a wandering scholar, a fashionable man, and even in drag as a voluptuous woman. His final appearance, complete with horns, tail, hoofs, and scaly red skin, settled in about the time of the Inquisition. The old horned god in drag.

Satan is very democratic, for he likes to wander among all classes of people in his recruiting campaign for souls, preying upon the unwary and the innocent who might be seduced by his promises. This medieval dirty-old-man-in-the-schoolyard image seemed effective enough until people started to take him seriously. At first, he was able to simply carry anyone off to hell, but later it became obvious that he would have to bribe people to sell their souls to his cause.

Satan reached the zenith of his power in the Middle Ages, when scholars spent years studying his habits and his life style in hell. Since even the devil cannot be everywhere at once, he is served by evil spirits, demons who serve the cause. Di Givry puts the number of hell's inhabitants at 7,405,926, divided into legions like an army, governed under a loose baronial confederacy. The leader of each legion is styled a prince. There is Astaroth, who guards the buried treasure; Lucifer (the old horned god in a new disguise), who governs sexual matters; Beelzebub, in charge of all matters of sorcery and occult matters; Bael, in charge of violence and death; Mammon, who governs all matters of greed and avarice. These are all names of pre-Christian gods, please notice . . .

In order not to disturb Satan, a diabolist might call on any of these princes or their subordinates; they are less likely to be angered at the disturbance and, unlike the master, they will be satisfied with the sacrifice of an animal rather than the surrender of the magician's soul.

Judging by the old broadsides and woodcuts, these demons are pretty gruesome in form and aspect. They also have a terrible problem with body odor, for it is frequently noted that they appear in a stink of sulphur and brimstone. They look like bits and pieces of humans, animals, and insects thrown together haphazardly. A typical demon might appear with three heads, tusks, two sets of horns, scales, and hair, with little faces on every joint and even on his buttocks.

Generally, these demons try to appear in a seductive form to their summoners, and many demonic conjurations include the codicil that the demon appear "in a form not frightful to behold, to cast off no foul stink or otherwise attempt to befright" the conjurer.

The Satanic pact is famous. The more sophisticated magician-scholars such as Faust and Agrippa used demons and spirits in their experiments. They controlled the actions of these supernatural beings, forcing them to do their bidding rather than being carried away to hell by them.

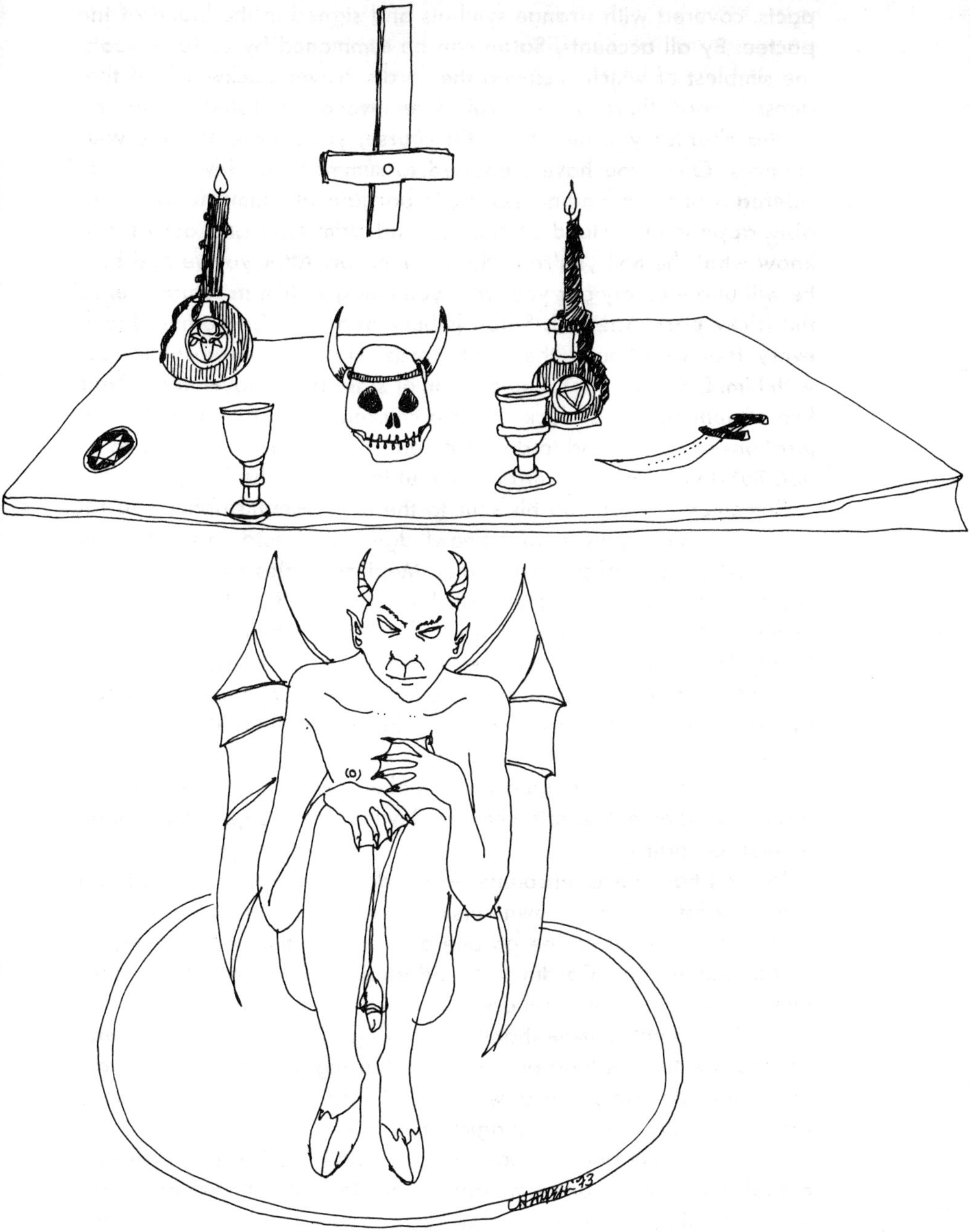

There are documents in existence that are supposed to be Satanic pacts, covered with strange symbols and signed in the blood of the pactee. By all accounts, Satan can be summoned by certain rituals, the simplest of which is saying the Lord's Prayer backwards. If that doesn't work, there are several other invocations listed at the end of this chapter you might try. Of course, you'll have to take your chances. Once you have managed to summon the devil, it is considered proper, indeed necessary, to bargain with him. He will probably appear in a cloud of sulphur and brimstone and demand to know what the hell you're bothering him for. After you've told him, he will undoubtedly ask you what you can give him in return. Here's the tricky part. After all, Satan is busy and can't be bothered with every fool who knows the right words. Try to maintain your cool with him. Don't ask for his autograph or stare at his cloven feet. Offer him something like a black cat or a chicken, or tie him up with conjurations so he's bound to do what you want whether he wants to or not. But don't sign the contract without looking at the fine print.

Remember, Faust sold his soul to the devil Mephistopheles in return for wealth, power, and knowledge that would last for seven years. At the end of the term, when Mephistopheles came to collect, Faust tried to welsh on the deal, locking himself in the study and praying. Around midnight, Faust's students heard a terrible noise issuing from the study. They tried to break in but the door held fast all night. As the light was breaking over the horizon, the door opened by itself. The students peered in and looked around. There was no sign of Faust, but his studio was a mess. Later they found Faust's body outside of town all mangled up. It looked as if it had been thrown from a great height. That's what the devil does to people who renege on their bargains.

While I have never encountered the devil in person, it is said that everyone has his or her own version of what it would be. I think he would look like an emcee on one of those daytime quiz shows, all tinted glasses and Cardin suits, offering me curtain, one, two or three . . . but that's my fantasy.

While I do not believe that card playing, gambling, and screwing around are sins, as long as you're not hurting anyone else, I do believe that you can bring down a lot of bad karma on yourself by fooling around with black magick. You may not get burned but you may get severely beaten about the head and shoulders. The devil is a dealer and he can get some rather fine ideas about trashing. When you're dealing with the devil, make sure your cause is bigger than your ego. There's still enough of the old Puritan in most of us to make an inadvertent bit of black magick come boomeranging right back.

In the Dark Ages, people believed that demons entered people's bodies and possessed their souls. Today we call this schizophrenic displacement and try to treat it with therapy. In the old times a person who fell into epileptic convulsions would have been considered possessed, and the demon would have been beaten, burned, or prayed out of the person. The demon who crept into an unwary victim could cause convulsions, the vomiting of pins, toads, snakes, and bugs, turn people into vampires and werewolves, make them blaspheme against God, speak in tongues, and cause poltergeist phenomena. A nun in the south of France reported that she had been possessed by a demon who happened to be sitting on a lettuce leaf she was eating. In Germany, a halfwit who was possessed by a demon took time out from his convulsions and pin vomiting to discourse on the finer points of theology with his exorcists—in ancient Greek. Blatty's novel *The Exorcist* has initiated a new wave of interest in possession, and it is interesting to note that both the Episcopal and Catholic churches still retain their rites of exorcism.

In Voodoo, possession is regarded as a sacred ritual, for in it the gods are talking through mortals. The Dionysians and other cults also regarded possession as a sacred ritual, one that was welcomed rather than feared. Are one culture's gods another's devils?

The Inquisition may have managed to suppress the old pagans and the peasant Satanists to some degree, but by the time the Reformation had begun, there was something new and different on the scene—the Black Mass.

Catherine de Medici is credited with the invention of the Black Mass. It was different from the old pagan rituals. The Black Mass was not just a bunch of country people trying to get rid of some loutish lord with black pins in a sheep's heart. The Black Mass was a parody of the Catholic Mass, dedicated to Satan, in the idea that anything that mocked God must surely please his opposite. It is impossible to tell how seriously Catherine de Medici and her courtiers took this new game they had invented. Catherine de Medici had probably been exposed to the occult all her life. The Medici family had strong connections among the hierarchy of the Church who were known to dabble in black magick. She surrounded herself with astrologers and necromancers, as was the fashion in Europe during the Renaissance, and she was a notorious dabbler in magicks and poisons. After the death of her husband, Henri II, the merry widow was free to indulge herself in her darker amusements as much as she wanted.

Perhaps she turned to the occult from boredom, as so many unhappy, wealthy idle people do. Perhaps she had some deeper motivation. She had tried adultery and gambling, the standard fashionable pursuits of her class, and found them boring. It is more likely that she wanted to see if even God would bend before her august person . . . or perhaps if the devil would grant her what God would not.

There is a form of deviation known as blasphemy, which means that someone gets a sexual thrill from profaning religious objects. This usually occurs with people who were raised in fanatically religious repressive backgrounds, such as Catherine must have had. Not only does the Black Mass produce this thrill, but it also has the added inducement of encouraging the enactment of most of society's other taboo preoccupations—incest, adultery, homosexuality, desecration, intoxication, fecal fascination, infanticide, sado-masochism, bestiality, and blood sacrifice. Catherine's Black Mass was a parody of the Christian litany. This may not seem like much if one is not Catholic or even a believer in the devil, but to someone who has been raised to believe in the power of both the Church and devil, it would seem like an incredible perversity, and if you were as jaded as Catherine, a lot of fun.

The Mass was (and is) conducted in a room hung with black and red tapestries, these being the colors of hell and carnal lust. Crucifixes and other religious objects are defiled by being displayed upside down or otherwise out of order. Artificial phalluses are glued onto statues of the saints and holes are drilled between the legs of the Madonna to represent a sort of crude vaginal passage. For the true decorator touch, skulls and bones are added, sulphur is burned in the censer, and the chalice and other paraphernalia are painted black or decorated with pornographic pictures of the saints. Black candles are burned and occasionally a live goat is present as a symbol of lust. It may be used for intercourse and sacrifice later. The total effect should be late Victorian or early Castle of Dracula.

A defrocked priest must say the Mass, and he should have been excommunicated for a carnal sin. His robes should be red and embroidered with obscene pictures. The Mass should be served on the body of a virgin, and a prostitute should serve as the acolyte.

Instead of the usual litanies, the priest will recite a long dissertation concerning the sex lives of the saints. The Mass should be read backwards with the name of Satan inserted every time the name of Christ, the Virgin Mary, or God appears. Hopefully, the priest will be able to do this in Latin, since that is supposed to be the most powerful magickal language. The wafers are supposed to be made from smashed up bugs, turnips, and a *merde*, while the chalice should contain a mixture of menstrual blood, urine, and semen. If there has been a sacrifice involved, the blood is mixed in the chalice so everyone can get a hit.

The virgin lies on the altar with her legs apart so that the congregation gets a good look at her vulva. At some point the priest throws open his cassock and deflowers the virgin while screaming what a rotten god God is and trampling a cross underfoot. While this is going on, the hooker takes on the entire congregation, who line up to denounce Christ and trample the cross, which signals the start of free-for-all orgy.

Anyone with the right amount of money and the proper connections can see a Black Mass in any of the major cities of the Christian world. While most of them are cheap tourist attractions staged for the benefit of the general public, and some of them could compete with German shepherds and Coke bottles in Juarez, there are others that are held privately for very select groups of true believers.

After Catherine de Medici, the Black Mass quickly spread in fashion all over Europe. It was something new to do for those with the money and jaded tastes, and it is doubtful that too many people took it seriously. No one knew it would lead to one of the most lurid scandals in history—the combined Profumo Affair and Watergate of its day.

The Chambre Ardente Affair reads like yellow journalism. It is pretty incredible, yet all the records document it as truth and we have no reason to doubt it.

Louis XIV believed himself to be ruling over France's golden age. He called himself the Sun King and remarked, "L'état c'est moi." But there was one scandal amid the peacocks and pleasures that even the Sun King could never quite forget. In those days it was common practice to consult card readers and fortunetellers. With a good line of patter and a thorough knowledge of poisons, it was possible to make vast fortunes off the unhappy rich. A simple scanning of the cards would disclose that a lady was married to a gentleman too many years her senior and had a poor but handsome lover on the side.

Such a problem could be solved for the right amount of money—gold was exchanged for a white powder to slip into the old husband's hock and presto, one more merry widow at court. One particular woman, Catherine Deshayes, known as La Voisine, started out as a fortuneteller and ended up running one of the best rackets in town. She trafficked in poisons, love philtres, and abortions on the side. La Voisine had a noble clientele who were willing to pay her prices. Since the lady herself was not above dabbling in a little black magick, it was not long before she was also offering Black Masses complete with the sacrifice of one of those unwanted infants. At her trial, she confessed to murdering at least fifty babies in such a way, and the remains of more than two hundred others were found in her backyard. She was not a nice lady, even for the times.

Nicholas de la Reynie, the King's Commissioner of Police, uncovered a poison-selling ring in 1677. It was like a bad novel. The heads of the ring were well-placed noblemen. De la Reynie, a good detective who originated many investigative techniques still used today, smelled something bigger as he tracked down the small-time pushers, the diviners who were making the future happy for their clients. The evidence was so overwhelming that he presented it to Louis in person. The King, shocked, set up the Star Chamber proceedings—quite sub rosa, for the room in which the chamber met was draped in black and lit with candles. At first it was just everyone in the nobility poisoning one another, which was bad enough, but the deeper de la Reynie got, the bigger and closer to the throne came the accused. The final horror story concerned his very own ex-mistress, Madame de Montespan, she who had been queen in all but name for years. When the King began to tire of her attentions, she turned first to aphrodisiacs, then to magick. The whole thing culminated in the incongruous sight of Madame de Montespan serving as the altar for a Black Mass. While it was bad for other members of the court to lie there and let a priest cut the throat of a baby over their bodies, it was horrifying when the King's own ex-mistress had performed such a rite for the King's affections to be restored, and, when that failed, a Mass was said for the death of the King and his new mistress. *That* was too close to home for comfort. Hurt and shocked, Louis ordered de la Reynie to stop persecuting the nobles and concentrate on the commoners. Madame de Montespan retired to a convent and Louis presumably put some extra food tasters on the payroll. Near the end of his reign, the Sun King destroyed the trial transcripts, but de la Reynie, more interested in truth than secrecy, kept his copies, leaving this last horror show on record for all the world to see, Satanism at the court of the Sun King.

The Black Mass reached its peak in the Thirties of this century and

continues to be a feature of magick. Because it was so sensational, it received a lot of coverage in the penny presses of the day. For instance, in the eighteenth century there was the Hell-Fire Club, the invention of Sir Francis Dashwood, an eccentric nobleman in England. The Hell-Fire Club was a parody of Satanism; most of the people involved certainly never believed that the devil ever existed. Dashwood inherited a huge amount of money from his father and used it to transform his country estate into a sort of underground pleasure grotto, where prostitutes dressed as nuns and bucks of the ton played devil-worshiping priests for weekend orgies. The British have always been more tolerant of their eccentrics than other nationalities and Sir Francis's monks included many of the most powerful men of the day. Benjamin Franklin was a member and probably used this chance to contact many of the influential people he was trying to influence for America's cause. But I doubt if anyone took all of that play too seriously as Satanic worship.

The Victorians limited themselves to sacrificing small animals and beating each other with wooden crucifixes in their rites, getting their kicks from breaking into churches and crucifying toads on the altars.

There is a story that two fashionable women were lunching in a restaurant in the Twenties when one of them glanced up from her dinner and noticed a strange-looking man wrapped in a black cloak striding through the tables. "Whatever is that?" she asked her companion.

The other lady looked over her shoulder and laughed. "Oh, don't mind that, dear, that's merely Aleister Crowley being invisible again."

Crowley is a contradictory figure in magick. On one hand he was a showman and a complete ham, a man with a huge ego and very little self-control; he died a drug addict in 1947 after spending his life trying to build an image of himself as the "wickedest man in the world." He styled himself the Great Beast of Revelations and managed to hurt or offend almost everyone he came into contact with. On the other hand, Crowley was a master magus, a man of great intelligence and skill with the occult arts. How much of his own writings we can believe is still hotly debated. Even the question of his involvement with Satanism is in question. Crowley was kicked out of one mystic-occult order; he formed several others that were painted up in the press to the worst degree, as orgies of sex magick and drug taking. He was supposed to have been a magnetic man; he was supposed to have been utterly depraved. As a Satanist, he was probably more literary than practical, for he delighted in anything that would shock the complacent middle class from whence he came. But Crowleyianity—the name of his self-proclaimed religion—has had an effect on many people who wish to worship the devil. Crowley advocated blood rituals, drug rituals, and sexual orgies as means of getting in touch with the powers that be. How be regarded the devil in this context is a moot point. I believe Crowley regarded Satan as a means to an end, for he was also involved with many other demons and experiments with elemental spirits. Crowley's effectiveness is sure; his methods are still under debate.

If one wishes to believe the Pope and certain members of various sects in California, the devil is alive and well today. Crowley's influence is strong in California, if not in Rome.

California has always been a haven for various cults and groups

—from those who practice sneaker fetishism to a group awaiting the reincarnation of Mary Baker Eddy. In the Santa Ana winds, the Mansonites made their weirdness manifest and I know of at least three Satanic groups that are flourishing.

My least favorite is a coven run by an ex-biker who proclaims himself the Incarnation of the anti-Christ and goes in for rituals involving the sacrifice of small animals. The release of living blood has always been considered an important part of certain magicks, on the principle of released energy and placation of the gods. This particular group imbibes animal blood laced with acid as part of their Satanic ritual. Satan, they say, is the Incarnate Evil who has inherited the earth, and all those who do not fall down on their knees at his sacred name will not be spared the fires of his wrath. Their rites are a combination of the Black Mass and Crowley's writings, lifted verbatim from his books. So far, their occultism hasn't been too effective. A death spell they cast on a universally unpopular cop in the Venice area hasn't worked yet, more's the pity.

As far as I know, the Church of Satan is the only non-Christian Satanist group around. It's legally registered with the state as a religious body, with fulll power to conduct weddings, funerals, etc. To accept the idea of the devil you must accept the idea of a monotheistic God and his diametric opposite, Satan.

For only the realization that each man is part God and part Satan will release the power of this strange red devil with his horns and tail. Is the devil as bad as he's been painted? Certainly he's a powerful occult force, and that may be the ultimate nature of his game . . .

SATANIC SPELLS, OR THE DEVIL MADE ME DO IT

The first thing to remember about asking Satan for anything is to protect yourself. Use the devil like a paring knife—always cast the spell away from yourself. In the next chapter, on ceremonial magick, we will take a look at what the adepts passed on to us about controlling demons and spirits, but you're not an adept yet, so it is wise to take every precaution to protect yourself should your spell backfire. When preparing for any Satanic dealings always carry an amulet or talisman on your body that represents the faith you were brought up in, like a cross or a Star of David or a Hand of Fatima, or something that has special magickal powers to you—a birthstone set in a ring, a pendant, your wicca necklace, or even your Brownie pin, if you feel that represents your faith in your higher self. A bloodstone is considered to be the best protection against nasty and unexpected attacks by demon forces. Here again, the magick circle is employed. It should be drawn in salt (a traditionally powerful demon repellent) and traced with a bit of iron or your bloodstone. Stand inside the circle during the entire spell, leaving it only after you have made the invocations for the departure of the devil. Remember, you may not see him appear in a burst of fire and brimstone. At first, you just get a creepy cold feeling that someone is there, watching in the darkness. If you're really going to pursue your Satanic rituals, you will probably start seeing some sort of ether-like being at first, then later, if you're really getting totally fanatical about it, the devil himself might appear in full regalia—just what you expect him to be. But by that time you'll be far beyond this book or any other . . .

SUMMONING THE DEVIL

This is the most difficult "summons" spell for an amateur to perform. I wouldn't suggest it unless you've got a really strong stomach and a fanatical sense of purpose. The person who gave it to me swears it works, though, if you can choreograph the whole thing and keep your mind on Satan as the most powerful Prince of Darkness. Get a black hen and a brand-new very sharp knife. Take yourself to a crossroad at midnight when the moon is in its last quarter. Put yourself and the hen and the knife inside the circle (draw it around you) and light three black candles. If you can't find a crossroad, try a place where someone committed suicide, murder, or some other horrible crime. Even a deserted house that's said to be haunted will probably work better than a crossroad. Place the candles at three points on the perimeter of the circle and, standing in the middle, slit the hen open with the knife, reciting the following incantation.

> Eheieh, Ioada,
> Tetrammatron Elhim,
> El, Elohim Gabor
> Eloah Va daath
> El Adoniai
> Shiel
> Shaddai.

While you are murdering a struggling chicken and incanting the above, let the blood run into the ground and call out to Satan that you wish a favor from him:

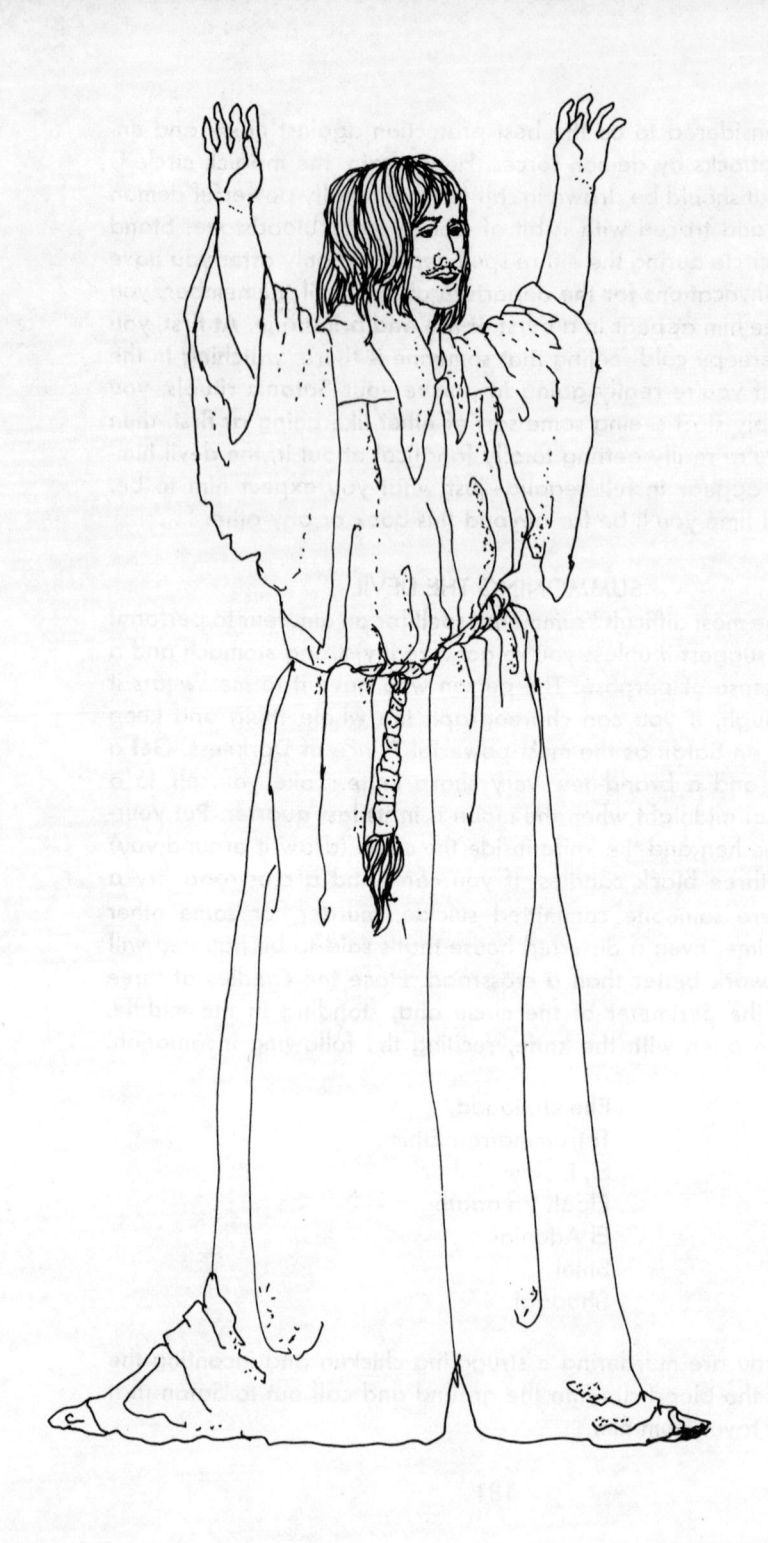

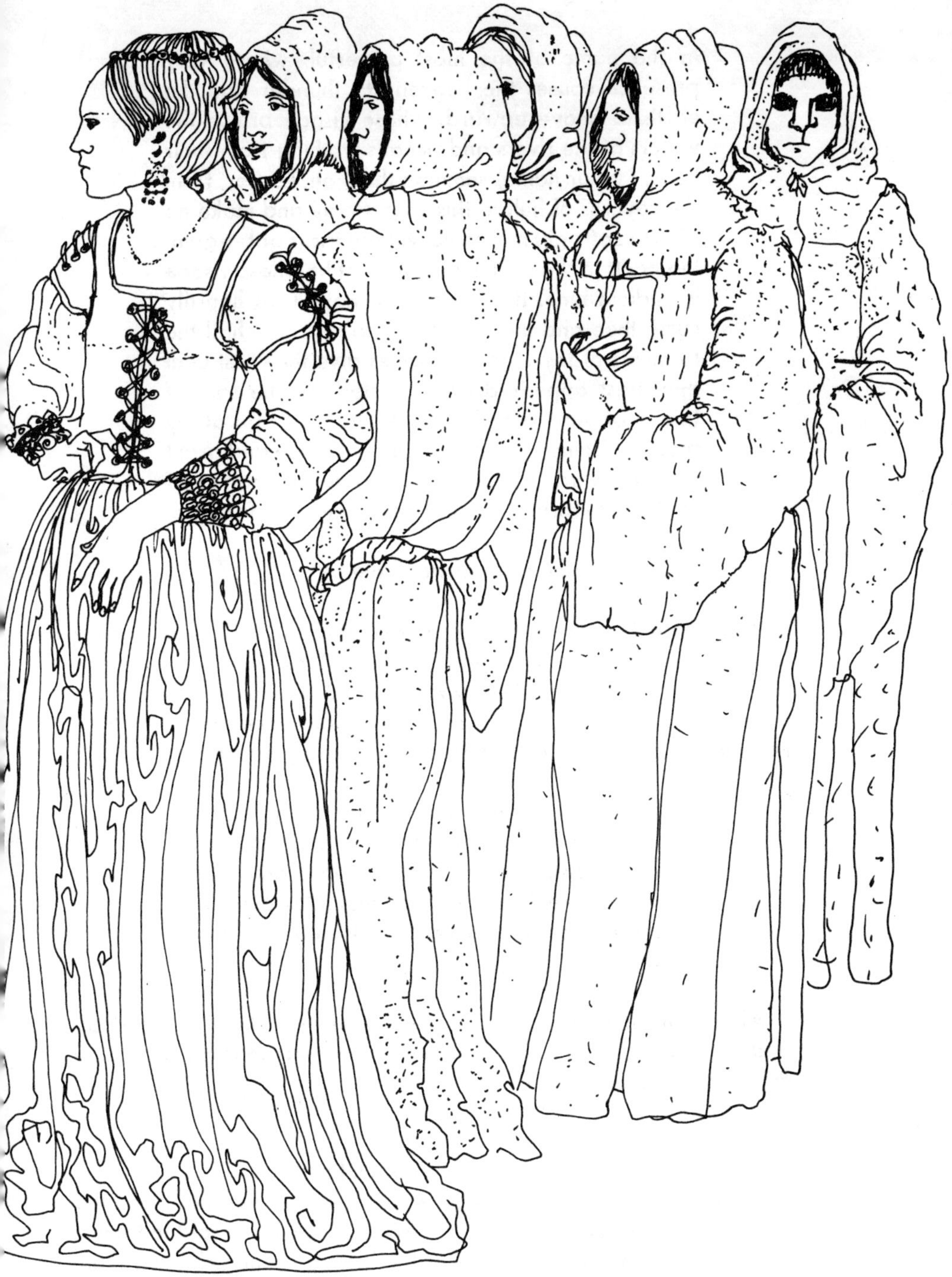

> In the name of the most powerful, whose very presence causes the heavens to thunder and the earth to heave upward; whose visage brings the waters of the rivers and oceans frothing from their beds, I (your name) summon thee, oh, Lucifer, from the caverns of hell to this spot. Come and make no effort to affright me, come without tricks or bargaining pacts to this spot in the name of he whose visage is endless time. If ye come not now, I do heartily curse thee and thou shalt see no rest nor shall the torments of thy eternal agonies give thee rest until thou hast appeared and granted me the soul of (name of your victim) that he/she might be at my bidding. Come without tricks or evil guide and grant me that which I demand. In the sacred names of Michael, Gabriel and Raphael, come thou forward.

And that damn chicken won't die. . . .

When you feel the presence of demonic forces it is as if they are entering your mind, as your conversations with them are carried out by telepathy. When you feel that you have reached the point of power, dismiss them by blowing out each candle in turn, reciting the following invocation at each extinguishing:

> Go ye, Oh Ancient Evil, back into the caves from which thou came. Suffer not and dwell in peace for I am satisfied with your actions and place thee in the realm of my goodness. Go now in the name of Adonai Elohim, who brought ye forth and commands thee yet.

After that, erase the circle with your left foot, leaving the dead and disemboweled hen in the middle of the circle to draw away any evil forces that might attack you.

INCANTATIONS FOR SUMMONING THE DEVIL

King Solomon was not only a powerful ruler, a wise man, and the husband of one hundred and some wives, he was also said to be one of the most powerful magicians in the history of magick, who managed to deal with demons and win—every time. This incantation is taken from his works:

I conjure you, oh, spirit, within a minute by
the power of great Adonai, by Ariel Johavan, Agala, Tagla,
Mathon, Oarrios, Alouzin, Arios, Membrot, Varvais,
Pithone, Magots, Silphae, Rabost Salamandre, Tabost,
Gnomous, Terraeae, Coelis, Godens, Aqua, Gingua
Juana, Eititmus.

After that, it's up to you . . . and when you get tired of your demons hanging around, Solomon suggests that you recite this formula:

>Lofaham
>Solomon
>Iyouel
>I Yoesfuel.

Exu

In Macumba, a form of Voodooism-spiritualism-Christianity, the devil is known as Exu, and he can be reasoned with and appealed to like any good Voodoo saint. If you have been wronged by someone else and desire retribution and rectification, take thirteen candles, a bottle of really good liquor (Exu likes rum in Brazil; but if you live in moonshine country, he'd probably take a Mason jar of good white lightning), and a fine cigar to a tree at a crossroad. Cast your circle around the tree (you're not a Macumba yet) and light your candles, talking all the while to Exu, as you would to a very powerful friend, telling him what your problem is and why you expect him to be able to solve it for you (he's powerful!). Pour the liquor into the ground for him and light the cigar, pointing out to him that you've bought the best there is, and you respect his power and need his help. Ask him to enjoy what you have brought him and to consider helping you out. Back away from the tree and out of the circle, still talking to him, leaving the candles burning and the cigar smoldering; then turn and walk away without looking back.

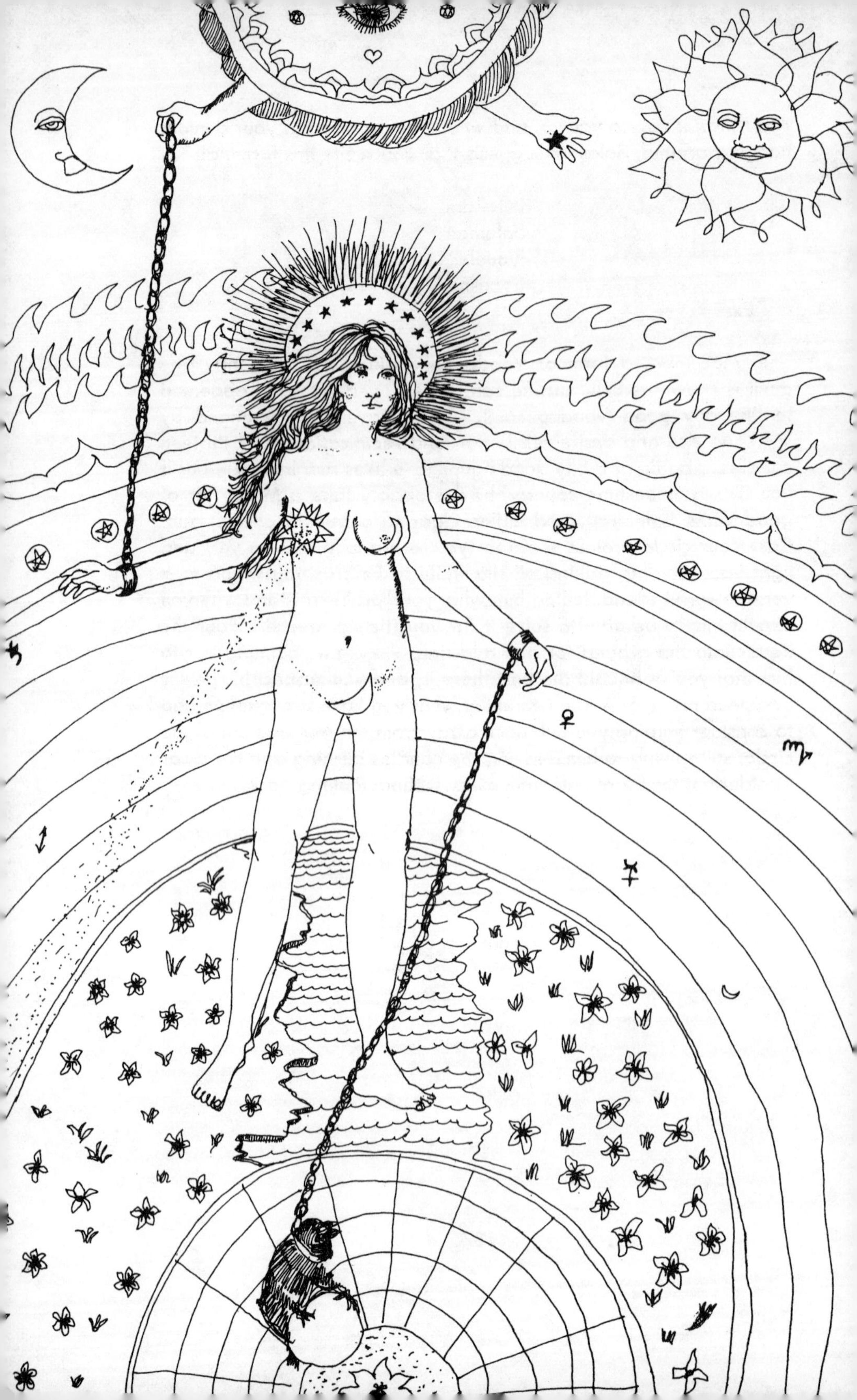

RITUAL MAGICK—ANGELS AND DEMONS IN THE CIRCLE

> Go forward, Faustus, in that famous art,
> Wherein all nature is contained
> Be thou on earth as Jove is in the sky
> Lord and commander of all these elements!
>
> CHRISTOPHER MARLOWE,
> *Doctor Faustus*

"... magick is an internal spirit within us, which can very well perform whatsoever the monstrous mathematicians, the prodigious magicians, the wonderful alchemists, and the bewitching necromancers can effect." So said Cornelius Agrippa, master magus of the Renaissance. It is a bitter statement, made at the end of a life spent in the study of magick and philosophy, and yet it mirrors the discovery any student of magick must find as a private revelation. The internal spirit within has all the power that we seek through ceremonies and chants and candle-burnings—that silent, lost spirit, the psi factor, the unknown quality of yearning that produces god and devils, magick and miracles.

From the very beginnings of the world, human beings have always believed that the *visible* world is surrounded by an *invisible* world populated with spirits of every sort. There are good spirits and bad spirits, spirits of snakes and trees and even stones, spirits of thought and spirits of action, spirits of good and spirits of evil. Depending on their whims, these spirits can be benign, malevolent, or indifferent. It is the earliest function of religion to placate these spirits, and to seek control of them so that the magus can control his own destiny. This is magick as an attempt to wrest power from nature; this is the magus as god.

To play around with the powers humanity invests in its deities is dangerous and immoral; if God had wanted man to fly, he would have given him wings, right? The idea that even a wise and holy man would even think of playing god is somehow unappetizing to society. The magician is regarded with a mixture of fear and respect for his attempts to call upon the spirits to do his bidding. Once invested with the power, the gods are not anxious to see man try to take it back from them. To assume control over destiny by the use of supernatural efforts and aids has always made less hungry people slightly uneasy, indignant, or outright paranoid. It implies that their lives are affected by a potential dictatorship from the unknown, invisible world, spirits under the command of another human being. You can't send a kid up in a crate like that. This moral judgment has weighed against the magus since the first shaman sat down and impatiently started to yell at the gods and got results.

Of course, control over the invisible world would mean ultimate control over the visible. Isn't everything governed by some spirit, some twist of fate in destiny? These were living beliefs to our ancestors; they still linger today. The whole science of ritual magick is devoted to incantations, charms, and ceremonies that control those spirits that are invested with such miraculous powers as finding buried treasure and imparting secret knowledge of higher mathematics. If the ritual magician employs the correct gestures, incantations, and secret names of the spirits and gods, he can alter nature to suit himself. Of course, these things are all esoteric and carefully veiled in symbolism; it would not do for the unenlightened to have such power in their grubby little fists. If knowledge is power, then this would be true power. And very few have mastered it.

There is an ancient belief that to know the secret name of anything is to control it. The name and the soul are one, inextricably bound together. In some societies, a child will be given a name that is used by everyone and another secret name that only he and his father and mother may know. This is done to prevent anyone from seizing control of his soul. If the soul of a human being is so important, think how much more sacred the secret names of the spirits and gods must be. Thus, in pagan teachings, the secret name of the goddess is known only to a few, and early Hebrews would never pronounce the secret name of God, Yahweh, substituting Adonai instead. To use the secret name of the god is to call upon its power and invoke its physical presence.

Which of course is what the magus wants to do. But first he must protect himself with ceremony and ritual, for spirits can be angry when forced to appear at some fool's bidding against their will. To fail to observe the proper rituals would be disastrous; the slave would turn on the master and destroy him utterly.

Having summoned the spirit, the magus must also know the proper form of exorcising it; otherwise the spirit will hang around indefinitely, embarrassing the magician in front of his guests and generally making a nuisance of itself. It has always been one of the rules that, when summoned, the spirit must appear, but it cannot depart safely without the proper ritual.

Between the summoning and the departure, the spirit is bound to do the magus's bidding, but only if the requests made are done with the proper ceremony and handled within the spirit's province of power. To call up the spirit of buried treasure and bid it to tell the future would not only be a serious lapse in taste, it would also give the spirit the excuse to tear the magus into tiny pieces.

Ritual magick is the most scholarly of all the arts and one of the most complex. Ancient kings were wont to surround themselves with magi as accepted members of their retinue. The Three Wise Men who came to Bethlehem were master magi who studied the heavens and took the sign of the star as an omen of some inner light. It is significant that they recognized the birth of Christ as the beginning of a supreme magus's life, for many non-Christians, not only Jews and Moslems, but witches and sorcerers also, regard Christ not as a messiah but as an important magus.

The Greeks and Romans recognized the importance of the magus's magicks, and Aristotle, Socrates, and Appollonius of Tyana, philosophers all, were considered magicians by their contemporaries. Their theory of natural science was based not on experimentation but on inductive reasoning. Supernormal phenomena were a direct offspring of the universal mind. Instead of seeking a reason, they framed their views in poetic, if primitive, logic. The ancients believed that the entire world was composed of four elements—earth, air, fire, and water. While we know now that there are at least one hundred different elements in nature, these four elements form the basis of magick.

The Platonic influence on ritual magick might have astounded Socrates. Plato believed that the universe is an animal, with a soul and mind. Since it contains everything within itself, it has no need of any of the usual appendages or any of the five senses; its shape is a perfect sphere. The world soul is linked to the stars; their influence upon earthly matters should be carefully studied, for each member of the animal, vegetable, or mineral kingdom contains some of the essence of the divine world soul within itself, and therefore some inherent perfection, some ability to attain divinity.

This theory was to gain great popularity throughout the period of the Roman Empire and to continue into the Middle Ages. While there were always laws against the practice of black magick, the magi seem to have been left pretty much on their own, and, as said earlier, they were often powerful figures in the political sphere. Merlin is such a magus; in fact, he may be the archetype wizard-scholar who combines the study of natural history, astrology, philosophy, and divination in a search for perfect knowledge. Merlin was a prophet and a clairvoyant, which no doubt added to his reputation.

In the eyes of the Church truck with any kind of spirit was truck with the demons of hell. Regardless of whether or not a spirit was good or bad in the pagan world he was definitely considered to be up to no good by the Christians. Anyone who had dealings with spirits who summoned them by conjurations and incantations was playing around with his immortal soul and his place in heaven. Yet the fascination with power over the spirits continued. At least two popes are reputed to have been powerful magicians, perhaps in the tradition of King Solomon. Solomon's reputation as a magus is so powerful that he was said to possess a ring by which he could not only control the fowls of the air and the beasts of the earth, but also any spirit or demon in the universe. One old text has him forcing Beelzebub to saw marble slabs for him. Every once in a while Beelzebub takes a rest break and Solomon and the demon converse on the powers and principles of demonology.

Originally demons were supposed to have been the spirits of dead heroes who carried messages between the gods and the magus. Spirits were the souls of the animals, plants, and rocks, or the souls of the dead come back for no good. This attempt at classification relates to the Platonic theory. While medieval thinking respected the Greeks, it tended to see all spirits as demons under the direction of Satan and made no distinction between good and bad. Demons existed and, as such, were against Christ and therefore for Satan. So the magus who summoned demons to do his bidding was automatically making a pact with Satan. The division between the powers of God and man was very sharply drawn, and as the Church extended its influence, the line grew ever more rigid. The magus was lumped together with the witch, the Moslem, and the Jew as a heretic by the time of the Inquisition and treated accordingly.

However, with the arrival of the Renaissance, magick again found popularity. More liberal times are apt to breed more questioning minds, and in the world of the university magick became a respected study.

One of the most remarkable figures in occult history is Heinrich Cornelius Agrippa von Nettesheim, known to history as Cornelius

Agrippa. His contribution to the understanding of magick is vast. He was a scholar, a skeptic, a swashbuckler, and an idealist. He studied alchemy, theology, philosophy, and natural science. He was a liberal humanist who espoused women's rights and the free and open study of every subject "known or unknown." He was also grouchy, cynical, and morally puritanical. He was unpopular with the clergy, who saw his studies of the Cabala and his associations with the Jewish community as dangerously heretical. Because he had many patrons among the nobility, he was able to pursue his work without too much hassle.

Agrippa's students included the notorious Johann Faust. Agrippa taught magick in relation to natural history, astrology, Platonic theory, neo-Platonic theory, Judeo-Christian theology, and psychic science. Ultimately, Agrippa wanted to rise above the dreary quest for temporal power and find spiritual enlightenment, or the philosoopher's stone, which makes man's relation to his world and his god immortal. He saw the world's mysteries as something to be decoded through rational results and logical action. It was an age of secret societies, hidden codes, and marvelous wonders. Above all, Agrippa was a pioneer scientist.

Agrippa's most important contribution to magick is his *De occulta philosophia*. In this remarkable and informative text, Agrippa laid down the principles of practical magick. The art called magick is science, philosophy, theology, mathematics, natural history, and psychology. The occurrences on earth are directly influenced by events happening in the heavens. By a study of astrology, it is possible to determine the course of the future. Every natural object is infused with Plato's inherent virtue, but is also infused with an occult virtue that arises from its inherent virtue. Following me?

Agrippa further declares that the four elements of earth, air, fire, and water reflect the actions of the heavens and the spirits.

Just as a person is born under a sun sign, so an object is ruled by a sign and a planet. If a tree belongs to the earth element, and falls under the astrological house of Virgo, then that tree is in harmony with a quartz also under the influence of Virgo. That tree and quartz would then be compatible with a different tree and quartz falling under another earth sign, Capricorn. Or the tree would be in opposition to another tree/animal/stone governed by Aries, a fire sign. See, everything is either compatible or incompatible according to its heavenly counterpart's affinity or discord on the cosmic plane. These astrological influences would, of course, include the spirits.

Agrippa based his ideas not only on Platonism, neo and pure, but also on the systems of the Cabala, Arabian numerical magick, and the rituals of Egypt and Mesopotamian magick. Thus, each planet influences the markings of time in cycles. The minutes, hours, days of the week, months, and years are all governed by the planets. Each planet has its own spirit that can be summoned by the magus. Agrippa felt these were the keys of magick. But he realized, too, that they were the keys to empty boxes without the divine experience.

Therefore, even though the magus sought to clothe the magickal experience in reason and logic, he realized that it was still the old pagan ecstasy that opened the doors between the two worlds.

Imagine, if you can, Agrippa and Faust touring Rhine's labs watching controlled experiments with cards and dice. The use of the knife in surgery was forbidden by edict. In Agrippa's day such experimentation was frowned upon. People built science on their ideas of what things were. It would never have occurred to them to take things apart and study them to see how they worked. Agrippa, Della Mirandola, Paracelsus, Postel, Nostradamus, and Della Porta, the magi of the Renaissance, accepted the existence of the psi factor/extrasensory perception/psychokinesis/mind-over-matter power without question. They knew it was there and they knew that if one could find the key to unlock it it would transcend all magicks and unlock the world. The rationalists won out in the end, however, and only now, more than three hundred years later, are we beginning to explore again the mystery at the back of the mind.

The theories that Agrippa laid down in his *De occulta philosophia* are not simply quaint ideas; they are important to the magician, for

they explain many of the complicated rites of ritual magick. Each object used in the magick arts must be carefully prepared according to ceremony and rules of manufacture. Suppose you are preparing for a ritual that invokes the aid of moon spirits and you need a knife. You would forge the blade from silver, the moon-metal, with the proper incantations to the moon. The handle of the knife should be hawthorn or hazel wood rather than oak. Hawthorne and hazel fall under the influence of the moon. Now, if you had used oak, which falls under the influence of Jupiter, the knife would not work, for Jupiter and the moon are not compatible. It would probably fall apart anyway if you know nothing about metalworking or woodcarving, but that should give you an idea of Agrippa's theory.

When you begin to manufacture your own tools, try to remember what is compatible with what. The combinations must always be in astrological harmony. If you must purchase something, always buy a new object rather than a second-hand one.

Ever since the first caveman drew the first hieroglyph on the wall (probably pornographic), human beings have been writing down their thoughts and messages for posterity. The Sumerians left their prayers and incantations against diseases and black magick; the Egyptian *Book of the Dead* gives the proper responses and rituals the soul of the dead must heed in the underworld. But there is nothing in magick more interesting than the grimoires. Literally translated, a grimoire is a black book. These books were copied by hand from magician to magician, listing the spells and rituals to be used when summoning demons. The earliest one shows the essence, if not the accuracy, of King Solomon's expertise as a magus. *The Key of Solomon* is the most useful of the grimoires, for it gives the proper times for all magick operations and the individual powers of the planets. It presents the names by which the spirits are to be constrained, the proper setting up of magickal operations, talismans and their manufacture, and the proper way to make and inscribe all the tools of the art, the clothes to be worn in the ritual, and the equipment needed to exorcise the spirits. *The Grimorium Verum* deals with the Faustian Pact and the summoning of lesser demons and spirits. *The Secrets of Albertus Magus* is merely a collection of the occult virtues of herbs, stones, etc., and the somewhat incredible miracles that can be performed through these virtues. *The Grimoire of Honorius the Great* is a who's who in the spirit world, together with the proper manners of conjuration and evocation. *Le Poulet Noir* and the *Red Dragon* are similar recipe books of demons and spirits.

These grimoires enjoyed a good circulation in the underground. There were periods in history when the simple possession of one of these books was sufficient evidence to convict someone for heresy. Yet with the invention of the printing press, more people began to read them and today some are even available in paperback.

How much has been lost by countless transcriptions, translations, and time is in question. Their accuracy may be dubious, for it has long been a practice of magi to leave out one crucial step, assuming that a trained magus would know the step and automatically be

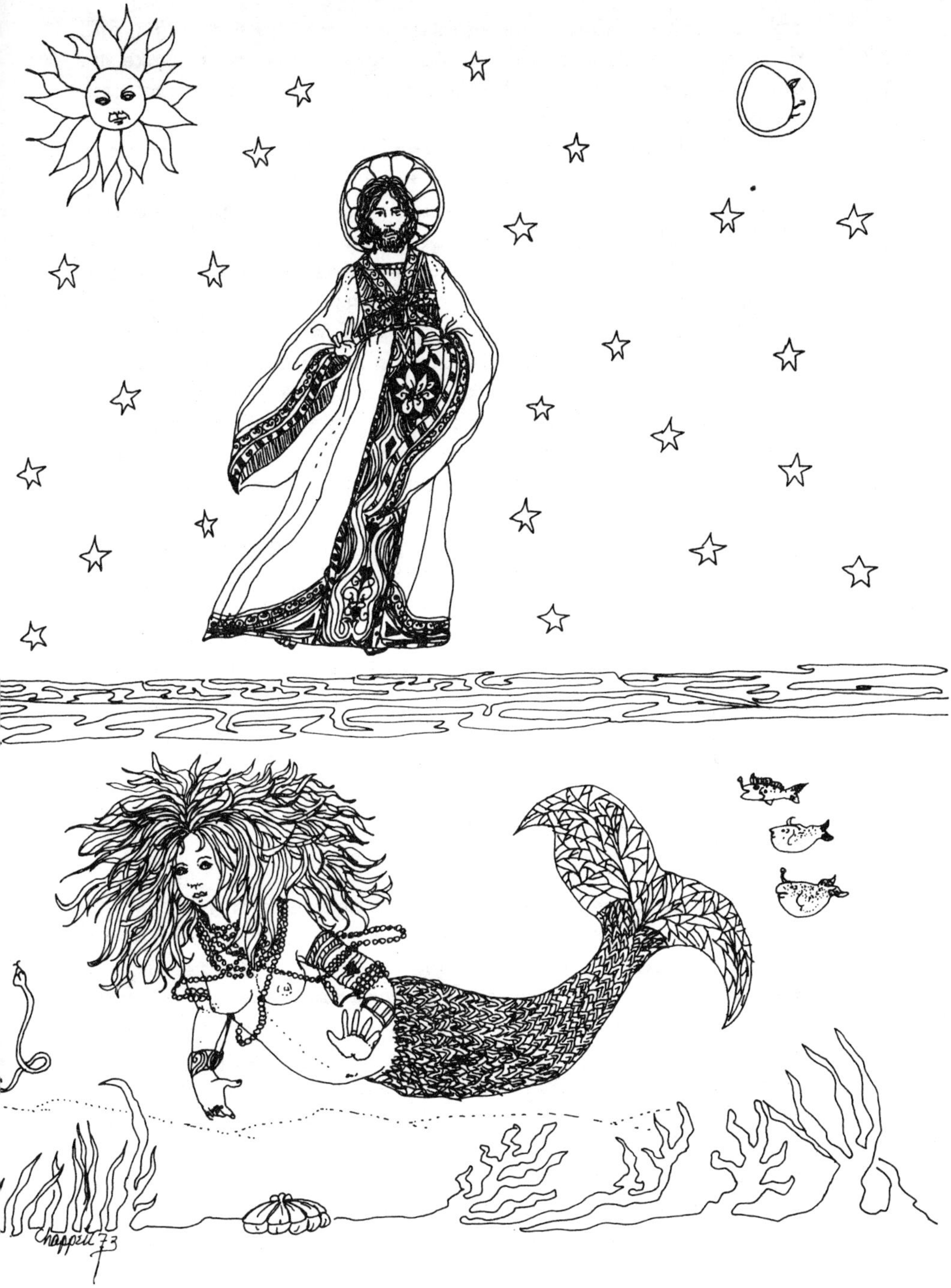
Chappell 73

able to put it in. Many of the rituals are of pre-Christian origin, and there are constant reminders to the magus that he must invoke the all-powerful constraints of God in order not to lose his souls to these pagan beasts and beings.

But the books are fascinating reading and I would recommend them to anyone with the patience to plow through their rhetoric.

There are two ways to look at ritual magick and both are equally valid. The rationalist (there is a reasonable explanation for everything) school says that ritual magick is a kind of theater production where the magician is both actor and audience. He goes through all these rituals and puts himself into a sort of trance where the spirits that appear to him are figments of his imagination—parts of himself that manifest themselves to him in ways he can comprehend. Hallucinations of his own creation. They say that each human possesses the innate capacity of knowing all things from past, present, and future, and that the ritual merely draws from within him the knowledge that lies buried in his mind.

The imaginative (everything is possible) school says that these rituals actually do summon discarnate spirits. The possibility that such spirits do exist, maybe in another dimension that coexists in time and space with ours and can cross over the borders without effort. As discussed earlier, there is an ancient tradition that spirits can be constrained by secret words of power, by the correct names, the correct gestures. The theory is that by the performance of these magicks, an opening into the "other world" is created, so that mortals and spirits can communicate—sort of like direct dialing on the telephone. The ritual is the connecting line between the visible and invisible worlds.

To a Renaissance magus, it may have been easy to run down to the corner blacksmith and hammer out a silver knife or find a virgin to weave him a robe to wear in the art, but try it today. And the ritual killing of a black chicken in the living room may not only upset your roommate, but will also probably not make any sense to you or the spirit you're trying to reach. Selective eclecticism is the key to raising the spirits. So, feel free to experiment within the limits of your capabilities. If it doesn't feel right, don't do it. Find a ritual that does feel right. After all, the best tool of magick is your own mind. While ceremonial magick requires a great deal of paraphernalia, preparation, and self-control, it can be a rewarding experience simply because you are practicing a full ritual. And that is good theater. The

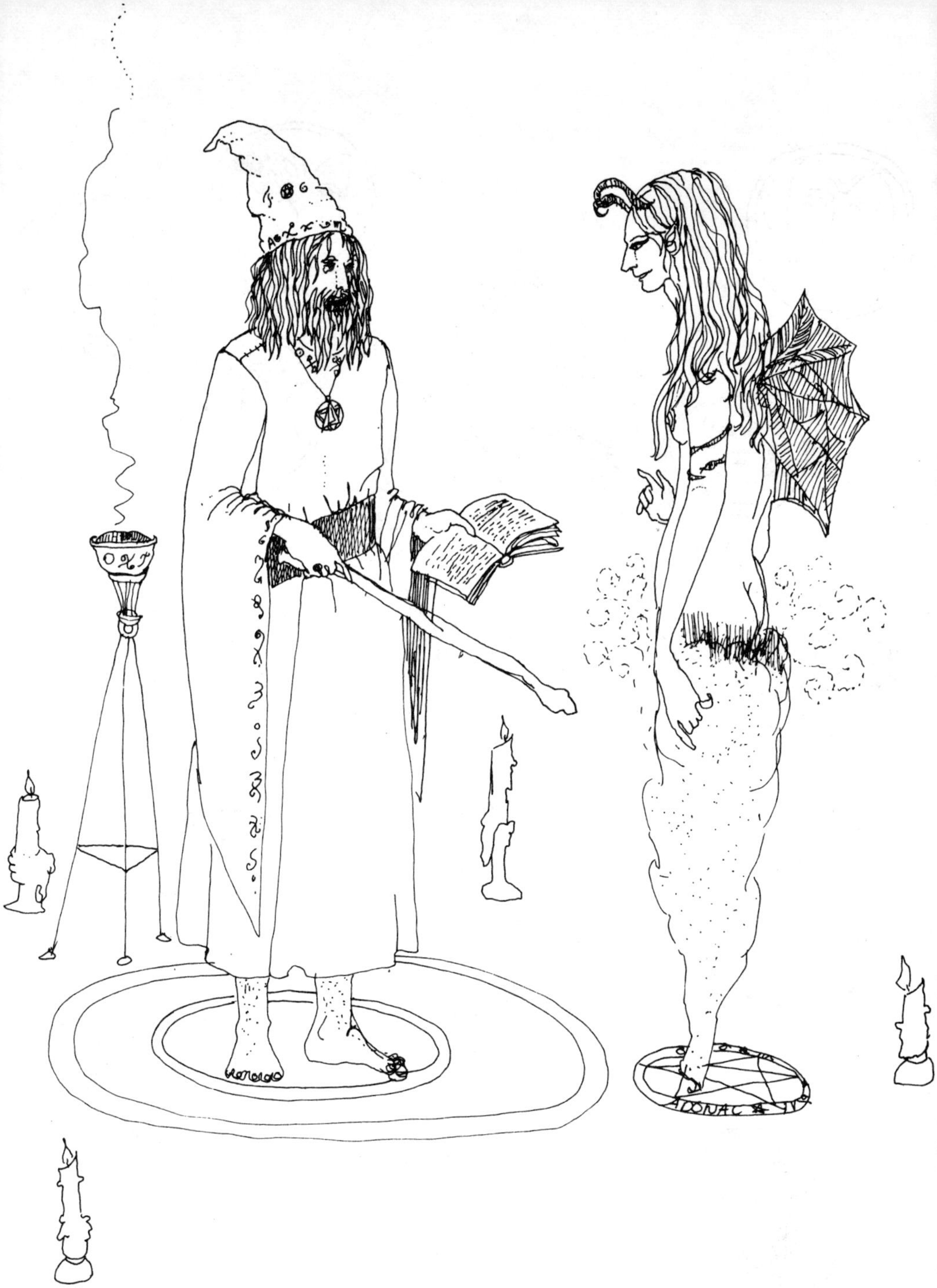
ADONAC

MARS
MERCURY
SATURN
URANUS
♀ Venus
☉ SUN
☽ MOON
Jupiter
Pluto
Earth
Neptune
Apollo

following is a literary magick, and deserves more time and understanding than a brief chapter in this book can give. But it's rewarding because it puts you on a one-to-one basis with your desires.

To begin with, focus your mind on what you want. Take about two weeks to gather your goodies, meditate on your spiritual harmony, and raise your cone of power. You should refrain from eating meat, drinking alcohol, and indulging in drugs. You are psyching yourself up to use your full mental powers, so that when the time comes you will be able to use every single iota of your being to fulfill your desires. You are wakening your sixth sense from its long sleep.

The ritual, as I've said before, is a dress rehearsal. As long as you've spent your time thinking positive thoughts, cleansing your mind, the less hidden paranoia and fear you'll step into the consecrated circle with.

Rather than overload you with all sorts of literary cautions, most of them being so symbolic to another age and place that they wouldn't have any meaning to a bright twentieth-century dweller, I've run down a simplified ritual that works for the getting of goodies —goodies being anything from a new blender to a trip to Nepal. As long as you're sure you want them with all your greedy yearning heart, and you've got a good mental picture of where you expect this windfall to come from (lottery tickets, etc.), and you know that you having X will not cause deprivation or harm to another person, then you may proceed.

Now, there are hundreds of spirits you can call upon, but the safest and most reliable spirits are the planetary elements, who are basically nice spirits who don't expect any hidden pacts and deals. To invoke the aid of these spirits you should know their names and sigils, the talismans by which they are symbolized.

Having picked the spirit that governs the area you're interested in, copy the sigil with ink on good white paper (parchment used to be de rigeur, but any good-quality paper will do).

Then consult an almanac to see when the moon will be in a house governed by that sign. Some magicians say the moon should be increasing, others say it doesn't matter. But just to be safe, wait until the moon is on the waxing. This may take a couple of months but no one said magick worked *fast*. Each day set aside a certain amount of time to think about that blender or that trip, even if it's the time between the six o'clock news and "All in the Family." Build up those positive vibrations. Believe that you are going to be grind-

The Signatures of the Spirits

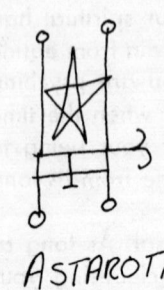

ASTAROTH
Knowledge of all things

ASMODEOUS
buried treasures

BAAL
invisibility

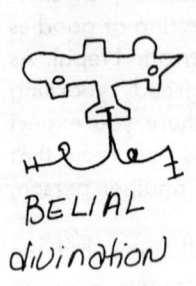

BELIAL
divination

Decarabia
gives familiar spirits

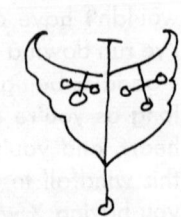

Flauros
protects against other demons

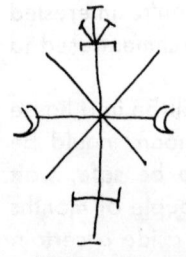

Murmur
for necromancy

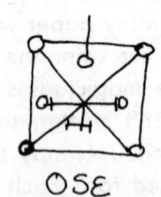

OSE
confers power on other humans

PROCEL
confers power in matters of love

SHAX
finds lost
or hidden
objects

VALPULA
confers artistic
talents

Zagan
for alchemy

Mersilde
opens all secrets

Sagatana
divines the
future

Lucifer
confers power over
the elements

FRUITIMERE
causes things
to grow

PETROPHY
the sorcerer's
companion

ASATAH
governs all
matters of philosophy
and mathematics

ing carrots in that blender. If you feel so inclined, read some passages at random from a book that inspires you. And keep yourself clean. Not only do you have to go through the soap-and-water routine but your living quarters should also be neat and tidy all the time. Get lots of exercise and take your vitamins.

And for the gods' sake, don't sit around the house and brood about how lousy your life is. Get out with your friends and boogie. Don't be afraid to dance and sing, see a good film or go to a party, but try to be celibate for at least a week before you start your spell. Sexual energy should be bottled up and saved for your ceremony. And wear your talisman. You are setting in motion a lot of forces and you will need all the protection you can possibly get, just to keep those little doubts and fears in the back of your head from becoming big hairy monsters. Gather your incense and your magickal tools together; reconsecrate them to exorcise the influences of any other magicks from them. They must be absolutely pure for this grand ritual.

The day and hour has come (three o'clock in the morning of December 18, even). Take a bath, prepare your talismans, prepare the altar. If you are working nude, make sure the room is warm enough. If you wear a robe, make sure that it is spotlessly clean. No wine stains from that brawl last Saturday night. Draw your consecrated circle and trace it with salt or a bloodstone, if you have one. Place your candles (of course, you've chosen the appropriate colors) at the cardinal points of the circle and light your incense.

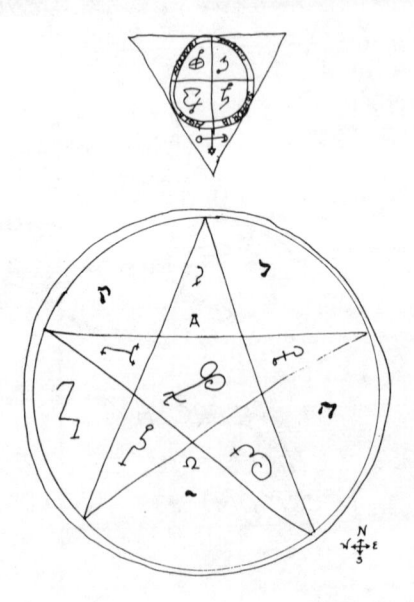

Ring your bell nine times to call the forces and recite your invocation to the spirit.

1st Conjuration

> I conjure thee, (N⁓N), in the fires of hottest hell!
> I invoke thy presence in my circle!
> Appear now forthwith, present thyself, (N⁓N),
> Now, I summon thee in thy true name by which Solomon
> Bound thee in all the fires of hell!
> Adonai, Sephoria, Rabuco!

Take the sigil of the spirit and pass it over the four elements (fire, water, earth and air) and hold it to the four points (north, south, east and west). Give the second conjuration.

2nd Conjuration

> (N⁓N), I conjure thee in the sacred names by which
> All things are bound forever!
> Adonai, Sephoria, Rabuco!
> Come to me now, by thine own sigil
> Thou art bound to come to me!

At this point you may start to feel another presence in the room. This is where you need all your courage. Spirits are rather like humans. They hate to be bothered by every fool who comes down the pike, and are apt to be a little disgruntled by all this commotion. Traditionally, spirits always appear in the north, so recite your third conjuration in that direction.

3rd Conjuration

> Adonai, Sephoria, Rabuco!
> (N⁓N), Appear to me now in a pleasing form
> Without monstrous shapes or foul odors.
> Bring me no great noises or delusions of fire
> Or snakes, nor any of thy hell's horrors
> By the sacred names of power I bind you
> to my will, command your modest and
> seemly presence here, to grant my wish!
> Adonai, Sephoria, Rabuco!

Now, having bound the spirit to your wishes, explain to him what you want, in precise detail. Remember how a mambo will reason with an impatient loa and adapt the same technique. Tell the spirit that you hate to bother him, and you wouldn't be going through all this rigmarole if you didn't have the greatest respect for his powers and the greatest faith in his ability to do you a good turn. When you are finished with your request, bid the spirit to depart with this conjuration.

4th Conjuration

By the sacred names of power I dismiss you (N.·.N),
You have granted my desires, (N.·.N), and I am
well pleased. Depart now, back to the hells from
whence you were called. By the sacred name of
He whose name causes worlds to end and all time
to cease, I command you to quit this place in peace.
Depart in goodwill, in no monstrous forms or vision
Torment me not in dreams or visions, but quit this
place utterly and return not.
Adonai! Sephoria! Rabuco!
Depart, (N.·.N), with my blessing!
ADONAI! SEPHORIA! RABUCO! AMEN!

Hold the sigil in your hand until you are sure the spirit has left. At this point it is not a bad idea to offer a little prayer to your gods to protect you and help the spirit for giving you his aid and succor.

By this time, if you've really been psyching yourself up, you should be totally exhausted, but you must repeat the whole setting-up process backwards, first dismantling the altar, then the circle, and lastly blowing out the candles...

Now sweep the floors, empty the wastebaskets, dust the furniture, and take another bath.

Now have a good stiff drink. You've deserved it for a week and now is the time to enjoy yourself. Go visit a friend or watch television or start repotting your plants or gesso a canvas. Anything that is real and a comforting part of the rest of the world will ease the pressure on your mind. Even a sorcerer should have plenty of other activities to keep him busy when he or she is not magicking.

Magick, after all, is only a wonderful extension of reality in the visible world, and a way to broaden your spiritual aspects. Basically, you get out of it what you put into it.

Blessed Be.

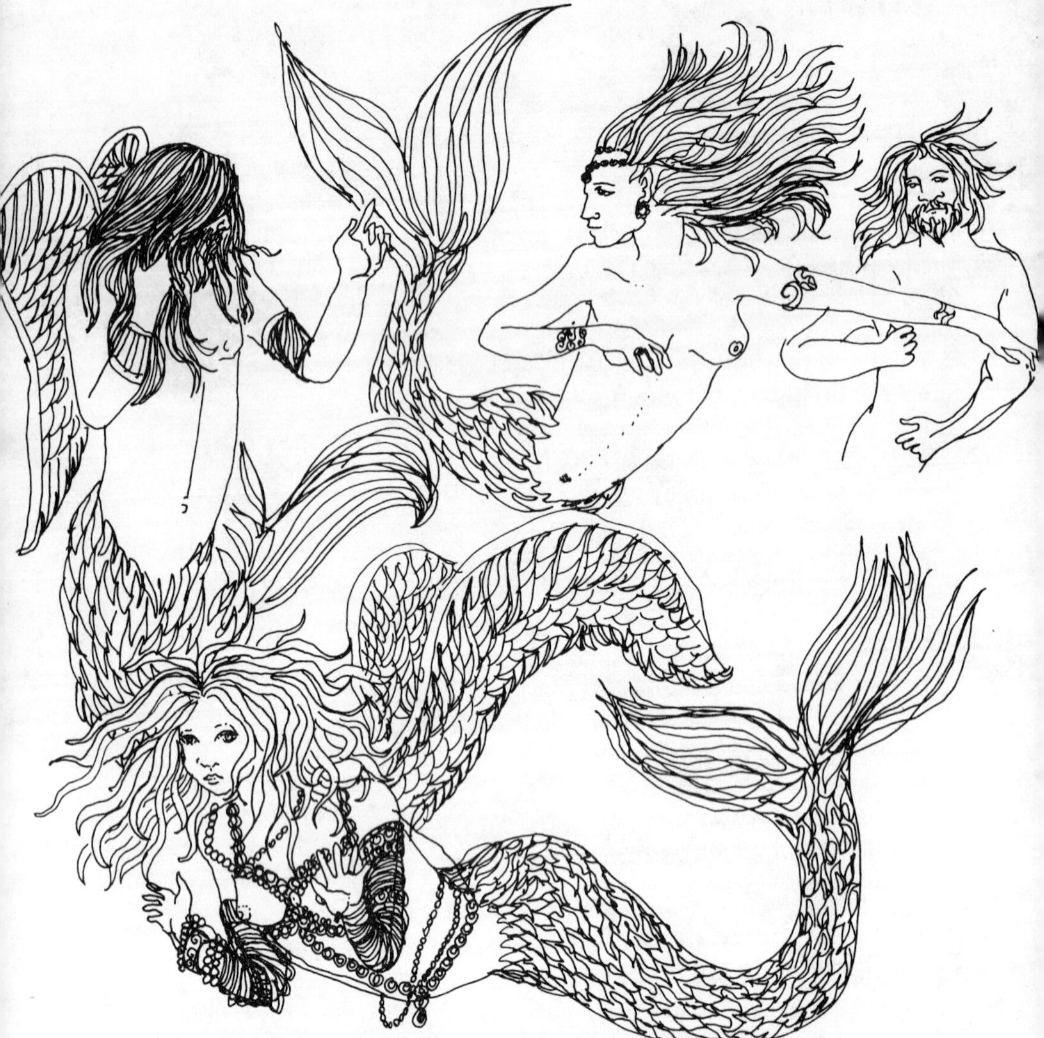

WHERE TO FIND IT

If you live near a large city, it's not hard to find stores that specialize in all the occult trappings from bats' wings to candles. Check out the ads in the local underground press and look in the yellow pages under religious supplies, botanicas, botanical gardens and the like. But if you live fifty miles from the nearest post office (and some people do) and you prefer to conduct business by mail, I've accumulated the following places that will ship and sell you Voodoo dolls and candles. Remember that what you can find or make is often better than anything you could buy, but give it a try anyway.

The number one place for all sorts of occult books is *Samuel Weiser, 734 Broadway, New York, N.Y. 10003*. Weiser's not only stocks all the cheap thrill paperbacks, they have the best selection of serious books on Oriental, Indian, European and every other sort of philosophy, the best editions of rare old volumes and their own reprints of works that would be unavailable to the general public otherwise. I love Weiser's. They have a circular that comes out several times a year listing their latest selections.

Tony Products, Box 783, Costa Mesa, California 92627 also handles books. One of their biggest sellers is a charming thing called Morgan's Tarot. It's amazing how these things get started.

The Warlock Shop, 300 Henry Street, Brooklyn, N.Y. 11201 has an interesting selection of objets d'art. I frequently shop there myself because it's in the neighborhood and Herman will take my checks. They mail a catalogue.

Oneida's Witchcraft Shop, 521 St. Philip, New Orleans, La. Oneida has a great selection of goods; being in the quarter doesn't hurt business either, I suppose.

The Wise One, 130 East Main Street, Norristown, Pa. 19401 was still getting started when I talked to Frank, but by the time you read this, I hope he'll be well on his way.

International Imports, Box 2010, Tuluca Lake, California 91602 does a rousing mail order business. They have a good selection of practically everything.

As does *The Cauldron*, PO Box 403, Rego Park, N.Y. 11374.

For herbs and spices through the mail, *Aphrodisia, 28 Carmine Street, New York, N.Y. 10004* is one of the best. This is another place I shop and love, even when they get uptight about the FDA and my activities.

If you want to grow your own, write to *Nichel's Garden Nursery, 1190 N. Pacific Highway, Albany, Oregon.* They have a great selection of herb seedlings, seeds, etc., for the country sorcerer's garden.

BIBLIOGRAPHY

This is a selective listing, and whenever possible the paperbound editions have been listed.

THE ROOTS OF MAGICK

Binder, Pearl. *Magick Symbols of the World.* London: Hamlyn; 1972.

Christian, Paul. *The History and Practise of Magick.* New York: Citadel Press; 1969.

Crow, W. B. *A History of Magic, Witchcraft and Occultism.* London: The Aquarian Press; 1968.

Crowley, Aleister. *Magick in Theory and Practise.* New York: Castle Books.

Fraser, Sir James George. Edited by Theodor H. Gaster. *The New Golden Bough.* New York: Anchor Books; 1959.

Haining, Peter. *Witchcraft & Black Magic.* New York: Bantam Books; 1972.

Hill, Douglas, and Williams, Pat. *The Supernatural.* New York: Signet Paperbacks; 1967.

Jung, Carl (ed.). *Man and His Symbols.* New York: Doubleday; 1964.

Seligman, Kurt. *Magick, Supernaturalism and Religion.* New York: Universal Library; 1968.

Wedeck, Harry E. *A Treasury of Witchcraft.* New York: Citadel Press; 1968.

Wilson, Colin. *The Occult.* New York: Random House; 1971.

HERB MAGICK

Aima. *Ritual Book of Herbal Spells*. Los Angeles: Hermetic Science Center; 1970.

Crow, W. B. *The Occult Properties of Herbs*. London: Aquarian Press; 1968.

Culpeper, Nicholas. *Culpeper's Complete Herbal*. London: Foulsham & Co.

AMULETS AND TALISMANS

Budge, E. A. Wallis (trans.). *The Egyptian Book of the Dead*. New Hyde Park, N.Y.: University Books; 1960.

Hohman, George. *Pow-Wows: or the Long-Lost Friend*. Hackensack, N.J.: Wehman Brothers.

Wright, Elbee. *Book of Legendary Spells*. Minneapolis: Marlar; 1968.

DIVINATION

The *I Ching* comes in three English translations; the most academic is the Richard Wilhelm edition; the most scholarly is the James Legge; and the best for divination is the John Blofeld edition. The Legge and Blofeld editions are available in paperback; the Wilhelm edition is, at this writing, generally available in an inexpensive hardbound.

Adams, Evangeline. *Astrology, Your Place in the Sun*, and *Astrology, Your Place Among the Stars*. New York: Dell Publishing Co.; 1972.

Carter, Charles E. O. *Astrological Aspects*. London: L. N. Fowler and Co.; 1968.

Chero, Count Louis Harmon. *You and Your Hand*. New York: Berkley Medallion; 1971.

Gibson, Walter B., Litzka, R. *The Complete, Illustrated Book of the Psychic Sciences*. New York: Doubleday; 1966.

Goodman, Linda. *Sun Signs*. New York: Bantam Books; 1971.

Leo, Alan. *Practical Astrology*. London: L. N. Fowler and Co.; 1970.

Martin, Kevin. *The Complete Gypsy Fortune-Teller.* New York: Putnam's Sons; 1970.

Rudhyar, Dane. *The Pulse of Life.* Berkeley, Calif.: Shambala Publications; 1968.

WITCHCRAFT

Buckland, Dr. Raymond. *Witchcraft—Ancient and Modern.* New York: H C Publishers; 1970.

Gardener, Gerald B. *Witchcraft Today,* and *The Meaning of Witchcraft.* New York: Samuel Weiser, Inc.; 1959.

Huson, Paul. *Mastering Witchcraft.* New York: Putnam's Sons; 1971.

Leland, C. *Aradia: The Gospel of the Witches.* New York: Buckland Museum; 1969.

Morrison, Sarah Lyddon. *The Modern Witches' Spell Book.* New York: McKay; 1971.

Murray, Dr. Margaret A. *The Witch-Cult in Western Europe,* and *The God of the Witches.* London: Faber & Faber; 1931, 1936.

GYPSY MAGICK

Clebert, Jean-Paul. *The Gypsies.* Middlesey, G. B.: Penguin Books; 1969.

Leland, C. G. *Gypsy Sorcery.* New York: Tower Books.

VOODOO

Anon. *The Life of Marie Laveau.* A pamphlet, 25 pp.

Densen, Mara. *The Divine Horsemen: The Voodoo Gods of Haiti.* New York: Delta; 1972.

Rigoud, Milo. *Secrets of Voodoo.* New York: Pocket Books; 1971.

St. Clair, David. *Drum and Candle.* New York: Tower Books; 1971.

Tallant, Robert. *Voo Doo in New Orleans.* New York: Collier; 1966.

SATANISM

La Vey, Anton Sanzdor. *The Satanic Bible*. New York: Avon; 1970.

Lyons, Arthur. *Satanism in America*. New York: Award Books; 1970.

Robbins, Russell Hope. *The Encyclopedia of Witchcraft and Demonology*. New York: Crown Publishers; 1958.

RITUAL MAGICK

Butler, E. M. *Ritual Magick*. New York: The Noonday Press; 1959.

Cavendish, Richard. *The Black Arts*. New York: Capricorn Books; 1968.

Jeannyne. *Magicks and Ceremonies*. New York: Lancer Books; 1972.

Shah, Idries. *The Secret Lore of Magick*. New York: Citadel Press; 1970.

Waite, A. E. *The Book of Black Magick and of Pacts*. New York: Samuel Weiser; 1972.